Scandinavian Studies
in Criminology, Vol. 13

Of Vice and Women:
Shades of Prostitution

Scandinavian Studies in Criminology
Edited by Annika Snare

**Books are to be returned on or before
the last date below.**

**7-DAY
LOAN**

12/12/09

Scandinavian Studies
in Criminology, Vol. 13

Of Vice and Women:
Shades of Prostitution

Margaretha Järvinen
Translated by Karen Leander

Scandinavian
University Press

The Scandinavian
Research Council
for Criminology

Scandinavian University Press (Universitetsforlaget AS),
N-0608 Oslo, Norway
Distributed world-wide excluding Norway by
Oxford University Press, Walton Street, Oxford OX2 6DP

London New York Toronto
Dehli Bombay Calcutta Madras Karachi
Kuala Lumpur Singapore Hong Kong Tokyo
Nairobi Dar es Salaam Cape Town
Melbourne Auckland

and associated companies in
Beirut Berlin Ibadan Mexico City Nicosia

British Library Cataloguing in Publication Data
A catalogue record for this book is available.

ISBN 82-00-21283-1

Printed in Norway by
Tangen Grafiske Senter AS, 1993

Contents

Foreword

By ANNIKA SNARE

Prostitution Research in the North

Over the past decade, quite extensive research on prostitution has been carried out in the Nordic countries. Earlier studies are available in the fields of medicine, law, history and the social sciences, of course, but current research distinguishes itself in several respects. Some of these features are international in nature, while others appear to be distinctively Nordic.

Much of the new prostitution research in the western world, including Scandinavia, has been feminist-oriented, and has invalidated traditional views or myths about women's «oldest profession». Researchers in many countries have gained insight through in-depth interviews and/or projects established to assist women in leaving the life of commercial sex. Scars on body and soul are more than amply documented in the literature, and these adverse physical and mental consequences for prostitutes have been one of the most thoroughly examined areas in the Nordic feminist studies on prostitution.

However, as a whole, the Scandinavian research orientation since the 1980s deviates from the work in most other countries by not focusing exclusively on the (female) prostitutes. A common ground is the strong emphasis on the role of customers: without demand, there would be no supply of prostitution services. From having represented the anonymous «forgotten» figure in past research, the prostitution customer surfaces as the principle subject of recent separate studies in several Nordic countries. By and large the customers are described as «ordinary» men in terms of age, civil status and occupation in relation to the general male population.

Likewise, the role played by the authorities controlling prostitution, instead of being ignored, has been the issue of serious concern in recent Scandinavian research. One of the central themes in the study Of *Vice and Women: Shades of Prostitution* is that the task of controlling sexual behaviour of ambiguous commercial nature has been translated and transformed into a societal control of women at large.

The overall focus on the control dimension is further a significant «trademark» of current Scandinavian prostitution research. This approach highlights the structural imbalance between men and women, that is, the gender-biased distribution of social, economic and political resources in society.

One might get the impression from the presentation above that total Scandinavian unanimity and harmony prevails in the prostitution research context. This is a false message, however. The relevant question is to what degree differences of opinion reflect variations which emanate from the different prostitution settings under study as well as from national contrasts.

Shades of Prostitution

A point of departure in *Of Vice and Women* is the discreet nuances of the Finnish prostitution picture of today. Commercial sex in Helsinki is not only small scale, but is also much less visible than its counterparts in Stockholm, Oslo and Copenhagen. The capital of Finland has no real street prostitution while the others all have notorious streets or blocks where contact with street-walkers can be made. If Finland is located at the low end of the scale, and Sweden and Norway somewhere in the middle, then Denmark should definitely be ranked at the top as to magnitude of prostitution. In addition, Danish commercial sex takes much more visible forms than in the rest of Scandinavia. Prostitution encounters in today's Helsinki are chiefly initiated via advertisements and at hotels/restaurants.

A goal of the present study is to delineate the specific Finnish character of the police-registered prostitution in the capital over a period of several decades (1945-1986). In which way does it differ from the forms of commercial sex described in the international research literature?

We meet the arrested street prostitutes of the 1940s and 1950s, and the young «ship girls», «truck girls» and «station girls» who caught the attention of the police and the public in the 1960s. We note how the nature of commercial sex changed in the 1970s and 1980s when those arrested for prostitution most often were mainly either socially marginalized women who moved in circles dominated by male vagrants or were hotel prostitutes and call-girls.

All the women were arrested on the basis of the 1936 Vagrancy Act (abolished at year end 1986). But it remains to be seen whether they in fact met the two criteria established by law: to engage in *paid* sex and on a *habitual* basis. Moreover, in the international literature five criteria have been adopted to define the phenomenon of prostitution. Are these fulfilled in the Finnish peripheral world of commercial sex?

Charged with prostitution, they were, but the «faces» of these women are frequently flushed with an innocent infatuation, love, romance, excitement, friendship and adventure. Interestingly, the clearest examples of commercialized sexual relations are found in the most private and exclusive prostitution environments. Yet, even among hotel prostitutes and call-girls, an internalized and consistent professional identity as prostitute seems to be missing.

Policing Prostitution - Controlling Women

Of Vice and Women tells the story of society's attempts to define and come to grips with multifaceted sexual relations, whether in the form of public or secluded encounters. In this borderland between downright commercialized deals and mutually gratifying sexual/social relationships, the policing of prostitution has functioned as an instrument to control women's sexuality and other life circumstances.

The author analyzes how, for many years, the authorities' control had the effect of a normative «curfew». Certain parts of the city - or spheres of urban life - emerged as almost forbidden territory for a woman who wanted to retain her status as «decent». At night, restaurants, the harbour or railway station and the streets became male domains. Women who ventured into these out of bounds areas had to be able to explain their presence to the police and to prove their «respectability». Failure to do so was, by the authorities, converted into sexual motives and alleged prostitution.

The Road to Knowledge

From a theoretical point of view, the study *Of Vice and Women: Shades of Prostitution* builds on and refines previous work. To start out, three general perspectives are used to classify earlier as well as more recent research on prostitution, and the content and implications of these different theoretical frames are analyzed. In particular, the systematization of the phenomenon of *controlling prostitution* as a «functionalist» approach, allows us to see more starkly the underlying assumptions of past (and current) strategies to control commercial sex.

Margaretha Järvinen fully acknowledges the «feminist» perspective of prostitution and its disclosure of gender-biased power relations in society. But as far as I can tell, it is her efforts to interweave «construc-tionist» thinking with a massive empirical analysis of the control of prostitution that merit special attention.

The usually abstract delimitations of concepts such as «social con-struction» and «relativity» are given a concrete empirical foundation in this book. Thus the discourse enhances the appreciation of prostitution, developed in a «social interactionist/control» perspective, by critically reflecting on the absolute or polar distinctions established in previous research.

Towards European Integration?

Finland's location on the geographical periphery of Europe explains, in part, the lingering touch of amateurishness in Finnish prostitution. In the not so far distant future, however, this might be a feature of the past.

The present European situation as a whole is characterized by an increasing international trafficking in women, particularly from East to West. Further, we are seeing a tendency toward a «professionalization» of commercial sex, that is, movements which advocate the right of wo-men to practise prostitution as a profession.

Here we are about to witness a head-on collision between these more southern European ideas and the full force of the Nordic prostitu-tion research. Reading *Of Vice and Women: Shades of Prostitution*, we find that we are also being confronted with a broad gap between conti-nental trends and the relatively «idyllic» nature of the prostitution mar-ket in the Finnish capital.

Author's Introduction

«Prostitution» in Helsinki during the period 1945 to 1986 is the subject of this study. Over these decades, prostitution was defined as a form of vagrancy and covered by the Vagrancy Act of 1936. The law was repealed at the end of 1986.

Before this study, the vice police's material on prostitution had only to a limited extent been analyzed. The 1936 Vagrancy Act provided us with an unique opportunity to study the control of prostitution over a period of five decades.

The early plans for this research project were met with considerable scepticism. Many fellow researchers maintained that prostitution did not exist in Finland, and others claimed that it was of such limited scope as to be without scientific relevance.

Commercialized sex in Helsinki was not an issue of much public debate in the early 1980s. In 1984, the Ministry of Health and Social Affairs published a short report on prostitution[1] where the conclusion was reached that commercialized sex did not constitute a widespread social problem. Thus, the Vagrancy Act was repealed in a situation when prostitution was defined as a small-scale phenomenon without visible social harms.

However, there were two earlier points in time when prostitution had been debated intensively: first, at the end of the 1800s and in the early 1900s when the regulatory system for prostitutes was the centre of controversy; and, second, in the 1950s and 1960s when prostitution was considered a serious youth problem. Since then, the topic of commercialized sex had been shrouded in almost total silence.

During the Vagrancy Act, prostitution was not criminalized, but

---

1 Rauhala 1984.

controlled administratively by the vice police and the social welfare authorities. Even though commercialized sex was not illegal, the measures set out in the Act were rather harsh. The law allowed long-term incarceration (institutional care or forced labour) as well as several other encroachments in the lives of prostitutes. The right to appeal these decisions was limited and rarely used.

The topic of this book is that of *prostitution known to the authorities*, and not prostitution in general. No indication is given here as to the dimensions of the non-registered prostitution or whether and how it deviates from the registered prostitution. The study is also limited to *heterosexual prostitution*, that is, commercialized sex where women are the sellers and men are the buyers of sexual services. Homosexual prostitution, with male sellers and buyers, is not included.

The main topic is not professional prostitution of the type we are familiar with from studies done in other countries. To a large extent, the women designated as prostitutes in Helsinki can be described as amateurs or semi-professionals. Thus, the focus in this study is on the gray zone between prostitution and mutually engaging heterosexual relations, and on society's attempts to deal with difficult-to-classify sexual liaisons.

The research project started out as a study in female deviant behaviour. Prostitution was defined as one of the classic examples of norm violations by women. However, what I will try to show throughout the book, is that prostitution is not a social deviation in the traditional sense but rather a *social construction*. Commercialized sex is a direct reflection of the gender structure in our society. The transactions between the prostitutes and their customers do not qualitatively deviate from «normal» and accepted heterosexual relations.

The work also began as a study of the control of prostitution. The measures taken by the authorities against commercialized sexual activities in Helsinki had not earlier been the subject of any systematic scientific analysis. It turned out though that the public measures enacted have not merely operated to control prostitution but also to control women in general. The anti-vagrancy measures have been used to prevent prostitution and to establish the boundaries between acceptable and unacceptable female sexual behaviour.

The Vagrancy Act is no longer in effect. The authorities, and in particular the police, who were obliged to uphold the Act, argued that its repeal would lead to a professionalization of commercialized sex in Finland. A street prostitution of the type found in other Western countries would take root in Helsinki. The level of social problems often accompanying prostitution - drug abuse, criminality - would rise. The effects of the repeal of the law naturally are difficult to determine, but there are many indicators (observations made during the project, information from the police and other authorities) that no significant change has occurred.

The study was financed by the Commission of Social Sciences at the Academy of Finland and the Finnish Foundation for Alcohol Research. Supervisor on the project was Elianne Riska, at the Åbo Akademi University. Together with Elina Haavio-Mannila, Helsinki University, Elianne Riska also served as pre-reviewer of my dissertation (which this book is an abbreviated version of). I would like to thank them as well as Hannele Varsa and Heikki Katajisto and other colleagues in Helsinki, and at the Institute of Criminology and Criminal Law in Copenhagen. Further, I am grateful to the personnel at the former Vice Police Division, the Central Register of the Criminal Police, and the Restaurant Division at the Alcohol Monopoly, in Helsinki.

I would in particular like to express my gratitude to those women who allowed me to interview them about their experiences in prostitution.

Finally, I thank Karen Leander for the hard work of translating the book, and Annika Snare for her inspiring editing and invaluable advice concerning the text. I am happy to be able to publish this work in the series of Scandinavian studies in criminology.

Margaretha Järvinen
Copenhagen, April 1992

1.

Prostitution and Control – Theoretical Approaches

Prostitution has been studied from a broad range of perspectives. There is an extensive socio-historical tradition of research focusing on, in particular, the early 20th century;[1] and a relatively comprehensive criminological-legal literature on prostitution;[2] in addition to the sociological and socio-psychological tradition in prostitution research.[3]

Within the sociological and criminological research literature, three principal theoretical perspectives can be distinguished: 1) a functionalist, 2) a feminist, and 3) a social interactionist/constructionist perspective. The last two perspectives are, in different ways, reactions against the functionalist approach.

In the following, the concept of *«prostitution»* is used to indicate a transaction where at least two trading parties buy respectively sell sexual acts (see Chpt. 1.3 for a discussion of various definitions of prostitution). The concept of *«prostitution control»* refers to those formal and informal measures which target the parties involved in the transactions (prostitutes, customers, procurers) for the purpose of combatting prostitution or channelling it into socially acceptable forms.

1.1. A Functionalist Perspective

The functionalist approach was the dominant perspective in prostitution literature for several decades of this century.[4] Though gradually becoming less pronounced in the research literature, it could still be traced into the 1960s and 1970s.[5] The functionalist tradition can be analyzed in terms of: 1) the view of prostitution and sexuality the literature advances; 2) the models used to explain the phenomenon of prostitution; and 3) the control measures suggested by the writers.

Prostitution and Sexuality: A Functionalist View

This perspective presupposes a specific understanding of sexuality, according to which prostitution is a normal and universal phenomenon, existing in all periods and all known societies. The functionalists consider prostitution as «women's oldest profession», a natural and unavoidable social phenomenon.[6] Prostitution is seen as a timeless institution, which is relatively independent of the societal structure and level of development.

The American sociologist Kingsley Davis (1937) is an oft-quoted representative of a Durkheim-inspired functionalist view of prostitution. He considered prostitution a necessary complement to marriage since family life both quantitatively and qualitatively limits the patterns of sexual relations. In his view, men have a natural «craving for variety, for perverse gratification, for mysterious and provocative surroundings, for intercourse free from entangling cares and civilized pretence» (p. 753). The alternative to prostitution would be total sexual liberation in society, which would obviously be incompatible with marriage and family life (ibid). Where the family institution is robust, there tends to be a well-defined system of prostitution, according to Davis. The opposite is true as well: when the family institution is weak, prostitution is vague and fluid. In this view, if one of society's goals is to preserve marriage and family life, it must also accept prostitution.[7]

Functionalist Explanatory Models

The functionalist research literature offers the following explanations for men's patronage of prostitution. The most important explanation is «sexual frustration» within marriage; the customer is assumed to have a greater sexual need than his wife, or «specific sexual desires» that the wife is unable or unwilling to satisfy.[8] Another common explanation is «sexual isolation». This deprivation may be temporary: some prostitution customers are men whose occupations (as sailors, travelling salesmen, and so on) necessitate long absences from their regular partner.[9] The sexual isolation may also be long-term: young single men, divorced men, and widowers are assumed to be overrepresented among prostitution customers.[10] Sexual frustration/isolation may also be related to the fact that some customers have difficulty succeeding on the non-commercial sexual market. According to functionalism, prostitution is needed to satisfy the sexual needs of physically, emotionally, or socially handicapped men.[11] Thus, prostitution seemingly fills important social functions in society.

The explanations for women's participation in prostitution are sought on many different levels in the functionalist-influenced literature. Explications may be found on the mental or emotional plane: prostitutes have been described as feeble-minded, mentally disordered, psycho-paths, and so on[12] - sociology has here freely borrowed explanatory models, not least of all from psychiatry.[13] Explanations may also appear on the sexual plane: prostitutes have been depicted as «hypersexual», or alternatively as «frigid» or «lesbians».[14] Sometimes, the reasons are of a social nature: women are assumed to become prostitutes as a result of traumatic childhood experiences, poor relationships with their parents, illness, alcohol abuse, and criminality in the home.[15] Or the explana-tions may be economic: prostitutes are described as women with high socio-economic ambitions but limited means for attaining them.[16] A common denominator in all these assessments is that the prostitutes are characterized as deviant, as mentally, sexually, or socially abnormal.

Prostitution Control: A Functionalist View

The functionalist view of the control of prostitution can be summarized in three theses. The first concerns the alleged immortality of prostitu-tion. Since prostitution is seen as a normal, universal, and functional phenomenon, the eradication of commercialized sex is deemed an unre-alistic goal for public policy. Strict control measures do not reduce prostitution in this view; they merely lead to the replacement of public prostitution with more discreet forms.[17]

The second functionalist thesis indicates that controlling prostitution may have direct negative consequences. Prostitution has traditionally been described as a societal «safety-valve».[18] If commercial sex did not exist, the loneliness and sexual isolation of some men would be total, according to the functionalists, and the resulting «sexual frustration» would lead to an increased number of rapes and other sexual violations. If married men were unable to go to prostitutes with their ungratified needs, they would instead turn to extra-marital relationships, affairs which would present a greater threat to family life than do the short-lived and superficial liaisons with prostitutes.[19]

Third, according to the functionalist perspective, control measures should be aimed not at prostitution itself, but at the trade's social dis-turbances. These may take the forms of venereal diseases, criminality, public disorder, and alcohol and drug problems. Combatting the ensu-ing social harms is seen to be much more realistic and necessary than eliminating prostitution. Discreet commercial sexual contacts between two willing, adult individuals are regarded as part of the private sphere. Prostitution that does not disrupt the public order is of no one's concern except that of the involved parties.[20]

1.2. A Feminist Perspective

The feminist perspective within prostitution research is primarily a product of the 1970s and 1980s;[21] however, its roots are in the turn-of-the-century debate.[22] This approach has also played a very important role in the modern Scandinavian research on prostitution.[23]

Prostitution and Sexuality: A Feminist View

The view that binds all feminist literature in this field is the notion that prostitution is linked to the inequality between men and women in society. Prostitution consists of a supply and demand for remunerated sexual services; in all periods, men have answered for the demand and women (or male prostitutes in homosexual transactions) for the supply. This is not coincidental, but rather reflective of the gender-skewed allocation of social, economic, and political resources in the society. The relative socio-economic power of men includes the right to demand sexual satisfaction even if this occurs at the expense of women. The imbalance of power between men and women is reflected in the sexualization of the socio-economically weaker gender. Women's position in the social structure is, in contrast to that of men, defined through their relationships to the opposite sex.[24] According to the feminist perspective, prostitution is not a natural and absolute phenomenon (as in the functionalist approach); on the contrary, it is seen as being defined by and changing with the power relations in society.

Another fundamental feminist point of view is that prostitution mirrors a patriarchal view of sexuality, where men are defined as sexual and women as asexual. According to the patriarchal sexual ideology which permeates the entire functionalist perspective, there is a fundamental and immutable gender difference in sexual needs. «Normal» male sexual needs are described as «natural forces» that cannot be subordinated to the constraints of marriage and family life or adapted to other societal interests. On the other hand, «normal» female sexual needs are seen as negligible or at least monogamous in nature and secondary to women's reproductive functions.[25] This lack of synchronization between male and female in the patriarchal view of sexuality results in the designation of a group of women as «public» and generally available. In contrast to «normal» women, these women are perceived as sexual beings, representing the dark, erotically exciting side - but also the most degraded and scorned side - of the female sex in male society.[26]

A third feminist point of departure is the thesis that prostitution reflects a tendency to view the female body as a commodity. In our patriarchal societies, women's bodies are commercialized in the extreme, and their societal value is, in a completely different way than the societal value of men, linked to youth and particular ideals of beauty. The status of the female body as a buyable, sellable, and exchangeable commodity constitutes the natural backdrop to a functioning commerce in sex.[27]

Feminist Explanatory Models

Within feminist research several models are presented for explaining why some women become prostitutes and some men customers. However, the common denominator is that the entry into commercialized sex is somehow related to the gender roles and the allocation of power and resources.

The most commonly cited reasons for why some women become prostitutes are economic. Historical works and studies of commercial sex today reveal that prostitutes are typically recruited from among the economically disadvantaged, the working-class, and poor immigrant families.[28] It is also shown that prostitutes often have poor educations, limited experience of working life, and thereby little possibility of securing a socially and economically satisfactory occupation.[29] For these deprived women, prostitution would then represent a natural and - in the opinion of some writers - «rational» alternative. Women assumingly prefer prostitution to badly paid, arduous female occupations with low status.[30]

Other common explanations for women's participation in prostitution are social rootlessness, loneliness, and social marginalization. Young prostitutes have been shown to be in the process of «drifting» away from the family, the school system, and the labour market for a long period prior to their participation in commercialized sex transactions. The prostitution setting, with its social network and well-defined system of norms, has been described as one of the few «deviant milieus» available to young women.[31]

A third explanatory model within feminist research maintains that, on the individual level, prostitution is linked to other forms of sexual exploitation. Some studies have revealed that experiences of incest and rape at early ages are common among prostitutes.[32] However, the research findings are contradictory on this point; other studies indicate that such violations are equally common among non-prostitutes.[33]

All these explanatory models are related to the basic premise of a linkage between prostitution and a patriarchal sexual ideology. The connection between economic problems, limited opportunities on the labour market, and social rootlessness, on the one side, and prostitution, on the other, is not direct. It goes via the gendered view of sexuality that defines the female body as a commodity and guarantees men the right to sexual services on demand. Following feminist reasoning, prostitutes are not mental or social deviants in the traditional sense of the word; they are normal women who choose prostitution from a subordinate position in which they face few attractive alternatives. However, this choice entails great costs for many prostitutes: further social and economic marginalization, psychological problems, and substance abuse are reported in many studies.[34]

The feminist-oriented explanations for men's patronage of prostitutes can be summarized by the following points. The common denominator is a questioning of the hypothesis about a direct link between sexual isolation/sexual frustration (in the functionalist perspective) and the purchase of sexual services.

First, according to the research literature, sexually isolated men and physically, mentally, or socially handicapped men are not particularly well represented among prostitution customers. On the contrary, it has been documented that prostitution customers on the average have more varied sexual experience than do non-customers.[35] Furthermore, customers are as likely to be married as non-married, and they come from all age groups and from all social classes.[36]

Second, research shows that the customers' motives for visiting prostitutes are not purely sexual. Of course, sexual release is one aspect of the transactions, but many other motives are indicated as well. The respondents attribute their sex purchases to: a wish to experience «excitement» and «the forbidden» or «sympathy» and «intimacy» in the prostitution setting; a search for «a one-sided, non-demanding relationship»; or the possibility to be «passive and subservient» with women. Thus, for a limited time and under well-preserved anonymity, some men buy themselves the right to be «weak».[37] Other men visit prostitutes «to dampen feelings of loneliness and isolation» - not only sexually, but also socially. They explain their sex purchases with the difficulties they have in starting and maintaining meaningful relationships with women; with uncertainty about their ability to satisfy women; or with general feelings of inferiority, poor self-confidence, and self-contempt.[38]

Third, according to the feminist literature, men's - like women's - participation in prostitution can best be explained by reference to traditional gender roles. As little as are the prostitutes, the customers are not physically, psychologically, or socially deviant. They are normal men struggling with a gender system which requires them to take command in the economic, social, and sexual spheres, at the same time that it limits their chances to display dependence and weakness. Prostitution offers them a temporary respite from the requirements of activity, mastery, and control. Or it may serve to convince them of their ability to take command, and to assure them that they still live in a society where the traditional gender roles are in good working order. Prostitution, so readily brandished by male society as a «safety-valve», is promoted as a solution to hardships, conflicts and the sensation of emptiness.[39]

Prostitution Control: A Feminist View

Finally, various specific approaches to the phenomenon of controlling prostitution distinguish the quite comprehensive feminist literature on this topic.[40] Here, two aspects will be discussed: prostitution control and deviant women; and prostitution control and female sexuality.

First, feminist research often analyzes the control of prostitution as an explicit control of *a group of women labelled as «deviant»*[41] In all described control systems, the primary target for control measures is the prostitute, not the male customers or procurers. Since female asexuality and monogamy are considered the norm, and the prostitute is depicted as sexual and polygamous, she is, by definition, deviant and thereby a natural object for punishment or treatment. In contrast, the customer does not deviate from the norms for his gender; his purchase of prostitution services is merely the result of sexual frustration, be it temporary or long-term. Therefore, the objective of prostitution control is to protect him against the trade's harmful consequences, such as diseases and criminality, and not to punish him or alter his behaviour.[42] Consequently, the ultimate purpose of prostitution control is to confine the sexual transactions within certain socially defined boundaries - by means of measures aimed at a group of «deviant» women.[43]

Several arguments have been cited in the literature in favour of gender-selective control policies.[44] One traditional argument is that the prostitute is «the active party» in commercial sex. Assumingly, she has more sexual contacts than the customer, and she, not he, offers herself for sale in public, thereby constituting a visible social problem. This is refuted though by reports confirming that male customers (in street prostitution) are equally prone to initiate solicitations as the prostitutes. The behaviour of customers often takes the form of so-called kerb-crawling where the man drives around the block for quite a while before selecting a particular prostitute.[45] This traffic can be disturbing and a problem for the people living in the area, for the prostitutes, and for other women subjected to advances by the potential customers.

Another argument used in favour of gender-selective control policies is that the prostitute, in contrast to the customer, is an integral part of an asocial milieu. Therefore, taking measures against the women would theoretically have a greater impact on overall criminality than would measures against the customers. Moreover, the prostitute represents that party in the sex commerce (along with possible pimps and other profiteers) who gains economically. She is the one who «exploits» the customer, and commercializes his sexual needs, according to this reasoning. In a control system with limited resources (that is, all control systems), a gender-selective control policy is thus viewed as rational and expedient.[46]

Second, the relevant feminist literature analyzes the control of prostitution as *a general control of female sexuality*. The purpose of prostitution control has often been not only to penalize or resocialize a group of deviant women, but also to establish the boundaries between permissible and non-permissible forms of female sexual behaviour.[47] There are two significant aspects of this control.

One aspect stressed by many commentators is that society generally exhibits greater interest in the sexuality of young women than of young men. In studies of so-called problem youth, it has been shown that girls' problems are depicted by the authorities in entirely different ways than are those of boys. Young girls running away from home, skipping school, committing minor crimes, or experimenting with drugs are automatically expected to be sexually active, promiscuous, and perhaps prostitutes.[48] In the Swedish Skå study, where an institution for problem youth is described, Gustav Jonsson (1977, p. 39) summarizes the authorities' interest in girls' sexuality as follows: «Expressed in simple and unadulterated Swedish: If we have to nail the boys, we take them as small-time thieves; but to really get at the girls, we take them as small-time hookers».

Another feminist basic notion is that the label of prostitution in many respects reinforces the traditional female role. When «deviant» behaviour among young girls is classified as prostitution, the girls are relegated to a stereotypical female category. Their absconding from home and school, their criminality, drug abuse, and probable promiscuity is sometimes perceived as a breach of the norms for femininity; but prostitution is rather an extension of the traditional female role. By classifying the girls as prostitutes, the society has categorized them, interpreted their behaviour, and warned other young girls who are «drifting» away from family life. The role as prostitute is - in contrast to female criminality and female substance abuse - «woman's oldest profession» (cf. the functionalist perspective). However disdained it may be, prostitution constitutes no threat to the social order.[49]

1.3. A Social Interactionist/Constructionist Perspective

As was the case with the feminist perspective, a social constructionist approach to prostitution,[50] inspired by classic interactionist theories,[51] has developed over the past two decades. This perspective and the feminist perspective are not mutually exclusive; on the contrary, there are many prostitution studies which combine the two approaches.[52]

The social interactionist/constructionist perspective could be described as follows. First, it stresses the relativity of the concept of prostitution.[53] Prostitution is apprehended as a social construction with contents and meanings that vary according to time period and society. Second, this perspective emphasizes the significance of social control for defining prostitution. The weight in interactionist studies is not put so much on the structural or individual causes of prostitution, or on the psycho- social consequences of prostitution, but rather on the interaction between the subject of control (the relevant authorities) and the object (the prostitutes).[54] Third, the interactionist/constructionist approach stresses the significance of an analysis of classifications. In the research discourse on prostitution, the central objects of classification are the prostitutes and their milieus[55] (the customers have been classified but only rarely). Fourth, within this research tradition, prostitution is often analyzed in terms of a career. The prostitutes' role is not perceived as something definitive or static; the duration and intensity of their involvement in commercial sex varies with many factors, including the control measures taken against prostitution.[56]

The Relativity of Prostitution

When prostitution is analyzed as a social construction, there can be no clear and under all circumstances applicable boundary between prostitution and non-prostitution. These two designations are seen as placed along a hypothetic continuum stretching from behaviours defined by everyone in a given society as prostitution to behaviours considered by no one to fall in that category. The passage from «normal» to «deviant» in this respect is hazy and is dependent on the criteria used in the definitional processes.[57]

The phenomenon of prostitution has traditionally been considered as difficult to define. The most important criterion used to define prostitution (in functionalist and other literature) has been *commerciality*. For a sexual relation to be called prostitution, the carnal knowledge must be linked to remuneration, in money or other forms.[58] Another criterion often used in definitions of prostitution is that of *promiscuity*: the sexual transaction is not supposed to be unique in the sense that the seller only has one customer.[59] A third criterion is *non-selectivity*: the prostitute is not assumed to choose her customers; all men who can and are willing to pay are serviced.[60] A fourth criterion is *temporariness*: the sexual transaction should not be a part of a long-term social relation,[61] and a fifth criterion is *emotional indifference*: the prostitution relationship is to be impersonal and neutral.[62]

The first dimension, *commerciality*, is a given in all definitions of prostitution: a sexual liaison without an economic element - in money or other forms - can hardly be labelled prostitution. In some definitions, attempts have been made to specify the criterion, usually by pointing out that the economic compensation is to be «directly linked» to the sexual services. This may imply that the amount of payment is determined by the fixed prices attached to the various sexual acts; it could also imply that the payment and the sexual services are linked in time or that they are related perceptionally - that is, that the link is clear to all parties involved.[63]

As for the second criterion, *promiscuity*, it is evident that the dimension refers to the prostitute rather than to the notion of prostitution. A woman who sells sexual services to one man exclusively is not a prostitute, according to some commentators. She is either a so-called «kept woman», if the relationship is long standing, or an «amateur», if the transaction is an isolated incident.[64] The tendency to bind the concept of prostitution to promiscuity seems to emanate from a traditional notion of women's matrimonial role; parallels are sometimes drawn between «kept women» and married women. A prostitute with many customers breaches societal norms to a much greater extent than a woman who sells herself to one man, regardless of whether the latter's prostitution income is greater or less than the former's.[65]

According to the third traditional criterion, prostitution is to be combined with *non-selectivity*. The decisive selection factor in commercial sex is the customer's willingness and ability to pay. Many studies reveal though that most prostitutes are relatively selective of their customers. This selectivity may stem from a desire for security, implying that customers perceived as dangerous are weeded out. It may be based on sexual requests, where customers' demands which are of too unusual a nature are rejected, or it may be based on social or ethnical background, where men of certain derivation are not allowed access. It is also true that many customers are selective in their search for prostitutes; the possibility to choose among various potential partners is certainly an important property of prostitution.[66]

The fourth criterion implies that to be defined as prostitution, the sexual relations must be *transitory and short-lived*. The function of this criterion has been (in part overlapping with the criterion of promiscuity) to distinguish prostitution from long-term, marital relationships or alliances resembling marriage. One problem with the criterion is that many prostitutes have regular customers, men who continually return to the same «hostess». It is difficult to see why these relations, highly commercial as they sometimes are, should not be labelled prostitution. In this sense, then, temporariness and freedom/unfetteredness are not imperative characteristics of prostitution relations.[67]

According to the fifth traditional criterion, prostitution is associated with *emotional indifference*; the liaison is supposed to be impersonal and neutral for both parties.[68] However, recent studies have indicated that commercialized sex is often linked to negative feelings (it is not always clear whether the concept of indifference in the definitions refers to the mere absence of positive feelings). Contempt, fear, repulsion, and humiliation are not uncommon sentiments among prostitutes and customers.[69] Moreover, in some cases (although these may be exceptional), prostitution is associated with positive feelings: friendship, infatuation, tenderness, and caring. This is especially true of relationships between prostitutes and regular customers.[70] Accordingly, if emotional indifference is a necessary criterion for prostitution, many paid-for sexual relations would fall outside of the definition.

As indicated above, the basic problem with the five criteria is that they are not helpful for distinguishing the phenomenon of prostitution from other sexual relations, in any definitive manner. The only tenable characteristic of prostitution is the economic one, but the relativity of this criterion inevitably leads to a vague definition. The other four criteria are important, not so much for a conceptual definition of commercialized sex, as for understanding the traditional research discourse as well as the control policies which have been implemented.

The five characteristics of prostitution should be defined as variables rather than as absolute categories (Fig. 1.).

Fig. 1. Characteristics used to distinguish prostitution from other sexual relations

non-prostitution relations		prostitution relations
low	commerciality	high
low	number of relations	high
high	selectivity	low
high	portion of long-term relationships	low
high	emotionality	low

The farther to the right on these scales someone's sexual relations can be placed, the greater the probability that the person in question will be defined as a prostitute or customer. Of course, the sexual relations need not have equally high or low values on all variables; a unique, selective, and long-term liaison may very well be highly commercialized (cf., above on «kept women»). This is also true for marital relations, conventionally defined as outside the spectrum of prostitution. If a marriage is commercial, with sexual services given in exchange for economic remuneration, this alliance, in the same way as non-marital relationships, could be defined as prostitution.

The five prostitution variables can be related to the concepts of primary and secondary deviance, a central theme in classic interactionist theories.[71] The phenomenon of commercialized sex - in the sense of primary deviance - can then be defined on the basis of a single variable, the economic component, whereas the other four variables determine how prostitution is perceived and controlled in the society, that is, prostitution as secondary deviance. As stated in one study[72] where this dichotomization has been applied, prostitution as primary deviance is difficult to identify, not because the concept of primary deviance is inadequate in this context, but because the normal female role itself encompasses many elements of commercialized sexuality, such as the use of sexuality to derive advantages, and signals which denote availability in the heterosexual interplay. This does not mean that all sexual relations between men and women comprise prostitution (an argument found in many prostitutes' working philosophy, cf. later). The point is merely that the distinction between the role as prostitute and the female gender role is not as clear-cut as is commonly assumed.

The German feminist researchers, Frigga Haug et al. (1987), describe the transition from a «normal» woman's role to prostitution by the phrase «slavegirl behaviour». The role as sexual object is characterized not only by passive acceptance of a subordinate position, in the opinion of Haug and others, but also by active participation. Women are expected to make their sexuality available to men, to «offer themselves», and to stimulate male sexuality - and many women accept this role as an important and rewarding part of their identity. In essence, prostitution is only a commercialized version of the widely accepted (by most men and women), heterosexual relations in society. Accordingly, the boundary between «normal» and «abnormal» is unclear, but the process of social definition and control involves continual movement towards a clearer distinction between prostitution and other sexual relations - and even more important: between prostitutes and other women.

The Significance of Social Control

The second integral feature of a social interactionist perspective on prostitution is the focus on control. The phenomenon of prostitution is seen as intimately linked to processes of definition, classification, and control. The designations «prostitutes» and «customers» do not apply to naturally given categories of individuals with particular social or psychological traits;[73] instead, they are the result of complicated social processes. The central question in a social interactionist analysis of commercialized sex is not why some people become prostitutes/customers, but how certain people become defined as such.

The definitional processes can be analyzed by use of the terms «action», «reaction», and «interaction».[74] Applied to prostitution, the concepts connote: a) the sexual encounter itself (action); b) society's definition of and measures against prostitution (reaction); and c) the relationship between those who control prostitution and those who are controlled (interaction). In an interactionist study of prostitution, the following questions could be asked:[75] a) what are the rules and norms that the prostitute breaches and why is prostitution seen to be a problem in society; b) which processes are relevant for a person to be identified as a prostitute or customer; c) how does the process of identification and control affect the individual prostitute and customer - and society?

The definitional processes in prostitution control can also be analyzed in terms of three distinctive features of the authorities' means of structuring their knowledge about various «deviants».[76] First, the process is characterized by simplification: persons, here prostitutes, who are subjected to the public measures are described in a summary and arbitrary fashion in the records and files. Registration is initially based on a few personal traits, patterns of behaviour, and social circumstances assumed to be significant for the «deviancy» (prostitution) while other pieces of information are excluded. Second, the definitional process is marked by negative expectations. Suspicion of prostitution colours the authority's entire perception of the arrestee; her social background, her life style and human relationships are all viewed with scepticism. Since she (probably) is a prostitute, she is also assumed to be morally inferior in other regards. Third, the definitional process automatically functions as characterization and categorization: the authorities form their overall moral judgement of the arrestees on the basis of comparisons. The arrestee may be categorized as a «newcomer» or as «hardened, practiced» in comparison with others, and she may be depicted as «weak and led astray» or «tough and determined» and is treated accordingly. However, the authority's vested interest in defining the suspect's conduct as prostitution, in simplifying and categorizing, is countered by the suspect's own interest in normalizing her behaviour or at least identifying mitigating circumstances for it. A focal counterweight to the authority's definitional process then becomes what has been called the «defence of meaning»:[77] to analyze the explanations and descriptions the «deviant», the prostitute, herself offers.

The stance taken by society to sexual «deviants» can further be investigated by using the concepts of bifurcation and ghettoization.[78] Controllers of prostitution often classify prostitutes by a simple dichotomy: women who prostitute themselves publicly and women who conduct their business privately (bifurcation). Of these two groups, the former is often viewed as the more pathological and deviant - and thus a given object for social intervention - whereas the latter group is considered to be beyond the authorities' jurisdiction. The discreet, private core of prostitution is thus surrounded by a ring of control measures, aimed at isolating certain forms of commercialized sex (ghettoization) and confirming the distinction between private and public.

The Significance of Classification

A third important theme in social interactionist/constructionist analyses is the classification system used in the prostitution discourse. The definitional processes vary according to prostitution type and milieu; some forms of commercialized sex are deemed more offensive than others - and thereby more susceptible to control.[79]

One prominent dimension used in the classification of prostitution is the *publicness* of the transactions. The concept of «public» can be interpreted here in at least two ways. Public (registered) prostitution may consist of sexual transactions which are in one way or another placed under state control. For example, public prostitution may be legalized or subject to regulation (state-regulated brothels or prostitutes otherwise registered with the police or health authorities). The opposite of these publicly registered activities then is «clandestine» (or «private») prostitution. The existence of clandestine prostitution may be the consequence of control priorities: authorities may desist from intervening in those forms of prostitution that are regarded as less disturbing or professional.[80]

On the other hand, the «publicness» of prostitution may simply refer to the degree of visibility of various forms of commercialized sex (whether they are legalized, criminalized, or decriminalized). The most frequent categories of prostitution - call-girl activities, hotel and restaurant prostitution, brothel and massage-parlour prostitution, ship prostitution, and street prostitution - vary considerably on the issue of publicness/visibility.[81] A relatively visible form of commercialized sex is street prostitution and a relatively invisible form is call-girl activities.[82] The degree of conspicuousness of these two forms may vary, though, according to the location and concentration of the activities; the methods used by the prostitutes and customers to come into contact with each other; and the prostitutes' (and pimps') life style in general - whether it deviates or not from that of their immediate surroundings.[83]

A central aspect regarding the publicness of prostitution is to whom prostitution is visible and to whom it is allowed to be exposed. The transactions may be invisible to everyone except those persons directly involved: the buyer and the seller. This is probably unusual, though. In the long run, prostitution requires a certain flow of information between prostitutes and customers/potential customers. Alternatively, the transactions may be invisible to everyone except a group of prostitutes, customers, procurers, and other persons who frequent these settings (hotel and restaurant staffs, neighbours etc.), while outsiders may remain unaware of the commercial nature of the contacts. A further possibility is that the activities are generally known in the community; some streets may be labelled as prostitution zones, and certain hotels and restaurants may be known as prostitutes' «hang outs».

Another important dimension in the classification of prostitution relations is their *exclusivity*. This concept largely summarizes the criteria of promiscuity, non-selectivity, and temporariness found in the definitions of prostitution. Exclusivity is linked to the degree of publicness/visibility of the transactions; an openly acknowledged, state-registered prostitution draws more customers than a discreet one.

In classifications of prostitution, the concept of exclusivity has been combined with other variables, for example, that of dependence/independence.[84] By combining these two dimensions, four types of prostitutes are identified: 1) non-exclusive independent; 2) exclusive independent; 3) non-exclusive organized; and 4) exclusive organized prostitutes.

Examples of the first type are unorganized prostitutes who operate on the street and in cheap hotels and bars - the stereotypical «whores». Characteristic of these women is the explicitness of their prostitution. The sexual contacts are uncamouflaged and without pretext, and it is clear to everyone that the women are working as prostitutes. Their clients are often numerous, the payment is made directly and in the form of money, and the contacts are short-lived and anonymous. Examples of the second type of commercialized sex are call-girls, often thought to represent the elite of present-day prostitution. Call-girls supposedly receive fewer clients, the contacts may be long-term and personal, and payment may be indirect and in the form of gifts, paid restaurant and rental bills, and so on. A crucial difference between prostitutes in this and the previous category is that street prostitutes operate on the principle of quantity - the more numerous the customers, the higher the income - whereas call-girls operate on the principle of continuity - the more customers who return, the better.[85] An example of the third type of prostitution in the typology is transactions at medium and low-status brothels and massage-parlours, where the prostitutes work for a «madam» or an organization, and where the operations are oriented towards a large volume of customers. In contrast to street prostitution, emphasis is also placed on establishing a regular clientele; therefore, the contacts are not as anonymous as they can be on the street.[86] Examples of the fourth and last type of prostitution are exclusive high-status brothels and bureaus from which call-girl activities are organized. The clientele is more exclusive than in the third type of prostitution, and the customer relations may be long-term and personal.[87]

A third dimension in the classification of prostitution is *social status*. This variable has been used to describe a) the socio-economic status of the customers;[88] b) the social background and living conditions of the prostitutes; and, linked to the above two, c) the price of the transaction. The economy of prostitution is dependent on two factors: the number of sexual transactions and the cost per transaction, and of these two factors, it is the latter which has more significance for the social status attached to the prostitute.[89] Thus, social status is directly linked to the dimension of publicness. The more private the sex trade, and the fewer with access to it, the more expensive it becomes. Customers of high-status prostitution do not only pay for sexual services; they also pay for discretion and for exclusivity.

In the literature on prostitution, the highest social status is often granted to call-girls, and the lowest to street prostitutes; in-between fall massage-parlour, hotel, restaurant, and ship prostitutes. Several studies show that the prostitutes themselves are very class-conscious: call-girls attach higher status to themselves than to street prostitutes;[90] prostitutes at massage-clinics assign higher status to themselves than to street prostitutes and in some cases than to call-girls.[91] On the basis of self-perceived class differences among American prostitutes, the following ranking order was developed,[92] from highest to lowest status: a) kept women; b) call-girls; c) brothel prostitutes; d) massage-clinic prostitutes; e) street prostitutes; and f) bar prostitutes. Many studies however, report great differences in social status within certain types of prostitution; among masseuses,[93] hotel prostitutes,[94] brothel prostitutes,[95] and street prostitutes.[96] The ranking order of types, therefore, cannot be seen as absolute, but only as indicating that some types of prostitution, as a result of their relative discretion, exclusivity, and similarity to marital alliances, tend to have higher social status than others.

The Prostitution Career

A fourth characteristic of the social interactionist research on prostitution is that the prostitute's (but seldom the customer's) participation in

commercialized sex is analyzed as a social career, divided into three
classic stages of roles:[97] the beginner; the occasional prostitute; and the
regular prostitute.[98]

The *beginner stage* covers the recruitment into prostitution in the
form of the women's first paid sexual encounters. Many career studies
of prostitution reveal that the recruitment phase entails a fluid transition
from non-prostitution into prostitution. The recruits have familiarized
themselves with the prostitution settings long before they engage in
their first genuinely paid-for contacts.[99] Sometimes they have long previously been labelled as promiscuous or as prostitutes.[100] They may
have skirted around on the periphery of prostitution via other functions,
such as strippers, dancers, or masseuses.[101]

The second stage - that of *occasional prostitution* - is often described as an apprenticeship period when the women fluctuate between
commercial sex and a more conventional life style. They learn how to
deal with customers, other prostitutes, and possibly procurers (pimps),
and they become adapted to their specific arena of prostitution - the
street, brothel, massage-clinic, bar, or hotel. Typical for this phase is
that the women do not perceive of themselves as «professionals»; they
view prostitution as a sport or a hobby, but not as work.[102] They claim
to be dabbling in prostitution for a while, until they have solved their
financial problems, until they find work, or until they get a place to
live. In this phase, the prostitutes often feel in control of their situation,
and confident that they could stop whenever they choose to. The contacts with customers are few and sporadic; the women receive men
when they have time and inclination - but the activities become more
extensive with time.[103]

The third stage - *regular prostitution* - is the phase when the sexual
transactions take on the systematic nature of a profession. By now, the
prostitutes are familiar with the rules of the game, the division of labour, and the competition pervading the milieu. Whereas prior to this
stage, prostitution had to yield to the women's other activities and
interests, the opposite is now true - prostitution has become the factor
that structures their everyday life. Typically, the women's self-image
has changed too, with most tending to define themselves as prostitutes
during this phase of their career, and to define their counterparts in the
sexual transactions as customers.[104] Thus, from having played a more
or less marginal role for the woman's identity, commercialized sex
constitutes the underpinnings of her identity and life style.[105]

The professional phase in the prostitution career can be analyzed
using four central themes in classic interactionist theories:[106] 1) prostitution as social relations, 2) prostitution as identity, 3) prostitution as
occupational ideology, and 4) prostitution as subculture. These themes

summarize the processes whereby the recruits are integrated into the social arenas of commercialized sex. The principal point of departure is that professions tend to standardize the behaviour and opinions of its members. A form of «esprit de corps» develops which legitimizes the common life style and supports the participants in their «deviant» careers. The beginners are socialized into the subcultures of prostitution, that is, into relatively distinct and structured systems of social roles and norms. The profession as organization is described as a system based on unity and reciprocity, where the parties help and support one another.

Social Relations in Prostitution

The professional stage in the prostitution career can be described on the basis of the social relations encompassed. The beginner learns how to relate to the other participants in the milieu, of which the most important are: the customers; pimps and other procurers; and, other prostitutes.

With regard to the first type of relationship - that between *prostitute and customer* - the socialization process primarily involves the prostitute learning a rational, economic approach for her enterprise, aimed at maximizing profits and minimizing efforts.

The maximization of profits requires learning to negotiate with customers, a skill that has been called «the art of talking the game».[107] When necessary, this implies playing an active sexual role: to approach potential customers, to discuss available services with them, and to control the course of events during the sexual encounter. According to some studies,[108] this «sexual aggressiveness» can be a problem for novices in prostitution, as it entails a breach of the traditional gender-role expectations. Many newcomers have little or no experience of taking the initiative in sexual relations. At the same time, the prostitutes must be able to come across as passive and humble, depending upon the customer's wants and needs. Thus, the deviation from the female gender role is illusory, with the transgressions tailor-made to the customer's expectations and desires; her behaviour must not threaten his standing.[109]

In professional prostitution, profit maximization is combined with a minimization of the seller's input. According to the literature, the involvement is minimized on several levels: time-wise, activity-wise, and experience-wise. A professional prostitute devotes as little time as possible to a sexual transaction. The more quickly she moves on to a new customer, or to another paid transaction with the same customer, the better. As documented in many studies, professional prostitutes try to invest a minimum of themselves, their feelings, and their thoughts in the interaction with customers. This minimization of personal efforts is not only economically motivated, it is also, and perhaps primarily, a vital defence mechanism. By sealing off the sexual transactions from one's personal sphere, the women protect themselves against the deleterious effects of commercialized sex. In fact, in the literature, this emotional defence is the best described of all aspects of professional prostitution.[110]

Some research depicts a clear-cut maximization of gains and minimization of involvement in the relationships between prostitutes and customers.[111] Other works show that the character of the liaisons varies by type of prostitution and by period of time.[112] The goal of minimizing personal efforts is complicated by the fact that certain types of prostitution entail continuity in customer relations. Call-girls, brothel prostitutes, and women in massage-clinics are expected to invest more time and personal involvement in the encounter if they want the customers to return. In these forms of prostitution, the gain maximization is constructed differently and less conspicuously than in forms built on temporary relationships with customers.

The relationship between the *prostitute and various types of procurers* is another category of social relations dealt with in the research literature. Of all the conceivable procurers (advertisers, landlords, proprietors and staff of hotels, restaurants, massage-clinics, and brothels), most attention is addressed to traditional pimps, men living off the incomes of one or more prostitutes. Pimps are found in most of the prostitution milieus described, such as among street prostitutes,[113] hotel prostitutes,[114] brothel prostitutes,[115] and call-girls.[116]

The link between the pimp and the prostitute has often been depicted as the most inexplicable and repulsive element of commercialized sex. To start out, the relationship seems to be based on unilateral exploitation, with one party, the woman, performing hard and demeaning labour, and thereafter surrendering most of her earnings to the other party, the pimp. What she receives in exchange is more diffuse and vague - security, belonging, and perhaps a better social standing in the prostitution world. Seen from the outside, her contribution and her involvement appear to be disproportionately great compared to his. Next, the relationship pimp-prostitute has elements of reversed roles. Here it is the woman who is gainfully employed and who brings income to the couple, while the man allows himself to be supported. Thus, the pimp is looked upon as a work-resistant «parasite», unwilling to live up to his role as breadwinner. Furthermore, the pimp relationships described in the research are sometimes polygamous: the pimp has simultaneous sexual relations with several prostitutes, and furthermore, the role of pimp is often associated with violence and criminality.[117] The social understanding of the pimp system is also imbued with a diffuse and possibly irrational antipathy. The pimp is seen as a mystical representative for an underworld of sin and unbridled sexuality. He obviously has free access to sexual services that customers have to pay for, and even worse, he can obtain delicate information about their identity and sexual desires.[118]

Pimp-prostitute alliances can be analyzed by means of the variables used to define the concept of prostitution: a) commerciality; b) promiscuity; c) non-selectivity; d) temporariness; and e) emotional indifference. Relationships with pimps vary, ranging from clearly commerical alliances - where the pimp functions as the prostitute's economic guardian, administering most of her earnings and supplying her with «pocket money» - to relationships where the parties on a more equal basis share home, household, and finances. They also vary on the issue of selectivity, duration, and promiscuity, ranging from connections where a «stable-pimp» has several women working for him, concurrently or successively, to alliances where a «live-in pimp» lives in a long-standing couple relation with one prostitute. Finally, the pimp relationships vary on the issue of emotionality, ranging from distant business-like contracts to liaisons based on mutual love, friendship, and respect. The social definition of the pimp system tends to follow the same pattern as the definition of customer relationships. The more pronounced the commerciality, the greater the promiscuity; and the weaker the emotionality, the more professional the pimp-prostitute alliance appears to be. The more it resembles a marriage, the more unique, long-term, and emotional it seems to be, the greater the probability that we would use another epithet than pimp relationship to describe it.

However, the definitions regarding professionalism are complicated by the fact that the liaisons are seldom one-dimensional from the perspective of the involved parties. From the prostitute's point of view, the traditional depiction of the pimp is an oversimplified stereotype that poorly reflects her reality. Where outsiders see a unilaterally exploitative relationship, she sees a unique and interdependent alliance. It is only natural that her pimp benefits from her labours, since they share a home and finances, or alternatively, since they are part of the same pimp-system, a family. In both cases, the prostitute shares more than financial matters with her pimp; he is an integral part of her social network, and perhaps of her security system.[119]

A decisive assumption, though, is that pimps play a crucial role in the professionalization of prostitution. Pimps with many prostitutes in particular may enhance the visibility of the prostitution milieus, and facilitate the recruitment of new prostitutes. They may also help detain women in commercialized sex. A woman who is emotionally dependent on her pimp may find it hard to turn her back on prostitution if this is her primary link with him. A prostitute with an economically dependent partner may also be compelled to expand and increase the profitability of her enterprise. Pimps obviously contribute to the creation of subcultures of prostitution, that is social systems with their own professional «ideology of prostitution».[120]

The third type of social relations within commercialized sex - those between *beginners and other prostitutes* - are also important for the process of professionalization. Friendships and acquaintances with other prostitutes play a central role for a woman's debut into commercialized sex; after pimps, other prostitutes are the most important port of entry. Typically, beginners associate with other prostitutes long before they make their definitive debut. This has been shown to apply to street prostitutes,[121] brothel prostitutes,[122] masseuses,[123] hotel prostitutes,[124] as well as call-girls.[125] The novices may start with a period of apprenticeship, during which the more experienced prostitutes supervise their transactions and assist them in establishing a clientele.[126]

The longer a woman works as a prostitute, the closer her connections to other prostitutes, regardless of how she was recruited. The level of contacts among the prostitutes, though, varies by prostitution milieu.[127] In certain forms (at brothels and massage-clinics, in street settings), prostitutes work side by side on a daily basis, whereas in others, for example among call-girls, the contacts are more sporadic. But this does not mean that the social networks among call-girls are unimportant for the structuring of their activities; typically, they refer customers to each other.[128]

In research reports, the links between prostitutes are frequently described in decidedly negative overtones. Many studies focus on competition and hostility among prostitutes,[129] and cite warm and functional friendships as the exception.[130] Assumingly, one factor leading to competition among prostitutes is the pimp system. Strong bonds of loyalty and cooperation among the prostitutes may not be in the interests of pimps (especially those working with many prostitutes) and other procurers. On the contrary, prostitutes are often forced to compete for the favour of a pimp. A prostitute's ambition to retain her position as «first lady» in the pimp-family is one of the system's most important components.[131] Differences in social status within the world of prostitution are also probably significant for the degree of competitiveness among prostitutes. A sense of professional community between, say, call-girls of high social status and street prostitutes, or between call-girls of different income classes, are improbable. The quality of the networks between prostitutes may also vary with the type of customer

relations (their commerciality, selectivity, and duration
indicate that the primary social reference group for f
their colleagues, or even their pimps, but rather their custo...
especially true of prostitution which is based on long-term liaisons w...
customers.[132] Naturally, supply and demand may also influence the degree of competition/collegiality among prostitutes. If the supply of sexual services exceeds the demand in a particular setting, any spirit of
cooperation among prostitutes may be hard-pressed.

Prostitution and Identity

The professionalization of prostitution can also be analyzed in terms of
identity, that is, the degree to which the involved women perceive
themselves as prostitutes. Having one or more paid sexual contacts is
not necessarily equivalent with defining oneself as a prostitute. Some
women with few such contacts may be labelled as prostitutes, by themselves or by others, while other women may receive customers for
years and still refuse to adopt an identity as prostitutes.[133]

The process of designation varies according to type of prostitution,
and according to the criteria for prostitution discussed above. The women's self-image in commercialized sex is influenced by the traditional
social definitions of prostitution. The more their customer contacts
resemble these definitions, the more likely they will define themselves
as prostitutes.

A common assumption in the research literature is that the woman's
identity as prostitute becomes stronger the closer her contacts are with
the other actors in the milieu.[134] However, her association with pimps
and other prostitutes could instead reinforce her shield against one-
dimensional labelling. Within the milieu, an alternative identity may
develop as a buffer against the disrepute. A collective defence against a
prostitution identity has, for example, been found among women who
prostitute themselves at massage clinics. These women may define
themselves as physiotherapists, entertainers, or even «hand whores»,[135]
but they do not regard themselves as prostitutes, despite the fact that
they offer sexual services for pay. A collective defence against the label
of prostitution has also been found among call-girls who may define
themselves as providing companionship, as therapists, or as private
entrepreneurs, but who unanimously dissociate themselves from the
traditional picture of «the whore».[136]

The identity as prostitute also varies with the woman's social relationships outside prostitution. Professional prostitutes are often described as isolated individuals: the longer their participation in the milieu,
the fewer their contacts and social roles outside of prostitution.[137] Wo-

men who succeed in preserving their social links to parents, siblings, children, relatives, and friends outside of the world of prostitution can use the socially acceptable roles as daughter, sister, mother, relative, and friend to counterbalance any process of labelling. On the other hand, women with severed external bonds are relegated to the other actors within prostitution: they are the customers' «whores», hostesses, masseuses, or therapists; they are the pimps' partners; and they are the other prostitutes' colleagues. To all or most of their friends and acquaintances, they are prostitutes, or at least masseuses or call-girls.

A woman who retains a job outside the milieu, be it conventional gainful employment, studies, or housework, is better able to fend off an identity as prostitute than is a woman without such responsibilities. This is also true for women who combine prostitution with semi-legitimate occupations such as naked modelling, striptease dancing,[138] or paid dance partner.[139] With alternative occupational roles, they can hold their own in the face of labelling, and dismiss prostitution as a mere hobby or as an extra source of income.

Finally, identifying oneself as a prostitute is linked to the labelling process itself. According to classic interactionist theories, social labelling is one of the most fundamental elements of the emergence of a deviant identity.[140] Women defined as prostitutes by those around them or by the authorities often face a momentous and disastrous process of stigmatization. The classification of women into «private, decent» women, on the one hand, and «public, depraved» women, on the other, is one of the most effective devices that is used against women in male-dominated societies. The role of prostitute is thus a deviant role similar to that of «master status» as used in social interactionist theory.[141] A woman perceived as selling sexual services is first and foremost «a fallen woman», «a whore», since this designation tends to overshadow any other social role. Furthermore, once a woman is labelled a prostitute, it is very difficult for her to shed the designation.[142]

The connection between label and identity has been analyzed by use of a model with four labelling categories: «complete labelling», «imagined labelling», «naive optimism» and «neutralized deviance».[143] Applied to prostitution, these categories connote the following. The first type refers to a situation when the definitional process influences both the social and the subjective identity: a woman has been defined as prostitute by her surroundings as well as by herself. In the second type of labelling, a woman designates herself as prostitute and assumes that her role as prostitute has had or will have social consequences. For example, she may refrain from seeking conventional jobs or friendships, since she anticipates obstacles derived from her role as prostitute. «Naive optimism» indicates a woman who has been labelled as prostitute but who denies the role herself (cf. the discussion on alternative roles above). The final category reflects the situation where no subjective or objective labelling has occurred despite the fact that a woman has participated in commercialized sex (ibid).

Occupational Ideology in Prostitution

The third core theme in social interactionist analyses of commercialized sex is «the ideology of prostitution». According to many researchers, professional prostitutes develop an occupational ideology, a way of reasoning that explains and legitimates commercial sex.[144]

In a study of the professional ideology among American call-girls, James Bryan (1966, pp. 443-444) quotes the following justifications offered by the women. One basic argument was that prostitution fills many important social functions in the society. Commercial sex was said to protect society and its institutions from the destructive male sex drive. The call-girls allegedly performed a vital psychotherapeutic function by providing companionship and sexual satisfaction to embarrassed and lonely men, who otherwise would live in complete isolation. Another argument was that prostitution is not morally different from other heterosexual liaisons. The call-girls maintained that all women manipulate men sexually, and therefore, prostitution should not be condemned - it is only a more honest form of manipulation. Housewives and other women who are economically dependent upon men also participate in commercial sex, according to these call-girls. «There are just different ways of being a whore», but unfairly society's control and contempt is saved for particular forms of prostitution.[145]

Albert Velarde (1975, pp. 261-262) analyzed the professional ideology among masseuses in the United States. Applying Sykes and Matza's neutralization theory (1957), he described three defence strategies used by prostitutes. First, the masseuses claimed that they did not hurt anyone; customers came to them voluntarily and their surroundings were not disturbed («denial of any real injury»). Second, the masseuses reciprocated society's scorn and condemnation by aiming sharp criticism towards their surroundings and the control of prostitution («condemnation of the condemners»). Third, the women redefined the social role of massage and asserted that the control of prostitution was based on erroneous premises («an appeal to higher authority»). As a counterweight to the surrounding's negative image of massage clinics, they depicted massage in a favourable light as constituting an important societal service.[146]

Finally, Tanice C. Foltz (1980) identified the following defence arguments among American prostitutes. The women argued that prostitution provides a sexual service with no strings attached: the prostitutes place no social/emotional demands on the customers. Thus, commercial sex poses no threat to the customers' marriages or other steady relationships; on the contrary, it may strengthen family bonds. Another argument was that prostitution satisfies the sexual desires of the customers, regardless of how «perverse» they may be, thus possibly thwarting sexual assaults on other - inexperienced and perhaps defenceless - women. Furthermore, the women viewed themselves not only as prostitutes, but also as sex therapists who deal with the customers' personal problems. A final argument was that society's stance with regard to prostitution is false and hypocritical. Here the prostitutes accused the male condemners of commercial sex as often being customers themselves. They also criticized other women who were unwilling to use their bodies, «women's most real source of power and control», to attain economic advantages.

To summarize, these statements simply stress the positive social functions of commercial sex (the women see themselves as satisfiers of sexual, social, and psychotherapeutic needs and not as prostitutes); they minimize its deviant properties (prostitution allegedly follows patterns similar to those of other heterosexual relations); and they cast doubt on control measures which target commercial sex (since prostitution is useful, it should not be eliminated). The valid question here is to what extent these statements can actually be said to constitute «a deviant ideology», that is a system of values in conflict with the prevailing values in mainstream society. In all essential respects, the defence ideology adopted by prostitutes resembles the traditional, functionalist and patriarchal view of prostitution as described earlier.

Prostitution as Subculture

In the research literature, prostitution milieus have often been described as subcultures.[147] The inspiration for these analyses has often come from a very masculine-oriented research tradition within sociology. Studies on subcultures almost exclusively deal with men, typically young working-class men.[148] The subcultures often seem to function as collective rites of passage, as manifestations of male identity and modes of behaviour. Girls are not necessarily barred from these settings, but they typically play a marginal role. So far, we have scarce information about all-women or women-dominated subcultures. Compared to the vivid descriptions of male youth cultures - with protest, excitement, macho, and violence as crucial ingredients - Angela McRobbie and Jenny Garber's (1976, p. 213) description of young girls' «bedroom culture» - with its «experimenting with make-up, listening to records,

reading weekly magazines, talking about their boyfriends, chatting...»
seems quite tame, an existence adapted to the requirements of the female gender role.

A typical feature of the subcultural studies on prostitution is that the
milieus are described as extremely male-dominated. The systems of
commercialized sex are not structured by the prostitutes but rather by
pimps and other male participants. The values and activities of these
men constitute the core of the systems, with the prostitutes playing subordinate roles.

Some prostitution researchers distinguish between varying degrees
of subcultural involvement among prostitutes. In a study of U.S. street
prostitutes, Norman Jackson and others (1967, pp. 139-143) identified
two groups: those belonging to «a criminal contraculture» and those
belonging to «dual worlds». The former group consisted of prostitutes
who strongly identified with pimps and other criminals. They adopted
norms and values that deviated from those of the surrounding society;
the professional defence strategies of prostitution also made the greatest headway in this category. The prostitutes in the second group disso-
ciated themselves from the subculture and placed their social frame of
reference elsewhere. Many of them lived conventional lives with husbands and children, and their life style was often very middle-class oriented. According to Jackman and others, the women's existence was
dichotomized so that prostitution was merely seen as a source of income in which they invested as little of themselves as possible.

In another study of American street prostitutes, Nanette Davis
(1971, pp. 318-319) identified three types of life styles: a hustler subculture, a dual-worlds culture, and a criminal subculture. The norms
and values of the women in the first category were dominated by pimps
and other participants in the milieu. Their life style was completely
structured by prostitution (a displaced daily rhythm, irregular living
patterns, an extensive abuse of alcohol and drugs) and by «hedonism
and a strong present-time orientation». Women in the second category
combined prostitution with family life, studies, and conventional jobs.
According to Davis, they had internalized the prostitution culture as
well as the American middle-class culture. Finally, women in the third
category primarily identified with a criminal subculture. They had often
been convicted of various crimes - drug offences, thefts, shoplifting -
and their main social group consisted of other criminals. It was primarily in this group, that «contranorms» could be found, that is, values that
explicitly flouted other societal interests.

These studies reveal that the women's involvement in the prostitution milieus is determined by two central factors. The first is their relationships to men (and to some degree, other prostitutes) within prostitu-

tion; active socializing with pimps and other men bind these women to the subculture. The other determinant is their ties to men outside prostitution; women living with partners (that is, men who are not pimps) and children tend to dichotomize their life situation and occupy a marginal position in the prostitution milieu. Thus, the studies clearly confirm the thesis that prostitution milieus are male subcultures where the prostitutes play secondary roles, which are perfectly suited to the interests of the pimps - as well as of the customers.

A question left to be answered is whether those prostitution milieus exist that can be characterized as female subcultures, centered around the friendship relations among prostitutes, and their norms and values. Is it possible to identify prostitution settings that are women-defined and women-dominated, or are they all, by definition, structured by, and in the interest of, men?

Notes

1   See, for example, Pearson 1972; Perry 1978; Finnegan 1979; Melby 1980, Schiøtz 1980; Walkowitz 1980; Bristow 1982; Rosen 1982; Otis 1985; Schaepdrijver 1986; Corbin 1987; Karras 1989.
2   Roby 1969; Geis 1972; Rosenbleet & Pariente 1973; Jennings 1976; Boles & Tatro 1978; Boyer & James 1979; Rowe 1979; Gibson 1980; McLeod 1980, 1983; Matthews 1986; Messerschmidt 1987.
3   Stein 1974; Heyl 1979; Prus & Irini 1980; Larsson 1983; Månsson & Linders 1984; Høigård & Finstad 1986; Miller 1986.
4   For example, Kemp 1936; Davis 1937; Kinsey 1948; Benjamin & Ellis 1954; Borelli & Starck 1957; Ellis 1959; The Wolfenden Report 1964.
5   Benjamin 1961; Benjamin & Masters 1964; Clinard 1968; Esselstyn 1968; Gagnon 1968; Goode 1978.
6   Borelli & Starck 1957; Benjamin 1961; Henriques 1963; Bullough & Bullough 1964; Brundage 1976, 1987; Ericsson 1980.
7   Davis 1937; Benjamin 1961; Clinard 1968.
8   Kinsey et al. 1948; Ellis 1959; Winick 1962; Benjamin & Masters 1964; Kleinman 1973; Stein 1974.
9   Benjamin 1961; Gibbens 1963; Bullough & Bullough 1964; Esselstyn 1968; Clinard 1968; Gagnon 1977.
10   Kirkendall 1960.
11   Gibbens & Silberman 1960; Benjamin 1961; Gibbens 1963; Esselstyn 1968; Velarde & Warlick 1973; Gagnon 1977.
12   Kemp 1936; Benjamin 1961; George 1965; Gagnon 1968; Martinussen 1969; Takman 1970.
13   Gibbens 1957, 1971; Choisy 1961; Hollender 1961; Maerow 1965.
14   Benjamin 1961; Greenwald 1970.
15   Kemp 1936; Takman 1968; Martinussen 1969; Greenwald 1970; Reckless 1973.
16   See, for example, Benjamin 1961, Esselstyn 1968.
17   Esselstyn 1968; Reckless 1973; Ericsson 1980.
18   Benjamin 1961; Benjamin & Masters 1964.
19   See, for example, Benjamin 1961; Trudgill 1976.

20   For example, The Wolfenden Report 1964; Clinard 1968; Reiman 1979.
21   Davis 1971; Rosenblum 1975; Jennings 1976; Millet 1976; Finnegan 1979; Gibson 1980; McLeod 1980, 1982; Barry 1981, 1984; James & Davis 1982; Pateman 1983, 1988; Dominelli 1986; Shrage 1989.
22   Lubove 1962; Riegel 1968; Pearsall 1972; Pearson 1972; Evans 1976; Trudgill 1976; McHugh 1980; Melby 1980, Walkowitz 1980; Musheno & Seeley 1987.
23   Melby 1980; Schiøtz 1980; Borg et al. 1981; Månsson 1981; Finstad et al. 1981, 1982; Finstad & Olsson 1983; Larsson 1983; Høigård & Finstad 1986; Varsa 1986; Prieur & Taksdal 1989.
24   Borg et al. 1981; Coward 1983; Finstad & Olsson 1983; Barry 1984; Dominelli 1986; Lerner 1986; Dworkin 1987; Musheno & Seeley 1987; Pateman 1988; MacKinnon 1989; Shrage 1989.
25   Dinnerstein 1976; Edwards 1981; Ortner & Whitehead 1981; Coveney et al. 1984; Jackson 1984, 1987; Snitow et al. 1984; Walkowitz 1984; Caplan 1987; Haug 1987; Kon 1987; Seidler 1987; Pateman 1988.
26   Rosenblum 1975; Borg et al. 1982; Finstad & Olsson 1983; Høigård & Finstad 1986; Dominelli 1986; McCombs 1986, Haug 1987; Karras 1989; MacKinnon 1989; Prieur & Taksdal 1989; Shrage 1989.
27   See, Rosenblum 1975; Laws 1979; Borg et al. 1981; Edwards 1981; Lerner 1986; Dworkin 1987; Haug 1987; MacKinnon 1987, 1989.
28   Davis 1971; Gray 1973; Perry 1978; Finnegan 1979; Walkowitz 1980; Rosen 1982; Bracey 1983; Larsson 1983; Butler 1985; Høigård & Finstad 1986; Schaepdrijver 1986.
29   For example, Gallo & Alzate 1976; Boyer & James 1979; McLeod 1982.
30   Walkowitz 1980; McLeod 1982; Rosen 1982.
31   Davis 1971; Gray 1973; Binderman et al. 1975; Boyer & James 1979; James & Davis 1982; Larsson 1983; Høigård & Finstad 1986.
32   James & Meyerding 1977; Vitaliano et al. 1981; Silbert & Pines 1983.
33   See, for example, Potterat et al. 1985.
34   For example, the Scandinavian studies by Fredriksson & Lind 1980; Borg et al. 1981; Månsson 1981; Finstad et al. 1981, 1982; Larsson 1983; Månsson & Linders 1984; Høigård & Finstad 1986.
35   Prieur & Taksdal 1989.
36   Simpson & Schill 1977; Månsson & Linders 1984; Høigård & Finstad 1986; Månsson 1988; Prieur & Taksdal 1989.
37   Stein 1974; Simpson & Schill 1977; Månsson & Linders 1984; Månsson 1988; Prieur & Taksdal 1989.
38   Månsson & Linders 1984; Prieur & Taksdal 1989.
39   Armstrong 1978; Borg et al. 1981; Larsson 1983; Månsson & Linders 1984; Olsson 1985; Høigård & Finstad 1986; Månsson 1988; Prieur & Taksdal 1989.
40   See, for example, Roby 1969; Rosenbleet & Pariente 1973; Women Endorsing Decriminalization 1973; Jennings 1976; MacMillan 1976; Boles & Tatro 1978; Gibson 1980; McLeod 1980, 1982, 1983; Eisenbach-Stangl 1983; Stallberg 1983; Barry 1984; Reynolds 1986; Musheno & Seeley 1987.
41   Gibson 1980; Greenwood & Young 1980; McLeod 1980, 1982; Edwards 1981; Dominelli 1986; Reynolds 1986; Shrage 1989.
42   Rosenbleet & Pariente 1973; MacMillan 1976; Borg et al. 1981; Høigård & Finstad 1986.

43   Rolph 1955; Lubove 1962; Riegel 1968; Geis 1972; Holmes 1972; Pearsall 1972; Pearson 1972; Anderson 1974; Brundage 1976, 1987; Evans 1976; Trudgill 1976; Walkowitz 1977, 1980; Perry 1978; Stopp 1978; Connelly 1980; Shumsky & Springer 1981; Symanski 1981; Weeks 1981; Carmichael 1982; Butler 1985; Matthews 1986; Rossiaud 1986, 1988; Schaepdrijver 1986; Corbin 1987; Mackey 1987; Karras 1989.

44   For example, Jennings 1976.

45   Roby 1969; Rosenbleet & Pariente 1973; Harrison 1975; Høigård & Finstad 1986; Prieur & Taksdal 1989.

46   For a more detailed discussion of these arguments, see Jennings 1976; cf. also Boles & Tatro 1978; Gibson 1980; McLeod 1980, 1982, 1983; Bracey 1983; Høigård & Finstad 1986.

47   Gornick 1971; Rosenblum 1975; Chesney-Lind 1977; MacKinnon 1989.

48   Armstrong 1977; Chesney-Lind 1977, 1979, 1989; Datesman & Scarpitti 1977; Feinman 1979; Bracey 1983; Gelsthorpe 1986; Campbell 1987; Messerschmidt 1987; Hudson 1988.

49   Dominelli 1986; Chesney-Lind 1989; Shrage 1989.

50   Gray 1973; Bryant & Palmer 1975; Velarde 1975; James 1977; Miller 1978; Foltz 1980; Prus & Irini 1980; Vitaliano et al. 1981; Potterat et al. 1985; Salomon 1989.

51   Such as Lemert 1951, 1972; Sykes & Matza 1957; Kitsuse 1968; Matza 1969; Schur 1971, 1979, 1983; Becker 1973, 1974.

52   See, for example, Davis 1971; Rosenblum 1975; Boyer & James 1979; James & Davis 1982.

53   Rosenblum 1975; Miller 1978; Peiss 1984; Messerschmidt 1987.

54   Jennings 1976; Gibson 1980; McLeod 1980, 1982.

55   Bryan 1966; Cavan 1970; Gray 1973; Stein 1974; Bryant & Palmer 1975; Prus & Irini 1980.

56   Davis 1971; Velarde 1975; James 1977; Miller 1978; Boyer & James 1979; Vitaliano et al. 1981.

57   Hawkins & Tiedeman 1975; Schur 1983.

58   Borelli & Starck 1957; Benjamin 1961; Henriques 1963; Benjamin & Masters 1964; Bullough & Bullough 1964; Esselstyn 1968; Winick & Kinsie 1971; Gagnon 1977; MacNamara & Sagarin 1977; Goode 1978.

59   Benjamin 1961; Hirschi 1962; Bullough & Bullough 1964; Clinard 1968.

60   Esselstyn 1968; Goode 1978.

61   Borelli & Starck 1957; Hirschi 1962; MacNamara & Sagarin 1977.

62   Cowan 1956; Borelli & Starck 1957; Benjamin 1961; Hirschi 1962; Clinard 1968; Bryant 1977.

63   Benjamin & Masters 1964; Clinard 1968; Takman 1968; Gagnon 1977.

64   See, for example, Benjamin 1961; Clinard 1968.

65   Davis 1971; Velarde 1975; Vitaliano et al. 1981.

66   Bryan 1966; Stein 1974; Exner et al. 1977; Janus et al. 1978.

67   Bryan 1965, 1966; Heyl 1977, 1979; Merry 1980.

68   Benjamin 1961; Hirschi 1962.

69   Stewart 1972; Gray 1973; Sheehy 1973; Millet 1976; Arnold 1977; Merry 1980; Silbert & Pines 1981.

70   Bryan 1965, 1966; Stein 1974; Gallo & Alzate 1976; Nelson 1987; Savitz & Rosen 1988.

71   Lemert 1972.

72   Rosenblum 1975.

73 Davis 1971; Velarde 1975; Boyer & James 1979; Vitaliano et al. 1981.
74 Plummer 1975.
75 Cohen 1980.
76 Hawkins 1981.
77 Cohen 1982.
78 Greenwood & Young 1980.
79 MacNamara & Sagarin 1977; Rasmussen & Kuhn 1977; Stopp 1978; Prus & Irini 1980; McLeod 1982; Bracey 1983; Miller 1986; Romenesko & Miller 1989; Salomon 1989.
80 Jennings 1976; Rasmussen & Kuhn 1977; Gibson 1980; Barry 1984.
81 Cavan 1970; Stein 1974; Velarde 1975; Bryant & Palmer 1975.
82 Roby 1969; Jennings 1976; Merry 1980.
83 Stein 1974; Merry 1980.
84 Miller 1978.
85 Miller 1978; see also Bryan 1965, 1966; Greenwald 1970; Stein 1974.
86 See also Exner et al. 1977; Rasmussen & Kuhn 1977; Heyl 1977, 1979.
87 Miller 1978.
88 Greenwald 1970; Stein 1974; Janus et al. 1978.
89 Stein 1974; Foltz 1980; Miller 1986.
90 Bryan 1966; Sheehy 1973.
91 Velarde 1975.
92 Janus et al. 1978.
93 Bryant & Palmer 1975.
94 Prus & Irini 1980.
95 Khalaf 1965; Gallo & Alzate 1976.
96 Exner et al. 1977.
97 Gray 1973; Rosenblum 1975; Heyl 1977, 1979; Prus & Irini 1980; Vitaliano et al. 1981; James & Davis 1982.
98 Becker 1973.
99 Bryan 1965; Gray 1973; Caplan 1984; Miller 1986.
100 Khalaf 1967; Shoham & Rahav 1968; Shoham 1970; Davis 1971; James & Meyerding 1977; Vitaliano et al. 1981.
101 Salutin 1971; Skipper & McCaghy 1971; Velarde 1975.
102 Davis 1971; Prus & Irini 1980.
103 Bryan 1965; Jackman et al. 1967; Bryant & Palmer 1975; Boyer & James 1979.
104 Hirschi 1962; McLeod 1982; Miller 1986.
105 Lemert 1972.
106 Sutherland 1937.
107 Samovar & Sanders 1978.
108 Bryan 1965; Heyl 1977.
109 Borg et al.
110 For example, Høigård & Finstad 1986.
111 Davis 1971; Coleman 1973; Gray 1973; Bryant & Palmer 1975; Millet 1976; Merry 1980; Larsson 1983; Månsson & Linders 1984; Høigård & Finstad 1986.
112 Bryan 1966; Roebuck & McNamara 1973; La Fontaine 1974; Stein 1974; Gallo & Alzate 1976; Janus et al. 1978; Karch & Dann 1981; McLeod 1982; White 1986; Savitz & Rosen 1988.
113 Cohen 1980; Merry 1980; McLeod 1982; Janus et al. 1984; Sereny 1984; Miller 1986; Romenesko & Miller 1989.
114 Prus & Irini 1980.

115   Heyl 1977, 1979.
116   Bryan 1965.
117   For descriptions of pimp-prostitute relationships which, to varying degrees, are thus characterized, see, for example Milner & Milner 1972; Coleman 1973; Hall 1974; Binderman et al. 1975; Merry 1980; Barry 1981, 1984; McLeod 1982; Girtler 1983; Caplan 1984; Miller 1986; Romenesko & Miller 1989.
118   See Young 1967.
119   For a description of the prostitute-pimp relationship from the prostitute's perspective, see, for example, Borg et al. 1981; McLeod 1982; Høigård 1985; Høigård & Finstad 1986; Miller 1986.
120   Milner & Milner 1972; Hall 1974; McLeod 1982; Miller 1986; Romenesko & Miller 1989.
121   Davis 1971; Gray 1973; Larsson 1983.
122   James 1973; Gallo & Alzate 1976.
123   Bryant & Palmer 1975.
124   Prus & Irini 1980.
125   Bryan 1966.
126   Bryan 1965, 1966; Heyl 1977, 1979.
127   Roebuck & McNamara 1973; Velarde 1975; Bryant & Palmer 1975; Heyl 1977, 1979.
128   Such as Greenwald 1970; Rosenblum 1975.
129   Gray 1973; Rasmussen & Kuhn 1977; Romenesko & Miller 1989.
130   Prus & Irini 1980; Saether 1988.
131   McLeod 1982; Miller 1986.
132   Such as Bryan 1966; Stein 1974.
133   Jackman et al. 1967; Davis 1971; Bryant & Palmer 1975; Velarde 1975.
134   Rosenblum 1975; Prus & Irini 1980.
135   Salutin 1971.
136   Hong & Duff 1976, 1977 on so-called taxi dancers.
137   Becker 1973; Plummer 1975; Schur 1983.
138   Cf. Becker's (1973) use of Hughes' (1945) concept of «master status» and «auxiliary» or «subordinate statuses».
139   Khalaf 1965; Roebuck & McNamara 1973; Arnold 1977; McLeod 1980.
140   Hawkins & Tiedeman 1975.
141   Bryan 1965, 1966; Velarde 1975; Miller 1978; Foltz 1980; cf. also Lemert 1951; Sykes & Matza 1957; Douglas 1977.
142   Bryan 1966.
143   Velarde 1975.
144   For a discussion of the concept of subculture, see, for example, Rubington & Weinberg 1973; Clarce et al. 1976.
145   See Hall & Jefferson 1976; Gill 1977; Willis 1978a, b; Corrigan 1979; Brake 1980, to give a few examples.
146   For example McRobbie & Garber 1976; Powell & Clarce 1976; Brake 1980.
147   Milner & Milner 1972; Gray 1973; Binderman et al. 1975; Janus et al. 1984.
148   Miller 1986; Romenesko & Miller 1989.

2.

Prostitution in Helsinki –
Issues and Data

2.1. The Nature of the Prostitution Control

This study deals with police-registered heterosexual prostitution in Helsinki over the years 1945-1986. During this period, prostitution was defined as a form of «vagrancy» and covered by the Vagrancy Act of 1936. The year 1945 was chosen as the starting point for the analysis, since the information on vagrancy for the years 1937-1944 is not directly comparable with that for the later decades. The new control policy did not properly take form prior to the Second World War. In addition, in light of all its special features and provisions, war-time prostitution would require a separate study. The archives of the vice police, the most fertile source of information in this study, stretch from 1945 to 1986, when the Vagrancy Act was abolished.

The theoretical background for the analysis is a combination of the social interactionist/constructionist perspective and the feminist perspective as described in Chpt. 1. A central issue is the relationship between prostitution (the alleged commercialized transactions per se) and prostitution control. It will be shown that the control measures have been based on a functionalist view of prostitution, whereby the foremost goal of the control policy has been to combat the «social harms» caused by prostitution. Various governmental inquiries, research reports, and articles have presented these disturbances in terms of health problems, social policy problems, public order problems, and youth problems. In contrast, prostitution has rarely been described as a problem in and of itself.

2.2. The Relativity of Prostitution

Another objective is to analyze the relativity of the prostitution concept, that is, to view commercialized sex as a social construction.

Throughout the period examined, prostitution was controlled on the basis of the 1936 Vagrancy Act. The criteria for prostitution were the same during all the relevant decades, but the targets of control shifted among milieus and modes of behaviour. The sexual relations, the living conditions and social problems of the women, and the confrontations between the authorities and the prostitutes vary considerably from setting to setting. The police-controlled prostitution in Helsinki is not a uniform and once and for all given category, consisting of a one-dimensional group of deviant and easily classified women.

The relativity of prostitution is analyzed by means of a detailed description of how prostitution was controlled in the different milieus, and of the interaction between the controllers and the controlled, the subject and object of control. The subject of control was a) the Helsinki vice police, who controlled prostitution under the provisions of the Vagrancy Act; b) the criminal police who investigated procuring, which was criminalized in the Penal Code 20:8; and c) the social authorities who, in conjunction with the vice police were responsible for controlling vagrancy (cf. later). The object of the control measures was primarily the women arrested for commercial sex during these decades, and secondarily the few panders accused of procuring. The prostitutes' customers were of little interest to the police. In a few cases, the customers witnessed against the arrested prostitutes or procurers.

2.3. Professionalism - Amateurism

It is clear that the control measures stipulated by the Vagrancy Act have not only been directed against the commercial, promiscuous, and anonymous sexual relations of professional prostitution. They have also focused on more selective and personal relationships. The control of prostitution seems to have been used for preventive purposes, that of controlling women who broke deeply ingrained social norms in society, and of establishing the boundaries between acceptable and unacceptable sexual behaviour.

The professionalism/amateurism of commercialized sex is dealt with under the four key words: prostitution as «social relations»; as «identity»; as «occupational ideology»; and as «subculture». Thus, the professionalism/amateurism of prostitution is analyzed first on the basis of its central social relations (the relationships prostitute - customer - procurer), and next in terms of the women's identity as prostitutes. How do the women define the terms «a prostitute», «a paid woman», «a whore», «a customer», «a pimp/souteneur/ponce»? How is their identity as prostitutes influenced by the measures implemented by the authorities? Further, the professionalism/amateurism dimension is studied from the point of view of the «esprit de corps» within the milieus. To what degree do the arrested women adopt an ideology that legitimates commercialized sex and questions the legitimacy of the control measures? Finally, prostitution is analyzed from a subcultural perspective. Can the prostitution milieus in Helsinki be described as social systems with their own norms and values? If so, are these subcultures male-dominated (by customers, pimps) or do they center around the friendships, interests, and values of the prostitutes? Is it possible for female power and dominance to take root in social systems created and sustained for the purpose of satisfying the needs of men?

2.4. Controlling Prostitution - Controlling Women

A distinct issue of the present analysis is the extent that the described control of prostitution has functioned as a generalized control of women.

According to the feminist perspective outlined in Chpt. 1, professional prostitution is legitimized by reference to a dualistic notion of male sexuality and female asexuality. Professional prostitutes are women at the disposal of the male society. They have no «right» to expect continuity in their commercial relationships. They are not allowed any personal demands (besides the economic ones), and their own sexual/emotional interests play no role. Professional prostitutes adopt an ideology claiming that the supply and demand of paid sexuality is part of the normal gender structure, and they view women's sexuality not as an end in itself but rather as a means for improving their socioeconomic position. Further, professional prostitutes, according to the literature, accept life in male-dominated subcultures, where they are supposed to subordinate themselves not only to the customers' wishes, but also to those of pimps and other procurers.

In this perspective, the shift from professional to non-professional prostitution becomes interesting. On the one side, we have the promiscuous and impersonal contacts of the designated «whore» - on the other side, there are the few and select contacts of the «amateur». In contrast to the professional prostitute's ideology, her subcultural involvement, and dependence on pimps, we see the amateur earning «pocket money», seemingly independently. In opposite to the professional prostitute's downgraded position in society, we find the amateur's sexual contacts which barely breach the female gender role of monogamy and passivity.

By definition, the gray zone between purely commercial relations and reciprocal sexual relations involves not only male but also female sexuality. A substantial part of this study deals with the cross-over area,

3 – Shades of …

and with society's attempts to come to grips with difficult-to-classify sexual relations. The measures provided by the Vagrancy Act have not only been aimed at professional prostitution but also at other forms of «undesirable behaviour» among women. These can be summarized in the themes: a) female sexuality, b) female use/abuse of alcohol, c) problems related to women's reproductive functions, and d) female poverty. The Vagrancy Act has been used against women who have broken prevailing norms regarding sexuality and drinking. It has also been implemented to control women «drifting» away from family life, and women - unemployed, homeless, marginalized - «drifting» away from other social security nets.

2.5. Interrogation Records of the Vice Police

The most important source of information has been the records on female vagrants interrogated by the Helsinki vice police during the period 1945-86. In the archives of the vice police, files for a total of 2 945 women were pulled: 50 randomly selected files for each year 1945-74 (with the exception of 1965, for which the records were pursued in their entirety)[1] and all of the individual files for the period 1975-86. After reviewing these 2 945 files, a total of 1 381 were extracted where commercial sex was indicated. The concept of prostitution was broadly interpreted; all files with notations about suspect sexual relations were included in the sample. A few such examples are: «A chases men in X-park»; «B strikes up acquaintance with men at the railway station»; «C is supported by men»; «D is suspected of commercial carnal knowledge».

Based on such a broad definition, the arrested women will be referred to as «prostitutes» - «street prostitutes»; «restaurant prostitutes»; «hotel prostitutes» throughout the book - instead of «women who the police suspect of prostitution». This does not mean that all the arrestees included in the sample were in fact professional prostitutes in the terminology used in the Vagrancy Act or under the criteria for prostitution already discussed.

In the quotations from the records, the women are referred to as A, B, C, D, and so on, in alphabetical order. For the women I interviewed (see later), fictitious names have been used. In order to guarantee the anonymity of the persons involved, minor revisions in background details have been made in the quotations, such as for exact age and hometown.

The comprehensiveness of the information found in the 1 381 individual files varies. Some records only contain the basic data required: name, age, place of birth, address, education, occupation, civil status, a short description of what the arrestee was suspected for, and which official measures were taken. Other files contain dozens or hundreds of pages, depending on how many times the woman had come in contact with the police; on how long the interrogations with her were; and on how many people were interrogated by the police in the current case. Some files include confiscated letters, date-books, diaries, address books, and photographs. In general, the records are more detailed for call-girls and hotel-prostitutes than for most of the others; the files on women suspected of procuring are also relatively exhaustive.

Most of the information about prostitution used in this book has been «filtered» through one authority: the police. To repeat, the study does not look at prostitution in general, but rather at prostitution registered with the authorities. What information is available has been influenced by two main factors: a) the police's attempts to establish the vagrancy status of the women (the prostitution criteria in the Vagrancy Act, facts about employment status, housing circumstances, and financial support); and b) the women's interests in normalizing their circumstances. The result is often contradictory, with some notations emphasizing «social deviancy» and others stressing «normality».

The responsibilities of the vice police have varied somewhat from decade to decade, but controlling vagrancy (and especially prostitution) has always been the core of their activities. The staff of the vice police division expanded somewhat during the study period: in 1950 there were 60 employees; in 1960, 69; in 1970, 71; and in 1980, 86 employees.

2.6. The Vagrancy Register

The records of the Helsinki vice police primarily cover arrests made in the city itself. However, when the vice police arrested a person for vagrancy, they often checked the nationwide vagrancy register for possible prior arrests in other towns. Any such prior arrests were entered into the Helsinki files, but, naturally, arrests in other towns after the last arrest in Helsinki were not noted. To obtain information about such later registrations, a check was run in the vagrancy register for 500 of the women in the sample (randomly selected among the 1 381).

2.7. Criminal Police Information on Procuring

To get data about procuring (pimping and other forms), the registers of the criminal police were checked for the period 1945-1986. However, it proved difficult to obtain exact data about the police-registered procuring in Helsinki. Persons suspected and/or convicted of procuring (with the exception of recent years when EDP had become available) were not registered separately by the vice or the criminal police. The only chance to find these individuals' files was to check through the annual reports of the criminal police on arrested persons 1945-1986. By this method, I found 49 individuals who had been arrested for procuring. This small group hardly represents all cases of procuring that came to the attention of the police over these decades. For the period 1975-86, though, I reviewed all of the individual files in the vice police archives and am able to state that, at least for these years, the two police sources accord well.

2.8. ALKO's Information About Restaurant Prostitution

Helsinki restaurants played a vital role in prostitution during the decades under study. In earlier years, the vice police were not the only authority controlling prostitution at the restaurants. They were joined by the Finnish Alcohol Monopoly (in the following referred to by its Finnish name ALKO), which controls all import, production, and sales of alcohol in the country. In the 1940s, 1950s, and 1960s, ALKO collected rather detailed information about the «sexual morality» of restaurant life. Inspectors sent out by ALKO periodically visited restaurants in order to check whether the establishments were being operated within the bounds of the law. They watched the sales on the premises, checked prices, ensured that alcohol was not being served to under-aged or intoxicated persons, and they controlled whether the «composition, status, and demeanour of the patronage» corresponded to the restaurant's price class as established by the Alcohol Monopoly. A prime measurement of the «status» of the patronage was the proportion of «unaccompanied women», that is, women not in the company of men at the restaurants. A high proportion of unaccompanied women was considered to lower the standard of an establishment[2]. The descriptions given by the inspectors of the «sexual morality» in the restaurant life of earlier decades include some mention of professional prostitution. However, these reports primarily permit, as do the police records, insight into the border area between professional prostitution and non-commercial sexual relations.

2.9. Interviews With Key Informants

To gain further insight into prostitution as defined by the authorities, interviews were conducted with «key informants» within vagrancy control, namely, representatives for the vice police (before and after the repeal of the vagrancy legislation), the criminal police, supervisors of vagrants and staff at the institutions. Since many of the homeless women in the study had lived or did live in lodging-houses/over-night shelters, staff from these institutions were interviewed as well. Moreover, interviews were conducted with representatives of the Helsinki out-patient clinic for venereal diseases, to which a majority of the arrested women had been taken for examinations. In all, 37 semi-structured interviews were held, lasting an average of 90 minutes.

2.10. Interviews With Prostitutes

To capture what the women involved thought about prostitution and its control, two groups of prostitutes were interviewed: sixteen call-girls and hotel prostitutes; and fifteen homeless women with experience of prostitution.

The call-girls and hotel prostitutes were interviewed in 1985. After a survey of the most recent police records under scrutiny, those women (32) were selected who the police suspected were still working as prostitutes. Sixteen of these were interviewed. The average age of the group was nearly 28 years. When certain social background factors (age, civil status, education, and employment situation) for the women I had an opportunity to interview were compared with those of the women not interviewed, no systematic differences between the groups were found.

This research method of contacting persons registered with the police is obviously problematic. The women could perceive the contact as a threat to their privacy and anonymity, in that they had not expected registration by the police to have such a consequence. I risked forcing them to recall difficult and negative experiences (police interrogation, arrest, and so on) which they might have preferred to forget. The fact that I learned about them from police records may also have influenced the information they were willing to give. Despite my reiteration that the police were in no way involved in the study, and that all information would be kept confidential, the women may still have been suspicious and restrained. They knew about my ongoing contacts with the police and for that reason could have tried to make as positive an impression on me as possible. Probably, this factor mainly influenced their responses about the current size of their circle of customers and about their total income from commercialized sex. To be on the safe side, they continued to downplay these features with me, as they had previously done with the police. In contrast, they obviously were quite open about their own past in prostitution, how they had gotten started, what consequences commercial sex had had for them and how they were affected by arrests and police interrogations. They also spoke willingly about the background of their customers and the men's reasons for buying sex.

Twelve of the interviews were face-to-face, at the women's home or at mine, and four were via telephone. The interviews lasted from between 40 minutes and six hours. In addition to these taped interviews, I had many opportunities for both short and lengthy discussions with the women on other occasions, at restaurants, cafés, on the phone, at their apartments, and during trials where they were called as witnesses. I also interviewed some of them anew in 1988, two-three years after the initial contacts.

In 1988, a total of 30 women were interviewed in a separate study.[3] Eight of them said they had some experience of prostitution and vagrancy control. By means of the snow-ball method, I came into contact with seven more homeless women with similar experiences (four lived at the shelter and three were entirely without housing). Thus, I interviewed a total of fifteen homeless women with explicit knowledge of prostitution.

The average age of the group was 41 years. For some, prostitution lay many years back in time; the oldest had been detained by the vice police during the 1960s. A few women were in very bad shape, both physically and mentally. They had difficulty describing their circumstances, and were unsure about how long they had been homeless, where they had lived during various periods of their lives, and how and why they had had contact with the police. Other women's accounts were clear and detailed about their housing situation, working experience, health problems, alcohol problems, relationships to men - and contacts with the vice police. The interviews lasted from one to three hours (I met with four of the women on several occasions), and most took place at the shelter: in the women's rooms, or in a meeting room.

2.11. Observations at Restaurants

About 30 visits to restaurants in Helsinki where prostitution was mediated were part of this project. The observations were made from 1983 to 1988, at intervals of varying lengths. Two main types of restaurants were targeted: local pubs/former sailor taverns, and nightclubs in hotels. The visits provided us with impressions of how extensive commercial sex was at these establishments, how visibly versus discreetly the liaisons were established, and what types of prostitution (as to social status and public order problems) were mediated.

Notes

1 See Järvinen 1987.
2 See Järvinen & Stenius 1985; Järvinen 1986.
3 Järvinen 1988.

3.

Controlling Prostitution

3.1. A Historical Review

The 1936 Vagrancy Act replaced three different systems for controlling prostitution: 1) the paragraph on prostitution in the Penal Code; 2) a system of regulatory venereal examinations of prostitutes; and 3) the then existing decree on vagrancy (dating from 1883).

Up until 1937, prostitution and procuring were prohibited under the provisions of the Penal Code, Chapter 20, Section 10, which was passed in 1889. The maximum penalty for prostitution was two-years' imprisonment, and for procuring three years in the house of correction. These provisions notwithstanding, the Penal Code was rarely applied to prostitutes. According to contemporary commentators, the burden of proof was difficult to meet in these cases;[1] furthermore, these provisions were primarily applicable to prostitutes working in brothels, and not to the more private forms of commercialized sex. Since the Penal Code's paragraph on prostitution partially conflicted with the decree on vagrancy (see below), a government commission in 1926 called for the repeal of the penal provision.[2] This occurred at the beginning of 1937 when the new law on vagrancy took effect. Remaining on the books, however, were the criminal penalties for procuring: «A person who maintains a house for the pursuit of illicit fornication or entices or induces another person generally to be used for fornication shall be found guilty of procuring and sentenced to the workhouse for a maximum of four years or to imprisonment. A person who for his own personal gain encourages or exploits another person's immorality, who generally is used for fornication, shall be sentenced as in paragraph 1. Attempts to these crimes are punishable offences» (Section 20:8).

During the early decades of the 20th century, prostitution was also controlled by means of preventive venereal examinations of prostitutes.

A so-called regulatory system was introduced in 1875 in the country's large cities,[3] though the Helsinki «examination bureau» for prostitutes was opened much earlier - in 1847. Under the regulatory system, all women known for or suspected of prostitution were registered by the police as public prostitutes, whereupon they were obligated to undergo regular examinations for venereal diseases.

The pros and cons of this regulatory system were keenly debated in the late 1800s. Encouraged by the international movements for abolitionism, the critics claimed that the system implied an official sanctioning of prostitution, that it was in violation of the Penal Code 20:10 (see above), and that the «preventive examinations» ensured no effective protection against venereal diseases, and more likely merely instilled a false sense of security. The system was considered unjust since the male customers were exempt from its provisions, and moreover, it was criticized for formalizing the public stigmatization of the women involved, thereby making it more difficult for them to leave prostitution.[4] In 1907, the Senate voted to abolish the regulatory system.

The third instrument for controlling prostitution prior to 1937 was the 1883 Decree on Vagrancy. In this legislation, vagrants were defined as «able-bodied persons without visible means of support, living a life of wandering or rambling, idleness, and immorality». Vagrants could be sentenced to public labour, for three months to one year for the first incident, and thereafter for six months to three years.

In the early decades of the 1900s, there was a widespread belief that vagrancy was on the rise throughout the country and that the implemented measures were ineffective. The Decree on Vagrancy was perceived as too narrow, since it required the three criteria of «wandering», «idleness», and «immorality» to be present at the same time. Additionally, the decree did not apply to all prostitutes, since many did not «wander» around and were obviously not «indigent».[5] In 1921, the Draft Legislation Committee was directed to make a proposal for a new law on vagrancy. The new law was passed in 1936 and took effect in January 1937.

3.2. The 1936 Vagrancy Act and Legal Criteria

The new vagrancy legislation introduced, according to its spokespersons, entirely new types of control. In a handbook intended for use by the police and health authorities,[6] it was stated that the control principles were borrowed from the fields of pedagogy and health care. The prime concern was to «restore the vagrant to a settled and decent life, and to convert him into a useful, productive, and responsible citizen». The means for achieving these goals were social training and supportive health services, including compulsory institutionalization when necessary. None of these measures were to be considered the equivalent of punishment. They were rather comparable with alcoholism treatment, even if confinement for vagrancy was of a somewhat harsher character. The Vagrancy Act was also perceived as a means for protecting society, by counteracting criminality, poverty, venereal diseases, and drunkenness.[7]

Four criteria were established for defining vagrancy.
The first was an assessment of the individual's ties to a specific domicile and the local labour market. Under the law, a vagrant was «an able-bodied person, idle and with insufficient means for his support, wandering from area to area, where the circumstances do not indicate that he seeks employment» (The Vagrancy Act 1936:1:1).
The second criterion reflected the individual's duty to support himself. A vagrant was «an able-bodied person accustomedly avoiding work and therefore in need of poor relief or at the risk of becoming an overwhelming burden to others...» (1:2).
The third criterion referred to begging. A vagrant was «a person accustomed to begging, using others for begging or allowing his wards under 18 years old to beg» (1:3).
The fourth criterion was related to prostitution and «other asocial behaviour not directly covered by the Penal Code».[8] Under this section, vagrants were «persons habitually obtaining income by morally reprehensible means or through their way of life otherwise imperilling the public order, security, or morality» (1:4).
Exempted from the provisions of the law were persons under the age of 18, as well as mentally ill and mentally retarded persons (Section 1).
In the above mentioned handbook[9] for the vice police, which was prepared by the social welfare authorities, the prostitution criteria were outlined as follows. Emphasized were a) that the arrested person had obtained income by means of carnal relations and b) that this behaviour had been practiced habitually. «Carnal relations» could be either «natural or abnormal» (no definition was offered for these terms), and payment could be in the form of money as well as «food, accommodations, clothes, jewelry, restaurant accounts, and the like». The amount of payment was irrelevant as was the issue of whether the recipient had explicitly requested remuneration or not. The crux was that the economic gain had been acquired as compensation for sexual relations, «in the form of a clear payment, an ostensible gift, or in the form of entertainment».[10]
The criterion of habitualness was as crucial as that of payment; in other words, «casual exercise of fornication» was not to be viewed as

vagrancy. Commercialized sex had to be definable as a way of life, which meant that only «professional fornication» could be considered as vagrancy under the terms of the law. However, the notion of professional sexual relations was not necessarily synonymous with full-time prostitution. Persons who were gainfully employed or who lived off of their capital, but who earned extra income by «immoral means», could be found guilty of vagrancy.[11]

According to the guidelines, the Vagrancy Act could also be applied to persons «not directly engaging themselves in fornication but supporting or promoting such activities». This primarily concerned persons providing rooms for prostitutes or procuring customers for them, presuming that this occurred habitually and for the express purpose of gain. Thus, the Vagrancy Act in part targeted the same behaviour as did the procuring paragraph in the Penal Code, but «nothing hinders a person from being criminally sentenced for procuring as well as processed as a vagrant».[12]

The Vagrancy Act was intended to cover both female and male prostitutes, but not customers of prostitutes who instead should «be regarded as instruments or objects in the exercise of fornication and therefore ought to be placed beyond all treatment and penal measures».[13]

Anti-Vagrancy Measures

The Act distinguished between four types of anti-vagrancy measures.

The first and mildest measure was the bestowal of warnings and - when warranted - expulsion to municipality of domicile. Besides warnings which were issued by the social authorities, a vagrant was «to be assisted in fleeing his adverse surroundings and in obtaining appropriate housing or work», and, when called for, hospitalization or other care (Vagrancy Act, Section 2).

If these measures proved to be insufficient, the vagrant was to be placed under supervision, generally for one year but possibly for up to two years. A person under supervision was obliged to comply with specific directives concerning his life style, dwelling, and employment (Sections 3-4). If the vagrant wished to move to another town, he was required to obtain permission from the social authorities (Section 1). If supervision did not help to «restore him to a proper and decent life style» or if he presented a danger to himself, to the safety of others, or to public order and morals (Section 5), harsher measures would have to be applied.

The third type of measure was incarceration in a workhouse or commitment to forced labour (Section 5). The initiative was to come from the social welfare board or the chief of police, and the final decision was to be made by the county administrative board (county administrative court of appeal after 1971) (Sections 24-26). While the case was being investigated, the detainee was to be held «in the workhouse or other municipal institution» (Section 38). Persons incapable of working could not be sent to the workhouse or to forced labour, and were instead processed according to the Public Assistance Act (Section 6). The decision to institutionalize a person or send him/her to forced labour could be appealed to the highest administrative court (Section 34). The maximum length of incarceration in the workhouse was one year (six months after 1971), and upon relapse, three years (one year after 1971) (Section 10). Forced labour was to be performed in public institutions specifically designed for the purpose, and lasted two years, although some recidivists could be retained for indeterminate periods (Section 15). Forced labour was abolished in 1971, and in 1984, the name workhouse was changed to public institution.

The fourth type of measure was a form of aftercare labelled «postsupervision». A person sentenced to institutional care could be released conditionally after three months had passed (one month after 1971), if it could be assumed that he would live «a proper and decent life» upon release (Section 10). A vagrant sentenced to forced labour could, on the same grounds, be conditionally released after one year (Section 16). Subsequently, the person was placed under supervision for one year (six months after 1971) if he had been discharged from an institution, and for three years if discharged from forced labour. During this time, he could be returned to the institution/prison if he violated the directives for supervision (Sections 10 and 16).

The social authorities and the vice police were the main agencies in the application of the Vagrancy Act. The responsibilities of the social welfare boards included holding the vagrant under observation (together with the police), making decisions with regard to warnings and expulsion to the municipality of domicile, ruling on supervision, proposing institutionalization and forced labour, and providing other support and guidance to the vagrant. The responsibilities of the vice police included detainment of persons suspected of vagrancy, interrogations and establishment of the arrestees' status as vagrants or not, and propositions regarding institutionalization or forced labour. A person could be detained if there were «probable grounds» for suspecting him of vagrancy. The initiative to the arrest could be taken by the social welfare board, the employment office, or the police themselves. Immediate interrogation was to follow detention (the same rules applied as for the interrogation of suspected criminal offenders). If the subject was found to be innocent, he was released directly after the interrogation, and if found guilty, the police sent the case to the social welfare board for further measures, in the form of warnings, supervision, or expulsion to municipality of domicile. In serious cases, the police jailed the vagrant, whereupon the county council board (later, the county court) was responsible for the final disposition of the case.[14]

A nationwide central register on all vagrants was set up.[15] Information was submitted by the police, the social district boards, and the county administrative courts of appeal, on all persons subjected to anti-vagrancy measures (warnings, supervision, institutionalization, forced labour), as well as on persons merely suspected of vagrancy (Section 2).

3.3. Criticisms Against the Vagrancy Act

Throughout its entire duration, the 1936 Vagrancy Act was the subject of severe criticism.

One issue consistently raised was the relationship between the care and punishment aspects of vagrancy control. In the legislative history to the law, it was stressed that controlling vagrancy would be based on treatment principles and that the social welfare board - in cooperation with the police - would be the central authority. However, it soon turned out that the anti-vagrancy measures were perceived as punishment, not treatment, and that the police continued to play the dominant role in the control of vagrancy.[16]

Another issue debated over several decades was the appropriateness of institutionalization for combatting vagrancy. The workhouses did not function according to legislative intention: these municipal institutions, originally built for the poor relief system, greatly varied in character, and the urban vagrants were poorly suited for work training which was primarily in the areas of agriculture and forestry. The assignment of clients was random, with first-time internees being housed with recidivist vagrants. Furthermore, the results of these measures were not very encouraging, with a large proportion of the vagrants resuming their asocial lives after their institutional sojourn.[17]

A third point of criticism was aimed at the use of forced labour. According to the Vagrancy Act, forced labour was to be performed in public institutions specifically designed for such purposes (Section 13), and the forced labourers were not to be confined together with prisoners (Section 18). The planned institutions were never built, and forced labour was performed in the prisons - in contravention of the law. Also, vagrants awaiting decisions from the county boards with regard to workhouse sentences spent weeks or months in general prisons. Several governmental commissions criticized these practices at the same time that they condemned forced labour as an unreasonably harsh penalty incompatible with the treatment philosophy of the vagrancy legislation.[18]

A fourth area of criticism concerned the legal rights of the vagrants. The criteria for vagrancy set out in the law were unclear, and at worst the law's enforcement could be very arbitrary. The law allowed long-term incarceration (institutional care or forced labour) as well as several other encroachments in the lives of vagrants (supervisor's directives as to the vagrant's work, dwelling, and life style). The right of appeal was limited and rarely used. The issue of legal protection eventually became the most decisive point of contention in the debate on the vagrancy legislation.[19]

A fifth negative aspect was the fact that the anti-vagrancy measures only embraced certain forms of vagrancy. An important objective with the passage of the 1936 law was that the concept of vagrancy was not only to encompass prostitution, but also the traditional male forms of vagrancy: begging, refusal to work, and an unsettled life style. Notwithstanding, prostitutes were long the primary target of the anti-vagrancy policies, while male vagrants were processed under other laws.[20] At the same time, the Vagrancy Act was considered ineffective and unjust even within the area of commercialized sex. Some prostitutes - the ones who were marginalized and alcoholics - were hit much harder by the public measures than were other, more socially integrated women. Furthermore, the authorities only focused on one of the parties in prostitution, the seller, and ignored the other, the buyer.[21]

Many commentators were also critical of the division of jurisdiction between anti-vagrancy measures and the system for alcoholism treatment. The critics maintained that most vagrants could be defined as abusers of alcohol and that the assignment of clients to the two jurisdictions was vague and arbitrary.[22] Thus, it was no coincidence that the Vagrancy Act was repealed at the same time that a new law on the treatment of addicted persons took effect in 1987. Now, the vagrancy problem was defined as an issue of substance abuse to be handled within the sphere of addiction treatment.

3.4. Prostitution as Societal Problem

Five approaches to the problem of prostitution can be discerned in Finnish govermental commission reports and in the research literature. Prostitution has been conceptualized as an issue for public health policy, for social policy, for public order policy, for protecting youth, and for gender policies.[23] In these approaches, various aspects of commercialized sex and different characteristics of the prostitutes are singled out as the core of the prostitution problem. Also, the five viewpoints result in fairly different suggestions regarding official intervention in prostitution.

A Public Health Problem

Traditionally, prostitutes have been defined as a significant source for the spread of venereal diseases. The responsibility for controlling prostitution has been assigned to the health authorities - with the police as assisting agency when necessary. The health-risk perspective was prominent around the turn of the century and during the early 1900s. It was used in Finland as well as other countries for justifying the «preventive examinations» of prostitutes under the regulatory systems.[24] The perspective can also be seen in the 1894 decree on the prevention of syphilis which legitimated discriminatory treatment of prostitutes up until the Second World War, thus long after the regulatory system had been abolished.

Under the provisions of the 1936 Vagrancy Act, preventive health examinations of prostitutes continued, as the arrestees were «required to submit to medical examination and all necessary treatment on command of the proper authorities» (Section 7). Up until the 1970s, the vice police in Helsinki transported a majority of the arrested female vagrants to the municipal out-patient clinic for venereal check-ups (cf. Fig. 2, later in this chapter).

The health-risk perspective on prostitution was clarified in many early research reports.[25] Venereal diseases were especially common among prostitutes registered during the 1930s and during the Second World War.[26] Immediately following the war, the studies reported a declining prevalence of the diseases, which was attributed to a new law on V.D. (taking effect in 1943) and more effective police surveillance - in the first years after the war, much tighter reins were placed on vagrants.[27] During the 1950s, venereal diseases continued to decrease among prostitutes. At the same time, the diseases, gonorrhea in particular, were reported to be more frequent among young prostitutes than among older ones. For that reason, continuing the «preventive venereal examinations» of female vagrants was deemed necessary.[28]

After two decades' intermission, the discussion about a possible correlation between prostitution and the spread of venereal diseases was resumed in the 1980s. In 1984, a study was published on 200 men seeking treatment at the Helsinki municipal out-patient clinic for venereal diseases.[29] Of the 173 patients who claimed to have been infected in Finland, only one (1) identified a prostitute as the source. Among the men infected while abroad, the majority cited prostitutes as the probable source. The study concluded that domestic prostitution was no longer relevant as a source of disease, but that contacts with prostitutes abroad presented some health hazards.[30]

With the emergence of HIV/aids, the traditional health-risk perspective on prostitution regained status. The argumentation has been much the same as during the period of the regulatory system in the 1800s. Thus, prostitutes are defined as a significant source of infection, due to their frequent and anonymous sexual contacts. Besides, their life style is often depicted in terms of irresponsibility and carelessness, caused by substance abuse, economic difficulties, and other social problems.

A Social Policy Problem

Underlying the 1936 Vagrancy Act was the view of prostitution as a manifestation of poverty and scarcity. Prostitutes, beggars, work-resisters, and ramblers were viewed as social losers, persons who had grown up in poor and broken homes, or in families blighted by alcoholism or criminality. Vagrancy was said to be linked with inadequate economic, social, and psychological resources.[31] According to the proponents of this perspective, it was society's obligation to intervene in the lives of the vagrants and to resocialize them, not punish them, since they were not fully responsible for their actions.

The social policy perspective was especially prominent in research projects which focused on the family background and personal problems of prostitutes. For example, in a study from the 1940s, various social background variables were compiled for 100 female vagrants incarcerated in a workhouse.[32] Half of the women had come from broken homes, where divorce or the death of one or both parents had split up the families, and many came from working-class homes characterized by poverty, overcrowding, and alcohol problems. About half of the women had left home at a very early age (15 years or younger).[33]

Another study of women arrested for prostitution in the city of Tampere in 1938, 1948, 1958, 1966, and 1967 noted that the social backgrounds of the arrestees from each of these years were very similar.[34] Almost all came from the working-class or lower middle class. In most cases, the parents as well as their daughters lacked any vocational training. Many of the women had dropped out of school and their work experiences were quite fragmented. At the time of first detention, almost half were unemployed, and nearly one-third were homeless.[35]

The social policy perspective gained in popularity during the duration of the 1936 Vagrancy Act. Eventually, it was concluded in research reports and government commissions that unemployment, homelessness, and alcohol problems were the main contents of vagrancy. Simultaneously, though, grew the general acknowledgement of the ineffectiveness of anti-vagrancy measures in dealing with these societal problems.[36] The ultimate recognition of the social policy perspective came with the 1986 commission report on vagrancy.[37] In this, vagrants appeared as «socially deprived individuals without means» whose lives were rife with curtailed opportunities and accumulated social misfortune. The remedy for social deprivation was not anti-vagrancy measures, but rather an improvement of the living conditions of these down-and-outs, that is, work, housing, and treatment.[38]

A Public Order Problem

The social policy perspective was often combined with the notion of prostitution as a problem of public order. Official intervention was deemed necessity since the «work-resistant», «rambling», and «indigent» vagrants could be expected to resort to criminal activities. Commercialized sex was viewed as a negative phenomenon since prostitutes and their associates were suspected of procuring, selling spirits, violence against the customers, and other illegalities. The Vagrancy Act was to be a sort of crime-prevention law, a function already stressed in the legislative history and commentaries to the 1936 law.[39]

The relationship between vagrancy and criminality was analyzed in many studies. A review of police and other public records for 100 women incarcerated in a workhouse 1945-47 revealed that 69 per cent had earlier been registered for violations of the penal law and 11 per cent had served prison sentences.[40] The most typical crimes were shoplifting and minor thefts, possession of illegal alcohol, disorderly conduct in public places, and resisting arrest. Another study of penal violations in a sample of female vagrants detained by the Helsinki vice police in 1982-83 confirmed that more than half of the women had been registered for criminality.[41] In most cases, the entries were for shoplifting and theft, while a few had been sentenced for fraud, violence, and drug offences.

For decades, the assumed correlation between vagrancy, criminality, and public order problems was used as the principal argument for continuing anti-vagrancy measures. It was claimed that the Vagrancy Act awarded the police with unique opportunities to combat procuring, drug traffic, and other organized criminality, and that the anti-vagrancy measures forced prostitution into discreet and less offensive forms.[42] Notwithstanding the criticism discussed above, the Vagrancy Act remained in effect until 1987 thereby assuaging people's fears that outright repeal of these provisions would lead to public order problems of unmanageable proportions.

A Youth Problem

The fourth perspective found in official and research reports is the notion of prostitution as a youth problem. Controlling commercialized sex was seen as a necessity since young girls were recruited to prostitution. Young boys selling - or buying - sexual services were seldom mentioned during the period under study. The negative concomitants of prostitution (an unsound life style, a displaced daily rhythm, and substance abuse) were especially harmful for young, vulnerable girls who ought instead to be investing their efforts in an education or work experience. Young prostitutes also risked exploitation by adult customers and procurers. Further, they were less able to anticipate the marginalization, degradation, and psychological problems that often accompanied commercialized sex.

There is no scarcity of research analyzing prostitution as a youth problem. One study surveyed the age distribution among female vagrants detained by the Helsinki vice police during the 1940s, 1950s, and 1960s.[43] In the 1950s, considerable mass media attention had been directed towards young prostitutes, particularly towards «ship girls» and «truck girls». Youth prostitution was defined as a new phenomenon or at least as a problem beginning to assume alarming proportions. However, the mentioned study of young vagrants in Helsinki did not bear these worries out. During the war-years (1942-43), almost one-fourth of the female arrestees were under the age of 20, compared to an average of 13 per cent for the period 1945-57. Thus, contrary to the mass media alarm, youth prostitution did not increase during the early postwar years.

In another survey, the age distribution of all persons recorded in the nationwide register on vagrants in 1983 was analyzed and compared to earlier findings.[44] The mean age of first-time detainees had remained the same since the Second World War, that is, about 26 years for women and 31 years for men. A total of 28 per cent of the women and nine per cent of the men had been under 20 years of age at the time of their first detention, while 11 per cent and two per cent respectively had been under 18 years.

Although a considerable number of young girls participated in prostitution over the years, this was not used as a justification for continuing anti-vagrancy measures in more recent decades. The interventions specified in the law (institutionalization in particular) were not considered as suitable for young vagrants. Under-age prostitutes were primarily the responsibility of the child welfare authorities. Since the 1960s, these authorities have not reported any large-scale youth prostitution.[45]

A Gender Policy Issue

During the period under study, a feminist perspective on prostitution was not especially noticeable in Finnish commission and research reports. In the 1980s, however, there was a breakthrough for a feminist understanding of commercialized sex.[46] In many aspects, this represented a revival of arguments glimpsed in the debate about the regulatory system at the turn of the century (see above).

The feminist approach to analyzing prostitution control in Finland
can be summarized in three points.

First, the proponents of this perspective challenged the legitimacy of
defining prostitution as a form of vagrancy. Throughout the period
1937-86, prostitutes were subjected to the same control measures as
«beggars», «ramblers», and «work-resistant individuals». For this reason, only some types of prostitution, those connected with social marginalization, were controlled, while the more private forms remained
beyond the area of official interventions. Further, the gender selectivity
of the control policies was heavily criticized; the customers and procurers of prostitution received negligible attention by the authorities.[47]

Second, it has been maintained that controlling vagrancy was ineffective even with regard to the most public portions of commercialized
sex. Public prostitution was closely intertwined with serious social
problems such as unemployment, homelessness, and alcoholism, and
these cannot be solved by means of the disciplinary measures specified
by the Vagrancy Act: warnings, supervision, and institutionalization.[48]

Third, according to feminist commentators, repealing the vagrancy
legislation would not imply that the Finnish society was sanctioning or
tolerating prostitution. On the contrary, efforts should continue to
thwart commercialized sex, but this ought to be done by increasing the
equality between the sexes in society, by a dismantling of obsolete gender roles, and by more research and information about the phenomenon
of prostitution. It was felt that the prevention of prostitution had received much too little attention in earlier decades.[49]

3.5. Developments Within Vagrancy Control

The Vagrancy Act was energetically enforced during the 1940s and
1950s. During those decades, each year between 1 000 and 1 700 vagrants were subjected to warnings, supervision, or institutionalization.
The corresponding figures for the 1980s were 300-500. Initially, the
Vagrancy Act was implemented primarily against women. In the 1940s
and early 1950s, three-fourths of the measures taken concerned women.
After 1970, men dominated in the anti-vagrancy measures and in 1985,
women constituted only one-fifth of the registered vagrants.[50]

Simultaneously, the anti-vagrancy measures used became less severe.[51] Institutionalization was the most commonly adopted measure in
the 1950s, when about 500 women yearly (40 per cent of the registered
vagrants) were sent to workhouses. By the 1980s, fewer than ten women (about five per cent of the registered vagrants) were institutionalized each year, while the majority left with a warning (49 per cent in
1985) or supervision (24 per cent in 1985).

«Professional fornication» (in other words, prostitution) stood out as the most frequent vagrancy charge entered against women up until the 1970s. In 1940, 87 per cent were registered for prostitution, whereas in 1970, the corresponding figure was 57 per cent, and during the 1980s, less than one-fifth were registered as prostitutes. The next most frequent vagrancy charge against women during the period 1937-1985 was «refusal to work»: in 1945, 16 per cent were registered as «work-resistant» and in the 1980s, the figure was 48-57 per cent. The remaining criteria found in the Vagrancy Act, those of «begging» and «rambling», were seldom used in the entries for female arrestees.[52]

Data from the nationwide register on all persons suspected of vagrancy (not only those receiving further measures) indicate that prostitution continued to be a major criterion during the 1980s. According to the register, two-thirds of all women detained for vagrancy over this decade had entries for prostitution. The register also reveals that 57 per cent of these female arrestees had entries for «inebriation» despite the fact that drunkenness was not an explicit criterion in the vagrancy legislation.[53]

The development of vagrancy policies in Helsinki from the 1950s to the 1980s is depicted in Figures 2 and 3.

Fig. 2. Female vagrants detained by the Helsinki vice police, and number of visits to the out-patient clinic for venereal diseases 1952-86.[54]

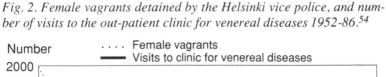

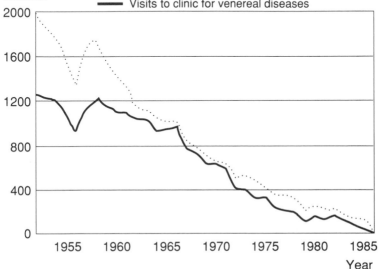

As shown, the total number of female vagrants (new detainees and recidivists) in Helsinki has decreased dramatically. In 1952, about 2 000 cases were registered by the vice police, while during the 1980s, less than 250 were arrested each year. The number of visits to the municipal out-patient clinic for venereal diseases in connection with arrests can be used as an approximate indicator of prostitution, since it was almost exclusively women suspected of commercialized sex who were escorted by the police to the health clinics. Up until the mid-1960s, more than 1 000 venereal examinations of female vagrants were reported annually. From the end of the 1970s, this figure fluctuated between 100 and 200 each year (Fig. 2).

The decrease in vagrancy arrests can also be seen from the next figure, depicting the number of first-time detentions only.

Fig. 3. First-time detentions of female vagrants by the Helsinki vice police 1952-86.[55]

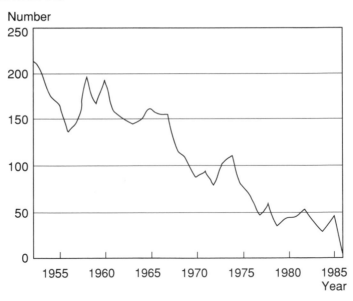

The decline seen in Fig. 3, however, is not as steep as for the total number of vagrancy cases. The number of newly registered female vagrants was 150-200 each year in the period 1953-67. During the 1970s and 1980s, the number was generally between 30 and 100 each year.

3.6. Background Information About the Prostitutes

This section covers data on certain background factors for the 1 381 women in this study who were registered as «prostitutes».

Age and Length of Time in Police Records

The average age of the women was 23.7 years at the time of their first arrest for prostitution. The age distribution fluctuated somewhat over time, with a higher average age at the beginning and at the end of the study period (25.1 years in the 1940s, and 26.3 in the 1980s), and a lower average age during the 1960s (20.4 years). At the time of their first arrest, 42 per cent were under 20 years old, 40 per cent were 20-29 years, and 18 per cent were 30 or older.

The period of time from the first to the last arrest by the police («registration period») varied greatly for the women. Of the 1 212 women entered into police records from 1945 to 1979 (the 1980s are excluded here since the follow-up period would be so short), 41 per cent were arrested only once for prostitution. The average length of the registration period for women arrested more than once was 4.4 years. Thus, police-registered prostitution was limited to a particular phase of most of these women's lives, a phase that ended before their 30th birthdays. Nevertheless, a minority engaged in commercial sexual relations over a relatively long period: ten per cent had registration periods of ten years or more.

In order to establish whether the women had been arrested in other areas of the country, the nation-wide vagrancy register was checked for 500 of them. Of these, 24 per cent had been arrested in other districts, either prior to or following their arrests in Helsinki. The typical pattern was for the women to be arrested first in other districts and then in Helsinki, a pattern related to their moving into the capital city. Of the total of 1 381 women, 25 per cent had been born in Helsinki, whereas a high 73 per cent had moved there from other parts of Finland. Only two per cent, that is 29 women, had been born in other countries, of which 14 in Sweden and ten in the then Soviet Union.

Education and Gainful Employment

As is the case in the general population, the level of education in the group of women studied improved over the decades. The proportion with only a compulsory school education (of eight years) decreased from 78 per cent during the 1950s to 57 per cent in the 1980s, and the proportion with low-level vocational training (typically, clerical training or hotel/restaurant school) increased from six per cent to 29 per cent. Three per cent of the women had some form of higher vocational training (typically within commerce or nursing).

The women's level of education (proportions of compulsory school and vocational training) did not deviate from that found among the general female population of Helsinki. However, direct comparisons are difficult due to incompatible age and educational categories in the statistics. The proportion of persons with a high-school diploma though was lower than among Helsinki women in the same age groups.[56]

In contrast, the employment status in the group diverged substantially from that of the general population. For the women studied, there was a strong correlation between prostitution and unemployment, because they were arrested under the provisions of the Vagrancy Act referring to «refusal to work» and «inactivity». But not all of these female vagrants were unemployed. Of the total of 1 381, 28 per cent were classified as gainfully employed, 57 per cent as unemployed, and nine per cent as students at the time of their first arrest. The proportion of unemployed was especially high in the 1970s when 84 per cent were classified as «work-resistant» or as «persons without occupation».

Most of the police files (97 per cent) contained entries about occupations (the woman's job upon first arrest or, if unemployed, her most recent job). The largest occupational category over the decades was that of maids/nursemaids: 24 per cent were registered under this category. The next largest categories were salesgirls at shops/cafés (18 per cent) and factory/ construction workers (17 per cent). The common pattern throughout the period was for the arrestees, if they had gainful employment, to work within low-waged female occupations with little chance for advancement. This feature was repeated for those women registered as students - they were typically being trained to become office or health care workers, cosmeticians, hairdressers, and waitresses, occupations hardly likely to guarantee the «good incomes» and the «right to self-determination» that some of these women, according to the records, had imagined.

Marriage and Children

As regards the women's civil status, 72 per cent were registered as unmarried, eight per cent as married, 13 per cent as divorced, and two per cent as widows at the time of their first arrest. Altogether, 29 per cent were reported to have children. Of these (399 children for which the information was relatively complete), 15 per cent lived with their single mothers throughout the registration period, 21 per cent with their fathers, five per cent with both parents, and 22 per cent with grandparents. The remaining children (37 per cent) were in some kind of institutional care or had been adopted by other couples.

The addresses found in the police files and other entries about actual living arrangements revealed that only six per cent of the women were in fact living with men at the time of their first arrest. Of these men, more than half were absent - temporarily or for protracted periods of time - when the women were arrested. Some were away due to their jobs as seamen or businessmen, others were serving prison sentences, still others were in treatment facilities. Thus, the police material contained very few potential «live-in pimps», or, in other words, men who co-resided and cooperated with prostitutes.

In fact, many more men reported their wives to the vice police. For example, X wrote to the police in 1945: «Honoured authorities! I implore you to imprison my wife immediately. She has been engaging in sexual relations while I have been at war. I hope that she will be punished severely for doing this against a man at the front. I do not want her to use my name any longer.» Another man, Y, wrote in 1959: «I have experienced one of the worst things that can afflict a man. During the time I have been at sea, my wife has received other men in our home. I request an immediate intervention by the police.» And Z wrote in 1960: «My wife, even though it feels alien to call her that... abuses alcohol and spends the night in strange men's accommodations ... What good is the vice squad if not to intervene in such cases.» What is salient here is the ambiguity as to whether these alleged extra-marital liaisons were commercial in nature at all. The writers of these letters expected the police to put a stop to their wives' unfaithfulness, regardless of whether the extra-marital sexual relations could be defined as prostitution or not. They wanted severe measures to be taken against the women: «Send her to the workhouse immediately»; «A year in prison would do her good.» (records, 1959, 1960).

There was only one case in the entire police material where a man contacted the vice police «in order to help» his wife. For 20 years, the woman had shifted between prostitution in Helsinki, arrests, supervision, sojourns in workhouses, and living with her husband in the north of the country. The man corresponded with the police throughout the whole period. In 1967, he wrote: «My wife, who you have now known for 20 years, is in Helsinki again and is spreading her venereal infection. Please, vice police, see to it that she receives medical attention and send her home as soon as possible... Despite everything she belongs here at home.»

Notes

1   For example, Komitébetänkande... rörande prostitutionen (Commission Report) 1891; Betänkande i prostitutionsfrågan (Commission Report) 1892.
2   Ehdotus irtolaislaiksi (Commission Report) 1926.
3   Decree on Regulated Prostitution 1875.
4   For a discussion of the advantages and disadvantages of the regulatory system, see, for example, Betänkande afgifvet till Finska läkaresäll-

skapet... (Commission Report) 1888; Heikel 1888; Pippingsköld 1888, 1890; Betänkande i prostitutionsfrågan (Commission Report) 1892; Betänkande... om... särskild kontroll... av prostituerade (Commission Report) 1896; Boldt 1897.

5   See, for example, Sarlin 1916; Ehdotus sukupuolitautien vastustamiseksi (Commission Report) 1924; Ehdotus irtolaislaiksi (Commission Report) 1926; Huttunen 1926; Simonen 1937.
6   Toivola 1943.
7   Ibid.
8   See, for example, Simonen 1937.
9   Toivola 1943.
10   Ibid., pp. 203-204.
11   Ibid., p. 204.
12   Ibid., p. 205.
13   Ibid., p. 206.
14   Ibid., pp 175-184.
15   Decree on Register over Vagrants 1945.
16   For example, Pakkotyölainsäädäntökomitean mietintö (Commission Report) 1948; Huolto-ohjelmakomitean mietintö (Commission Report) 1949; Irtolaishuoltotoimikunnan osamietintö (Commission Report) 1969.
17   Huoltolakien tarkistamiskomitean mietintö (Commission Report) 1946; Kasvatus- ja työlaitoskomitean mietintö (Commission Report) 1947; Huolto-ohjelmakomitean mietintö (Commission Report) 1949; Työlaitostoimikunnan mietintö (Commission Report) 1968; Irtolaishuoltotoimikunnan osamietintö (Commission Report) 1969; Lanu 1970.
18   Pakkotyölainsäädäntökomitean mietintö (Commission Report) 1948; Huolto-ohjelmakomitean mietintö (Commission Report) 1949; Irtolaishuoltotoimikunnan osamietintö (Commission Report) 1969.
19   Sosiaalihuollon periaatekomitean mietintö (Commission Report) 1968; Työlaitostoimikunnan mietintö (Commission Report) 1968; Irtolaishuoltotoimikunnan osamietintö (Commission Report) 1969; Taipale 1982.
20   Huolto-ohjelmakomitean mietintö (Commission Report) 1949; Taipale 1982.
21   Irtolaislain kumoamisen vaikutuksia selvittävän toimikunnan mietintö (Commission Report) 1986.
22   Työlaitosten ja kunnalisten huoltoloiden kehittämistoimikunnan raportti (Commission Report) 1977; Päihdeasiainneuvottelukunnan mietintö (Commission Report) 1978; Taipale 1982.
23   See Järvinen 1984.
24   For example, Kölli 1982; Drake 1983; Nygård 1985; Tuulasvaara-Kaleva 1988.
25   See for example, Jokivartio 1946.
26   Pätiälä & Mäkikylä 1948.
27   Pätiälä & Mäkikylä 1948; see also Jokivartio 1946.
28   Härö 1961; Härö & Kilpiö 1961.
29   Pönkä 1984.
30   Ibid.
31   Ehdotus irtolaislaiksi (Commission Report) 1926; Pakkotyölainsäädäntökomitean mietintö (Commission Report) 1948; Huolto-ohjelmakomitean mietintö (Commission Report) 1949.
32   Soikkeli 1949.

33   Soikkeli 1949; see also Paasio 1956; Koivusaari 1958; Penttilä 1965;
      Turunen 1965.
34   Tolkki 1969.
35   Tolkki 1969; see also Nissi 1965; Turunen 1965; Sandberg 1970; Golo-
      win-Salonen 1974; Grönholm & Laine 1976; Lukkariniemi 1980.
36   Työlaitosten ja kunnalisten huoltoloiden kehittämistoimikunnan raportti
      (Commission Report) 1977; Päihdeasiainneuvottelukunnan mietintö
      (Commission Report) 1978.
37   Irtolaislain kumoamisen vaikutuksia selvittävän toimikunnan mietintö
      (Commission Report) 1986.
38   Ibid.; see also Taipale 1982.
39   Ehdotus irtolaislaiksi (Commission Report) 1926; Huttunen 1926; Böök
      1936; Simonen 1937.
40   Koivusaari 1958.
41   Rauhala 1984.
42   See, for example, Irtolaislain kumoamisen vaikutuksia selvittävän toimi-
      kunnan mietintö (Commission Report) 1986.
43   Härö 1961; Härö & Siivola 1965.
44   Varsa & Heinonen 1984.
45   See Irtolaislain kumoamisen vaikutuksia selvittävän toimikunnan miet-
      intö (Commission Report) 1986.
46   See, for example, Irtolaislain kumoamisen vaikutuksia selvittävän toimi-
      kunnan mietintö (Commission Report) 1986; Varsa 1986.
47   Irtolaislain kumoamisen...(Commission Report) 1986.
48   Ibid.
49   Ibid.
50   Statistics from National Board of Health and Welfare on anti-vagrancy
      measures 1937-1985; see also Taipale 1982; Varsa & Heinonen 1984.
51   National Board for Health and Welfare statistics on anti-vagrancy
      measures 1937-1985; see also Mäkinen 1979.
52   National Board of Health and Welfare statistics on anti-vagrancy
      measures 1937-1985.
53   Varsa & Heinonen 1984.
54   Source: Annual Reports of Helsinki Police Department 1952-1986.
55   Source: Annual Reports of Helsinki Police Department 1952-1986.
56   See General Population 1950, 1960, 1970, and 1980.

4.

Prostitution Environments:
Streets, Restaurants and Youth Hang-Outs

4.1. Introduction

Although the concept of prostitution in the Vagrancy Act was the same throughout the period 1945-86, the phenomenon was defined in very different ways at different points in time. Furthermore, the definitional processes and the control of commercial sex took different forms in the various prostitution environments.

Figure 4 gives a first impression of where Helsinki's prostitution took place during the period under study. Here it is shown where arrests were made or which prostitution environments were mentioned in the police records. The data consist of a total of 3 305 arrests, divided by type of prostitution. This figure is higher than that of the prostitutes in the random sample (1 381 persons), since many women were registered more than once.

Street prostitution was especially prominent during the 1940s and the first half of the 1950s. During that period, 15-25 per cent of the arrests were for street prostitution. By the end of the 1960s, this type of prostitution had almost entirely disappeared from the records.

As shown in Fig. 4, harbours, restaurants, and the central railway station were significant prostitution environments in earlier decades. The proportion of all arrests for harbour prostitution decreased from 25 per cent in the early 1960s to less than five per cent by the end of the 1970s. Simultaneously, arrests for prostitution at the central railway station decreased from 35 per cent at the beginning of the 1970s to five per cent in the early 1980s.

The most important form of police-registered prostitution during the 1970s and 1980s was sexual transactions between socially marginalized women and their male counterparts. This type of prostitute, typi-

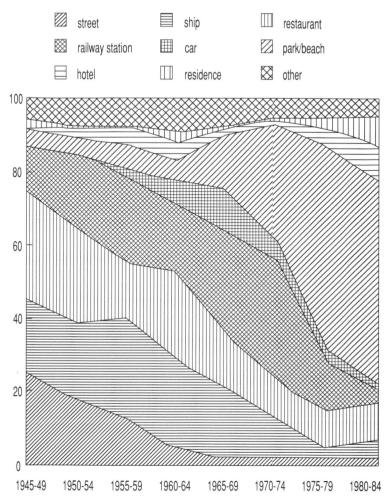

	street		ship		restaurant
	railway station		car		park/beach
	hotel		residence		other

Fig. 4. Arrests of female vagrants in Helsinki, by location (percentage distribution during five-year periods)

cally arrested in parks or public squares, constituted nearly 60 per cent of all registrations after 1975. Two other forms of prostitution increased their share among arrests, that of hotel prostitution and call-girl activities in residences.

4.2. The Street as Prostitution Milieu

Helsinki today is a city without street prostitution of the type found in most Western countries, that is, commercial sex concentrated in specific areas where prostitutes gather in search for customers. Thus, Helsinki lacks the kind of prostitution often considered to be the most public and least exclusive one, and the kind that entails purely commercial, easily classified relationships between customers and prostitutes. The city is thus without one of the most regulated, stigmatized, and despised forms of prostitution - the prototype of professional sexual relations[1]

The Helsinki police records from the 1940s and 1950s nevertheless reveal that once street prostitution did exist in the city. The records for 123 women (9 per cent) out of 1 381 refer to street prostitution; nearly all (114) of these are from 1945-59. During this period, two major streets in the absolute center of the city were in focus: Mannerheim Street and the Esplanade, with 38 per cent and 24 per cent of the arrests, respectively. All other streets mentioned in the police records account for less than ten per cent of the arrests.

The presence of prostitutes on the two major streets of Helsinki was described in the following manner:

«A wandered around the center of town for about an hour and spoke to various men. Finally, she made contact with a stranger; the couple apparently intended to go to the man's home» (records 1950).

«B was observed in the center of town... She was intoxicated and tried for 1 1/2 hours to make contact with men, in all likelihood in order to earn money. She asked six-seven men how much money they had. If the men looked well off, she asked them for taxi fare. She chased after one man she was sure had money. When the man asked if he could also get something for the taxi money, she replied 'yes'» (records 1959).

«C wandered back and forth... for more than two hours, swinging her umbrella and swaying her body... A whole flock of men followed her but they all kept their distance since her price was so high. Several men said that she cost 10 000 marks» (records 1954).

These prostitution activities seem to have been concentrated around carriage and taxicab stands. Some of the street prostitutes were referred to in the police records as «carriage girls», after the horse-drawn cabs still in use in the 1940s and 1950s. It is evident that street prostitution in the center of Helsinki in particular emanated from the taxi stand on the Esplanade:

«After strolling Mannerheim, Mikael, Central, and Alexander Streets, D came to the taxi stand on the North Esplanade... She tried to climb up into the carriage where an elderly intoxicated gentleman was sitting» (records 1947).

«In order to get a catch, E climbed into a carriage... The man inside denied knowing E to the police but admitted that she seemed willing to accompany him for indecent purposes» (records 1946).

In some cases the transactions seemingly were a product of cooperation between the prostitutes, the coachmen or drivers, and the customers:

«F and another girl had told the carriage driver from Mikael Street where he could find them if customers came along. The carriage arrived and one of the girls quickly jumped in, leaving the other at her post... F had birth control devices in her purse when she was arrested» (records 1952).

«The taxi drove once around the Old Church Park; the driver apparently had an agreement with G. Three men from (the city of) Lahti sat in the car. They asked her to come along... G was hesitant about joining so many men. But when they said that all three had lots of money, she quickly conceded and got in the car» (records 1953).

Of 123 records involving women suspected of street prostitution, about one-fourth included notes such as «H has been seen negotiating with carriage drivers», «J seems to know the drivers quite well», «K hovers near the taxi station», or «L lives in a hostel where the drivers come when they have suitable customers» (records). That the prostitution described - including the cooperation between the drivers/chauffeurs and the prostitutes - was general knowledge during the 1940s and 1950s is obvious from the newspaper articles in the police press archives. The vice police maintained (in newspaper interviews and in my own interviews) that they definitely intervened in «the procurement of girls» if it was conspicuous. However, they also admitted that it was extremely difficult to prove this type of violation on the part of the drivers. A review of the criminal police's procurement cases reveals that no carriage/ taxi station «girl-procurers» were ever prosecuted (see Chpt. 6).

Controlling Street Prostitution

Most arrests of street prostitutes were the direct result of vice police patrols in the relevant areas. In the following extracts from interviews, three vice policemen recall how this social control was organized:

«The Esplanade was sort of a central point for us then (1950s, MJ), when carriages were still in use in the city. There were always about 10 girls around. They hung out at the Swedish Theatre. When a customer came from a restaurant or the like, they left with him, in a taxi, a carriage, or on foot» (interview 1985).

«They chased men on the streets then... And we stood and waited for them... the carriage-girls. We patrolled, stood in doorways, at shop-windows, and waited... and froze... We watched them for a while... when we were sure, we broke up the transactions. Sometimes we arrested the girls at the hostels where they often took their customers» (interview 1985).

«I remember once... in the beginning of the 1960s when I was new here... I was one of the first women police officers... We stood there on the Esplanade and watched the girls. I went into a doorway... was going to look in a shop-window and suddenly a women snarled at me: 'Go to hell, whore, these are my hunting grounds'... I did what she said (laugh) and left» (interview 1985).

Some of these arrests were based on reporting from informants. Occasionally, the women's parents or husbands pointed the police towards them:

«My wife has left her home and work... I found out she was in Helsinki... She is sick and is spreading infection... Her description is: She has a green coat... brown-green or yellow-green, not clear green... and black dress with white lace collar» (letter 1952 to vice police).

Dissatisfied customers could also act informant:

«A man who wishes to remain anonymous states that a couple of days ago he, in intoxicated condition, accompanied a woman of the streets and spent the night with her. In the morning he noticed that the woman had open sores and scars on her arms and legs. He now fears he has been infected with a venereal disease» (records 1947).

«A man relates that he met two women on the street and that he took them to his office 'for indecent purposes'. In the office, he gave each of the women 350 marks, whereupon they suddenly disappeared. He caught one of the women down on the street» (records 1947).

Sometimes the spouses of prostitution customers informed:

«M is arrested in the home of couple X. Mrs. X explains that her husband brought M home, kept her there night and day, and drove out his wife» (records 1945).

«N says that last night she met an unknown man on the street. He invited N to his home and said that his wife was gone. In the morning, the wife suddenly returned home. She called the police immediately» (records 1951).

The police records contain very limited information about the customers of street prostitutes during the 1940s and 1950s. As was specified in the directives of the Vagrancy Act, the object of control was the prostitutes, not the customers, and the latters' requests to remain anonymous were respected by the police. However, the few references that do exist indicate that the clientele was heterogeneous in age and social status. Some customers are described as «gray-haired men», others as «two whipper-snapper boys, one drunk», or «three young men that O called students, none of whom who wore their class cap». Other descriptions include «properly dressed gentlemen» and «men in dirty work overalls», and in a few cases, direct references are made to the customer's occupation: «P was arrested at the home of a fur dealer»; «Q was found at Y's automobile garage»; «R's circle of customers seems to consist of labourers and sailors» (records).

Professionalism in Street Prostitution

To what degree then did the sexual contacts described in the police records fulfil the criteria in the Vagrancy Act that a) the sexual acts were to be linked to monetary compensation, and b) that the compensated sexual acts were to have developed into a life style (Chpt. 3.2.)? How was the phenomenon of commercialized sex defined by the vice police and how did the arrested women themselves depict their actions on the streets?

The arrestees' most common explanations for their mere presence on the streets during the evenings or at night were «visiting friends» and «going to the movies»:

«S claims to have visited a family. On her way home, she took an extra swing around town looking for a place to buy cigarettes» (records 1948).

«T maintains that she had gone to the movies, the 9 o'clock showing. She unfortunately cannot remember which cinema she visited, nor the name of the film» (records 1950).

Other explanations used by these «single women» (that is, women unaccompanied by men) were «taking a walk while waiting for a train/bus/tram» or «looking for a taxi after missing the last bus home». Less common and less legitimate reasons included:

> «U claims that she was walking back and forth along Mannerheim Street because she didn't dare go home drunk, since her landlady Mrs. X doesn't condone drinking» (records 1948).

> «V says she has a weak heart, and that her doctor has recommended fresh air as often as possible. Therefore, it is not so strange that she wanders around on her own in the evenings» (records 1961).

According to police comments, many of the women's stories were fabricated. The woman who claimed to have just left a movie theatre had been observed on Mannerheim Street for several hours. A woman who said she had just «arrived in Helsinki by train» had in fact lived in a hostel in the city for several weeks. Only two cases were found where the women apparently succeeded in convincing the police that they had been falsely arrested: «X seems to be an honest working-class women, and we allowed her to leave»; «Y was able to give us the name and address of the family she had just visited... she has a job and a place to live and has never before been arrested... she seems trustworthy» (records).

The women were also requested to explain why they spoke to men on the streets. Some denied having had contact with men at all:

> «Z asks us why she couldn't be left alone even on a Sunday evening. Even a cat can get impatient, she says... and disavows having been out with gentlemen, 'unless you can call the vice police gentlemen'» (records 1960).

Other women pointed out that it was the men who initiated the conversations, and not vice versa: «A complains that several men accosted her during her walk; she refused them all... and was relieved when the police came to her rescue, she says» (records). One woman's explanation runs as follows:

> «B states that she strolled up and down Mannerheim Street but that she wasn't out after men. She says she ducked into a doorway to rest, and that a man followed and spoke to her... She lifted up her skirt to adjust her garter, and not to show the man her legs» (records 1949).

Still other women claimed to be closely acquainted with the men in their company: «C says that the man she was seen with is her husband - in my own husband's company, I can go where I please, she declares»; «I have not spoken to men on the street other than relatives and old acquaintances, D explains; – that woman has a big family» (records). However, some of the men laid no claim to knowing these women:

> «E and F were watched... together with two men. The couples approached two taxis, whereupon the women were arrested. The men denied knowing the women. When they heard from the vice police that E and F were well-known vagrants, they said they wanted nothing to do with them» (records 1948).

Finally, many arrested women were asked to explain why they spoke with carriage/taxi drivers so often. One woman explained:

> «G claims that she got separated from her boyfriend as they stepped off the tram at the railroad station. So she walked around the center of town looking for him. On Mannerheim Street, she asked a carriage driver who knew her boyfriend if he had seen him. Later she looked in another carriage to see whether her boyfriend was sitting inside. It was then that she was arrested by the police» (records 1945).

When the police arrested women as street-walkers for the first time, it is often unclear whether the two prostitution criteria in the Vagrancy Act, «sexual acts for compensation» and «habitualness» have been met. What is clear from the interrogations is: a) that the women had difficulty coming up with a reasonable explanation for their wanderings along the Esplanade, Mannerheim Street, etc.; b) that they had been spoken to by various men and in some cases had discussed sex for payment with them; and c) that some of the women seemed to have some form of agreement with carriage/taxi drivers. However, it remains unclear whether the arrested women were professional prostitutes in the judicial sense, that is, if the sexual contacts for compensation had developed into a life style.

Among the 123 women who are indicated as street prostitutes in the sample, ten per cent had been arrested once by the vice police, and the rest, two or more times. The group's average number of arrests was 11 and stretched over an average period of 8.2 years. About one-third of the 123 women admitted at one point or another during interrogation that they had performed as prostitutes: «H says that she has had intercourse with men for money, at the men's homes, at their offices, or at the hostel»; «J admits that she was hunting men; men are my source of income, she says». One-fifth of the women persisted in denying they were prostitutes: «K claims that her husband's information is untrue, that it is based on jealousy and spite»; «L refuses to discuss sexual relations even this time; she views the questions as impertinent», and the remaining records lack any clear indication on whether prostitution was admitted or denied.

Some of the women had apparently acted as prostitutes previously but had ceased doing so: «M protests against the fact that all women registered by the vice police are forever suspected, no matter what they are doing in town»; «N is furious about being arrested; she has tried to live properly for several weeks, she says» (records). The arrests were nevertheless made in accordance with the law since persons under vagrancy supervision (both M and N above) were routinely instructed to keep away from certain street environments.

The vice police had the endlessly flexible Vagrancy Act at their disposal; if there was not enough evidence that a woman had acted as a prostitute, her behaviour probably still fell under one of the other criteria found in the law, such as «wandering from place to place» or «refusal to work». As many vice policemen stated in interviews, prostitution is an activity that seldom or never could be proven: «the nature of the phenomenon is such that you cannot be 100 per cent certain... we did not peek through keyholes at the hostels... in order to see what the man and woman did... or if the man paid... that's why we write in our notes 'suspected of commercial fornication'» (interview 1985 with vice police).

Could it have happened that some of the vice police's female clients during the 1940s and 1950s were innocently suspected of street prostitution, despite observations of the behaviour described in the quotations above? One vice police says:

«Innocently suspected... no, I don't think so. Or at least it was rare. We watched them for a long time before we arrested them... we didn't arrest any innocent housewives out shopping... And we were familiar with many of the girls... and the girls knew each other... and us... and gave us some bits of information... It wasn't innocent virgins we arrested, no» (interview 1985 with vice police).

However, the professionalism of the 1940s and 1950s street prostitution does not seem to have been as advanced as that found in street prostitution abroad. One woman who was arrested for vagrancy in the 1960s gave this assessment of the professionalism of the sex trade on the Esplanade and on Mannerheim Street:

«There were no paid women... I mean who would display themselves in windows or stand half-naked and wait... like you see on TV for example... There were only women who were... a little loose. If you went to a restaurant and didn't want to go home alone... and a man came along who didn't want to go home alone either... then you went with each other. That's not so strange... But you weren't allowed to do that... nor to go to the hostel, they spied on you there too (the police). You couldn't do anything in those days... not have lots of men... For money, if we got paid? Nah, you know... I don't remember anymore» (interview 1988 with Anneli, 58 years).

Control of prostitution by the vice police during these decades was not only directed at professional prostitutes (women who satisfied the criteria for prostitution in Chpt. 1.3. or those found in the Vagrancy Act). The control was aimed at women who violated important sexual norms by «wandering back and forth on the streets» at night; «behaving provocatively» and «swinging with their body»; «following unknown men home or to a hostel» and women who submitted ambiguous information about their working or residential circumstances - regardless of whether this was related to professional prostitution or not. Further, visible use/abuse of alcohol in some cases seems to have been sufficient cause for intervention by the police. Judging from stray remarks in the police records, the notations «sexually provocative» behaviour and «alcohol abuse» were used to create a «general moral impression» of the women. Apparently, it was this overall picture - and not whether the arrestees fulfilled the criterion of habitualness in the Vagrancy Act - that was decisive in the choice of official measures (warning, supervision, institutionalization).

Declining Trends in Street Prostitution

Five different explanations can be offered for the substantial decrease in street prostitution during the 1950s and 1960s (see Fig. 4).

First, the decline may be illusory, in the sense that there was only a reduction in police arrests while the sexual transactions continued as before. Women strolling alone on the streets of Helsinki in evenings and nights were more easily a target for police attention in earlier days than after the 1960s. This is undoubtedly the case, but obviously the women arrested were not always innocent strollers. All of them were not professional prostitutes as defined in the Vagrancy Act, but many were seemingly on the streets for a specific purpose: to make sexual, in some cases compensated, contacts. This was indicated not only by the police's observations, but also by many male strollers, who willingly submitted information about the negotiations they had with the women. Second, instead of decreasing, street prostitution may have spread out over a broader area and thereby become less visible in the city as a whole. Street walking may have expanded to areas with lower status in the city, streets that are not as sensitive to social disturbances as are the Esplanade and Mannerheim Street. The prostitution scene may also have shifted to other public places, such as the city's parks, the waterfront, and so on. The decrease in street prostitution is indeed accompanied by a sharp increase in arrests of marginalized women joining male drinking groups (cf. Fig.4). It is apparent though that the outdoor prostitution of the 1970s and 1980s has little in common with the street prostitution of prior decades. Today's marginalized women are seldom «public prostitutes» in the sense that some of the post-war street-walkers were. They are homeless and unemployed women, often with alcohol problems, who sell themselves to men in drinking gangs or other men from similar social strata. There is no specific park, beach, or other outdoor area in today's Helsinki where, for example, late-night male patrons of restaurants could go assured of finding companionship as there was in former times.

Third, the decrease in street prostitution may be real and a consequence of rigourous police measures against the previous sex commerce on the streets. The repeated arrests may have led to a general ghettoization and privatization of prostitution, forcing the women into less visible forms of paid sex relations, especially call-girl and hotel prostitution.

It is certainly true that the police arrested street prostitutes more often than women practicing the trade in restaurants, hotels, or in private homes. Moreover, some groups of prostitutes apparently believed that street prostitution - in contrast to other types of commercialized sex - was forbidden. This notion is found, for example, among Finnish women operating in Sweden: «In Stockholm, I walk the streets; in Helsinki, I visit ships because it is against the law to walk the streets here» (records 1962). On the other hand, it is difficult to conceive why police interventions against street prostitution would have such drastic effects in the 1950s. The authorities did not accelerate their actions during that decade (such as more arrests per woman, more institutionalizations) - on the contrary, the control measures de-escalated. In addition, the vice police actively intervened against other types of prostitution during that time, such as prostitution on ships, without having achieved a corresponding effect.

Fourth, restaurant prostitution may have replaced street walking when restaurants opened their doors to unaccompanied women in the late 1960s (see below). The fact is, however, that some establishments had been open for prostitutes throughout the period under study, playing an important procuring role in the 1940s and 1950s, although the general control of the female patrons was of the strictest nature. There was also a link between restaurant and street prostitution during these decades: «The arrestee says that she often makes contact with her customers on the street and then accompanies them to some restaurant»; «The girl always appears outside restaurant X at closing time hunting for customers»; «The arrestee hangs around restaurant Y; if she finds no one willing, she tries her luck out in the dark» (records). More than one-third of the records for women involved in street-walking indicate restaurant prostitution as well. Rather than replacing each other, some of the combined forms of street and restaurant prostitution disappeared from the 1950s to the 1960s.

Finally, the decrease in street-walking may be linked to a «generational shift» in prostitution which occurred during these decades. The Esplanade and Mannerheim Street continued as relatively important haunts for some of the older prostitutes, especially women recruited to commercialized sex immediately after the Second World War. Thus, according to police records, the average age of the street-walkers was higher in the 1950s than had earlier been the case. With a rising average age and increasing numbers of marginalized women, the street prostitution gradually changed character. The development can be illustrated by means of the following example:

O was arrested the first time in 1951, 20 years old, when a man complained to the police that she had infected him with a venereal disease. During the 1950s, she was repeatedly arrested for street and restaurant prostitution. In 1955, for example, she said during police interrogations that she spent her days and evenings at assorted restaurants and her nights on the streets - until she met appropriate company: «I have to go somewhere - I don't have an apartment where I can hide from the police». O had a favourite doorway on George Street where she waited for customers. At the beginning of the 1960s, she was totally excluded from the labour and housing market; she also had an alcohol problem. The police wrote: «O is one of the few of the old guard who is out on the streets every evening regardless of the weather». The trade got worse and worse though; O had difficulty finding customers and was sometimes so intoxicated that she forgot to take pay for her services. She was arrested a total of 42 times. In 1970, police records show that she lived with an old man who was supporting her (records 1951-70).

Eventually, the street lost its attraction for newcomers to prostitution. Other environments such as ships, some cafés, the central railway station (cf. Chpt. 4.4.) captured their interest. The street and its prostitutes did not fit into the youth culture and milieus generated in the 1960s. When new recruitment waned, street prostitution also lost its hold on the customers. With this shift, the circle was completed - the attention of the vice police turned away from the streets to other prostitution areas.

4.3. Restaurants as Prostitution Milieu

Traditionally, restaurants have played a central role in the sex commerce of Helsinki, being especially significant in the control of prostitution during the 1940s and 1950s (see Fig. 4). Of the total sample of 1 381 women, almost 40 per cent were suspected at one point or another of making contacts with customers at restaurants. Below, an analysis is made of the interplay between the prostitutes in various restaurants and the authorities who controlled restaurant prostitution: the Helsinki vice police and the state liquor monopoly (ALKO).

Restaurants under Suspicion

The number of restaurants mentioned in the police records was especially high during the 1950s and early 1960s. In that period, about one-third of all premises in Helsinki where alcohol was served were suspected of prostitution procurement. After the end of the 1960s, the number of restaurants in the records decreased substantially, in absolute numbers as well as in relation to the number of places with alcohol sales-on-the-premises. During the 1970s and 1980s, police records show that prostitution contacts were made at ten per cent of Helsinki's restaurants.

From all of the restaurants named in the police records during the entire period under study, 22 were chosen for closer investigation (establishments mentioned at least 15 times in the records). Of these, 11 were dance restaurants, six were hotel restaurants/night clubs, two were sailors' taverns, and the remainder were local pubs.

From the ALKO inspectors' reports, 15 restaurants were selected, premises where prostitution procurement was directly indicated. In the reports are also found (almost as many) restaurants described as «common hunting galleries» or «taverns with large proportions of unaccompanied women», but the information about sexual contacts at these establishments is too limited to be usable in an analysis of prostitution. Direct information about commercialized sex is primarily found in the inspectors' reports from the 1940s and 1950s. If we compare the reports of the ALKO inspectors with those of the police, we find that all 15 restaurants in the former are also mentioned in the latter. These two agencies joined forces in the control of restaurants, especially in the earlier years. Judging from the monopoly's archives, the cooperation consisted of the police informing the inspectors as to which restaurants attracted «criminal elements» or «loose women and ship girls». Naturally, the exchange of information contributed to the adoption of a uniform view of the restaurant problem.

The Restaurant Standards

The standard of the restaurants played a significant role in the principles of prostitution control. In the following letter from the Alcohol Monopoly to the Ministry of Social Affairs in 1961, the monopoly explains the link between prostitution and the standards of restaurants:

> «The restaurants' profit share, computed as a certain percentage of the alcohol prices, is greatest in the upper restaurant category and gradually decreases down to the fourth price category... The fourth price category consists of common restaurants, the third price category of lower-middle class, the second of upper-middle class, and the first is reserved for restaurants providing service of the highest quality... Unaccompanied women who patronize restaurants 'for a special purpose' lower the standard of an establishement. This is especially true of entertainment restaurants. Most of the unaccompanied women, according to general opinion, belong in the third-class price category» (letter 1961 from the Alcohol Monopoly to the Ministry of Social Affairs).

Accordingly, prostitutes were considered a natural part of the restaurant environment, but not in establishments of the first and second price classes. However, this rule was difficult to enforce in practice; as shown below, a wide range of restaurants were suspected of prostitution activities.

The ALKO inspectors described the atmosphere at one of the very known prostitution restaurants of the 1940s and 1950s, an establishment of the third price class owned by a subsidiary of the Alcohol Monopoly, as follows:

> «X resembles an underground tavern... with a clientele that would hardly be allowed in at any other restaurant in Helsinki. Ordinary citizens would not willingly go there to quench their thirst... The room is filled with drunken men and women... The noise is outrageous and isn't helped by the ear-splitting music from the loudspeakers... These people are definitely not nature lovers, as they can be seen sitting here sweating away even on Midsummer's Eve (reports 1947-56).

The facility that headed the monopoly's prostitution list during the 1950s was a dance restaurant in the third, and later the fourth, price category. The place was labelled in 1956 by an inspector «the most sinful restaurant in town»:

«The clientele is worse than at any other dance restaurant in town... The owner has abandoned any notion of dress code. 'There is no person in Helsinki who is too poorly dressed to be allowed in here', he says... The restaurant attracts foreign men who come 'for a special purpose'... we have observed Italians and Japanese, Negroes and mulattos... The majority of women belong to the round-heeled guard» (reports 1950-59).

The two sailor taverns in the police material were also described by the ALKO inspectors:

«The tavern is periodically the unruliest in town. It is a haven for ship girls and young vagrant women... the clientele otherwise consists of people from the lowest levels of the working-class... The harbour and the sailors draw suspect women here» (reports 1955-56).

«Half of the room is filled with young women, the other half with sailors... a real sailors' tavern... The proximity of the harbour means that it is often filled to the hilt... The general picture today is very unsettling. New ships arrive and customers exchange the latest news, sometimes in loud voices, in a genuine sailor fashion... Everyone knows each other, seamen, 'sea-women', and dock workers» (reports 1947-57).

Of the 15 restaurants suspected by ALKO for prostitution, five belonged to the first/second price classes (see above). Of the 22 restaurants in the police material, seven (including the night clubs of the 1980s) belonged to the first price class. Two establishments of the highest price class where prostitution transactions occurred received these words by the inspectors:

«The lighting is so dim that you cannot even read a newspaper... A quiet highball clientele... men and unaccompanied women... appear to be enjoying themselves... many men are sitting here in paletot and hat... A painting on the wall appeals to people's most prurient instincts, and it serves as a temptation for spineless individuals» (reports 1951-53).

«The overall atmosphere is bad. A typical hunting gallery... The clientele consists of businessmen and some so-called artist types, all in the same 'the day after' condition. Orders such as 'a boiled egg and two bottles of beer' indicate that this is place for recovery.» (reports 1956-63).

«Unaccompanied Women»

Women without male escort constituted a substantial problem for ALKO and the restaurants in the 1940s, 1950s, and 1960s. There was no general prohibition applying to all unaccompanied women, all restaurants, and all times of the day; women were accepted during the correct hours and if their express purpose was to eat. In the more expensive restaurants, unaccompanied women or «a company of women» were welcome if their clothing, appearance, and demeanour - in the eyes of the restaurant controllers - met the standards of the establishment. Dance restaurants, where women were an integral part, made up a class unto themselves. The combination of alcohol consumption and dancing made these restaurants especially troublesome from a moral perspective. Dancing facilitated sexual contacts, commercial and non-commercial, and unaccompanied women thus had to be closely supervised.

At more expensive restaurants, men were not allowed to approach women they did not know: «If the staff observe a man asking a woman at the next table to dance, they tell the head-waiter who then gives the man his bill» (report). The tables should not be too close to each other, to prevent «strangers making contact with each other at different tables» as well as «round-heeled women's activities» (report). Restaurant patrons who did not know one another were not to be placed at the same table: «Total strangers share tables at this common restaurant, something that does not promote moral propriety» (report). The dancing was to be performed discreetly and morally irreprehensibly:

«Among the couples on the dance floor, I took special notice of two Norwegian sailors in casual female company. One sailor kissed his partner on the dance floor... and the other twirled his partner around so quickly that she fell against a table. The sailor lifted her up but the girl sunk to the floor like a dish rag» (report 1948, second price class restaurant).

«About half of the restaurant guests were women and there was no mistaking the quality here... The dancing was uninhibited and not pretty to watch, to my eyes, and in no case were the circumstances suitable for a restaurant of high class» (report 1964, third price class restaurant).

The most important rule concerning the control of morals at restaurants, though, was that the proportion of unaccompanied women was not to be too high:

«The unaccompanied women make a bad impression. All of them, except two old grandmothers, seem to be on the chase after men» (report 1953, third price class restaurant).

«It is obvious that the restaurant today divides its guests into castes. The best clientele is placed in the dance hall and the worst, such as unaccompanied women, are placed in the bar... The proportion of unaccompanied women is greater here than at any other restaurant in this price class» (report 1956, second price class).

«Most of the women are fast. This attracts both foreigners and Helsinki's grass-widowers... The men are generally middle-aged, and seem to be resolute charmers. An improvement of the restaurant's standard is impossible as long as single women are admitted» (reports 1952-58, second price class restaurant).

Nonetheless, the share of unaccompanied women could not be allowed to shrink too low, in case this would have a detrimental effect on the finances of the dance restaurants:

«Not many customers. The most important reason is perhaps that the restaurant has tried to block entry to unaccompanied women. So now also the men have moved to other restaurants where they are likely to find dance partners» (report 1956, first price class restaurant).

If the proportion of single women was low, the competition for them could also lead to disorder: «The atmosphere was touch-and-go since all the men flocked around the few unescorted women's tables»; «They really wanted to dance; sometimes you saw three men bowing to the same woman»; «Of 60 guests, only... five unaccompanied women who were in great demand»; «The few women, regardless of age or appearance, attracted the men like magnets» (reports).

Some dance restaurants apparently tried to solve the problem by establishing a quota for the number of women admitted without male escort:

«The head-waiter volunteered that the restaurant management, after a period of declining patronage, ordered that unaccompanied women were to be admitted once again. However, these women are limited to one four-person table and two two-person tables» (report 1960, second price class restaurant).

«Often there are six tables with unaccompanied ladies. There seems to be a fixed quota to ensure the restaurant's reputation as a decent contact place and at the same time to assure a sufficient number of customers» (report 1964, second price class restaurant).

A fifty per cent quota of women was considered too high, the fear being that the women would «leave their mark» on the entire restaurant, with intervention by ALKO as the result. This was the case despite the fact that such a high proportion of women was described in some reports as a «calming factor»: «As many women as men; the atmosphere was very peaceful when there for once was no fighting over the women» (report).

Denunciations and Arrests

Some unaccompanied women had the bad luck of soliciting plain-clothes policemen: «A drunk woman approached me and asked me to come along, she said that she would treat me to this and that»; «One of the round-heeled ladies came up and said, 'a handsome man like you shouldn't be allowed to go home alone'» (records).

Other «suspect women» were pointed out to the police by the restaurant personnel: «P was arrested at the request of the doorman; she had gone from table to table in the restaurant after male company;» «According to the doorman, Q showed up at the restaurant every day, and the men swarmed around her»; «The head-waiter asked us to take care of R; the girl will go under if she doesn't get any help, he said» (records).

Sometimes, the women were arrested on the basis of outsiders' complaints:

«Miss S, originating from village X, spends all her time in restaurant Y. I certainly don't need to spell out how she makes her living! Arrest her, dear vice police.» (letter 1951 to vice police)

«...two beauties... the one has gonorrhea that she is spreading through various dance restaurants. The women have an address first here, then there. It is easiest to reach them at dance restaurant X which is their regular hang-out. With the greatest respect, from one who hates vagrant women» (letter 1948 to vice police).

The greatest number of unaccompanied women was nevertheless arrested as a result of raids at restaurants or of police patrolling immediately outside:

> T was arrested outside of a sailor's tavern. She had been banned from the tavern because she «day in and day out loafed around with foreign sailors». The police found an address book in her purse with the telephone numbers of dozens of different men (records 1965).
>
> U was arrested outside restaurant X where the following took place: She climbed into a car, «but refused the driver intercourse as he had no money». She got out again and stopped the first best car, which «happened to belong to the vice police» (records 1965).

In some cases, the police discussed the sexual morals of the women suspects with male restaurant patrons: «Everyone knows V, we were told by Mr. X who wishes to remain anonymous; she goes home with just about anyone who promises her something to drink»; «The man told us that he sat at Y's table and asked what her price was; the price though was so high that he left immediately» (records).

Professionalism Within Restaurant Prostitution

The restaurant inspectors' reports illustrate the classification system used to define unescorted women as prostitutes:

> «Two women, undoubtedly of the loose type... raise their glasses with all of the men in the restaurant... and finally someone accepts their offer» (report 1950, second price class restaurant).

> «One woman, who apparently longs for male company, is leaning back with her hands in her ulster pockets and one leg seductively crossed over the other. She starts a conversation with the men at the next table and lets them know how 'boring' it is to sit alone» (report 1953, third price class restaurant).

> «A bad impression, due to... the ladies. For instance, a woman around 40 years old has evidently been in a fight, and has a very bruised eye. She is sitting in the company of a 25-year old man, which does not hinder her from flirting with other men...» (report 1957, third price class restaurant).

Similar descriptions of the restaurants' «public women» are found in the police records:

«Z was discovered at restaurant X on the hunt for men. She meaningly cast a long look at the man at the next table. He responded and then left. Z hurried out after him... After a moment's negotiations they went to an alcohol shop and then to an empty railroad car» (records 1945).

Female restaurant patrons who «toasted with all the men in the restaurant», «looked longingly at the men», or «left the restaurant with strange men» were suspected of being prostitutes by the inspectors and vice police. Another sign of deficient morality among the women was to be familiar with restaurant personnel: «Those two women clearly are regular customers here; they don't even have to order food and are immediately each served a glass of spirits»; «The woman confers at length with the waiter, undoubtedly discussing the male patrons» (reports).

The ALKO inspectors and the vice police were trained observers who were quite familiar with the details of restaurant transactions:

«Seven unaccompanied women, all on 'fishing expeditions'. The women had a total command over the rules of the game. When the head-waiter approached, they sat as still as a candle. But as soon as his back was turned, they resumed their flirting... A pretty 22-23 year old focused her attention in one direction and then left. A man immediately followed. Despite her age, this woman was well initiated. A masterpiece in how to fool the head-waiter (report 1956, third price class restaurant).

Of the total 587 women in the sample who were at some time registered for restaurant prostitution, 24 per cent were arrested only once. The average number of arrests was 7.6 and the women's run-ins with the vice police extended over a period of about seven years. Of the 587 women, 20 per cent, at one point or another in their police recorded careers, described their sexual relations as prostitution:

«A claims that she preferably visits the finer restaurants... On the occasion in question, she sat down at X's table. X paid her restaurant bills and they proceeded to go to another restaurant. Once again, the man paid the bill there: 4 - 5 000 marks. A asked him for money for clothes: a pair of pants and a petticoat: 1 240 marks... A had intercourse with the man and received 1 000 marks for it» (records 1951).

«B relates that she normally goes to restaurants with a girlfriend, and that they seldom have money with them which is the reason why they strike up an acquaintance with men who are willing to pay.

She admits that it is understood that they will later follow the men home or to their workplaces. B says she seldom demands money from the men, but that she sometimes is given 20-30 marks for taxi-cab fare; a couple of times, she received jewelry from her restaurant acquaintances» (records 1965).

At least three circumstances complicated the efforts to control restaurant prostitution. First, very few of the arrested women came to the restaurants solely to earn money: «C says she goes to restaurants in order to eat, drink, and enjoy herself»; «D considers restaurant X as her home; all her friends sit here, she claims» (records). Second, many women did not define «sexual relations in exchange for restaurant entertainment» as prostitution, although the concurrent interpretation of the Vagrancy Act supported such a definition: «E repeatedly denies having been paid for her services; she admits though to allowing the men often to pay her restaurant tabs» (records). Third, the women's motivations for entering into these sexual liaisons appear to be entangled: «I went home with X because I wanted to drink with him, not because I wanted money»; «Can you believe it, two young handsome boys wanted me, an older woman» (records).

As with regard to street arrests, controlling prostitution at restaurants functioned as a generalized control of women's sexuality - and women's drinking. If women visited restaurants, if they intruded into male territory, they should at least refrain from demonstrating sexual interest and from breaking the norm of female temperance. Some protests from the women against these restrictions are found in the police records: «Suddenly a woman begins to perform: 'Look at me, a tipsy woman, now you don't have to go to the movies... why in hell do you always have to persecute drunken women'» (report); «F is totally hysterical. Why arrest me just because I like to sit at pubs, she is screaming. We do live in a free country, don't we?» (records).

Two women I interviewed about the control of restaurants during the 1960s recalled:

«You can't imagine what it was like at that time, crazy... If you wanted to go out dancing... or just to a bar, you got problems. So it was a matter of finding a man on the street. It didn't matter how shabby he was, just so he wore pants... Then we walked into the restaurant arm in arm... That's the way we did it at some restaurants but not all. At X pub, I knew the personnel so there was no problem» (interview 1988 with Raija, 62 years old).

«...It was after my divorce that I started going to restaurants alone. And I didn't even go very often... didn't want to. It felt like everyone looked at you, that they were thinking... you know, that everyone thought... I don't think that the women at the restaurants were very immoral. They were totally normal women... Maybe there were some restaurants, sailors' taverns, and the like... where the women were a little unusual... But not otherwise... It was just that it was so unpleasant to come to the restaurant... if you walked in with a girlfriend... Alone, no, I didn't go completely alone. I would never have done that» (interview 1988 with Gunnel, 51 years old).

Developments in Restaurant Prostitution

The control of restaurant prostitution remained largely unchanged right up to the middle of the 1960s. The number of arrests varied from year to year, and the focus of the control exercised by the vice police and inspectors shifted among restaurants. Nevertheless, the sexual contacts in restaurant life were described in similar fashion throughout the period.

Gradually though, the role of the Alcohol Monopoly as the guardian of women's morality changed from being an obvious task to becoming increasingly problematic. The control of female patrons was incompatible with the more liberal tenets of the 1960s both in sexual and alcohol attitudes. In addition, ALKO received some letters of protest from women who frequented restaurants:

«In the lobby, we were told that women (evidently women not in the company of men?) were not allowed into the restaurant bar... We were informed that 'available, hmmm, I mean unaccompanied women' are not supposed to visit the more expensive restaurants. We told him that we were not unattached women but rather customers. The head waiter replied, 'we will see how unattached you are later this evening'» (letter 1967 from three women to ALKO).

In 1967, the Alcohol Monopoly released a statement to restaurants to remedy «the seeming ignorance» pertaining to female visitors to restaurants. This statement stressed that there was no legislation that encouraged restaurants to discriminate on the basis of customers' sex. Further, it was noted that women without male escorts did «not in and of themselves lower the standard or price class of restaurants», and that ALKO did not take gender into account in its supervision of restaurants. Moreover, the Monopoly emphasized that men at the finer restaurants were expected not to accost the female guests who had come there seeking peace and quiet (letter 1967 from ALKO to the restaurants).

Subsequently, ALKO's archives covering the 1970s and 1980s contain no data relevant to the question of prostitution. According to police sources (records and interviews), the development of restaurant prostitution since the end of the 1960s can be summarized as follows.

To start, the sex commerce at sailors' taverns and other establishments frequented by seamen declined. A large part of the sexual contacts established in restaurants in earlier days were between sailors and prostitutes. Over the past two decades, this type of restaurant prostitution shrank substantially (sailors' pubs are further discussed in the end of section 4.4.).

Next, prostitution at dance restaurants (excluding night clubs) also declined according to the police records. These data do not necessarily reflect an actual decline in commercialized sex. While prior to the 1970s, the few «unaccompanied women» at restaurants were defined as a phenomenon obviously in need of control, in more recent times, the increasing proportion of female restaurant guests[2] has made it much more difficult to identify prostitutes. Identifiable or not, several of the prostitution contacts described in the early records were so commercialized that they would not have avoided police detection even in the 1980s.

Last, prostitution in the night clubs of the international hotels has rose, according to police sources (see Chpt. 5 for a discussion of hotel prostitution). In all probability, this reflects an actual growth in the sex commerce. It is difficult to imagine that hotel prostitution of the type later described could have been engaged in during the 1950s without intervention by the authorities.

4.4. Prostitution as a Youth Problem

There were three types of commercialized sex during the postwar period primarily defined as youth prostitution. One was harbour prostitution: judging from the police's press archives, public attention on the *ship girls* was most intensive during the late 1950s and early 1960s. Another type of youth prostitution was linked to hitchhiking: the *truck girls* were topical during the 1960s. A third type was prostitution at the central railway station: the *station girls* were in focus in the 1960s and early 1970s.

Ship Girls, Truck Girls, and Station Girls

Harbour prostitution (arrests for boarding ships and other contacts with sailors) was previously one of the most crucial forms of commercialized sex in Helsinki. The ship girls' share of all arrests was relatively constant (20-25 per cent) right up to the end of the 1960s. Since then, harbour prostitution has been of little significance (about five per cent of the arrests during the period 1975-86) (cf. Fig. 4).

Truck prostitution and the concept of truck girl emerged in the vice police's records in the mid-1950s. The term was used for girls who hitchhiked, typically with trailer-truck drivers, and who were suspected of paying for the rides with sex. As was seen in Fig. 4, this type of prostitution was a short-lived phenomenon; in the 1970s, again, truck-related prostitution was of little significance.

Entries concerning prostitution at the central railway station (contacts established in or immediately outside the main building, or in the station tunnel) appear in the records for the entire period under study, but especially at the end of the 1960s, when 28 per cent of all arrests were for station prostitution, and at the beginning of the 1970s, when the figure was 33 per cent.

To what degree then was harbour, truck, and station prostitution an actual youth problem? The average age (at first arrest) of the women registered for harbour prostitution alone (189 girls) was 20.9 years. The truck girls (89 girls only arrested for this type of commercialized sex) on the average were 17.6 years old, and the station girls (159 girls) were 20.5 years old at first arrest. The proportion who were under 18 years of age was 24 per cent of the ship girls, 40 per cent of the truck girls, and 22 per cent of the station girls. Thus, the prostitutes discussed here, especially the truck girls, belong to the youngest group in this study; the average age for the entire sample of 1 381 women was 23.7 years at first arrest.

The ship, truck, and station girls of the 1950s and 1960s were not only described as a youth problem in terms of the age factor but also in terms of the girls' family background. The police often located the cause for the the girls' wayward behaviour in their relationships with their parents. For example, at least one-third of these girls were cited as coming from homes that were split by divorce or death, and 15 per cent had lived with others than their biological parents at some time during childhood.

Information about divorce might be formulated as follows: «F, 14 years, has run away from home... after the divorce, her father remarried and F can't accept her stepmother»; «G came to Helsinki to meet her father... the father, who hardly knows G, refuses any contact with G or her mother» (records). Some of the records indicate that the girls' single mothers had severe social problems: «H, 16 years, left school to take care of her younger siblings. Her mother had gotten a job in Helsinki but couldn't take the children with her to stay in her small rented room... the children ended up living in a tent next to the church in their hometown» (records). Some of the girls remained when their parents moved abroad: «J's parents had left for Sweden. They had never even contemplated taking J, 18 years, with them. She moved to her grandmother's» (records).

In nine per cent of the records involving ship, truck, and station girls, entries about alcohol problems and illnesses in the family were found: «K, 15 years, ran away from home... father is alcoholic and mother is mentally ill» (records). In seven of the records, mention was made of incest between father/stepfather and daughter: «L, 18 years, hitchhikes with long-distance trucks. She says she can't stay at home because her father takes advantage of her sexually... for three years, her father has been forcing her to have intercourse two-three times a week» (records). Other records describe conflicts that involve the girls' boyfriends and use of alcohol: «Her mother kicked M, 15 years, out of the home. She told the police that the daughter is not welcome until she stops drinking alcohol and meeting boys»; «N, 16 years, refuses to return home if her parents won't accept her boyfriend. They say his hair is too long and his clothes are dirty» (records).

Controlling Youth Prostitution

The vice police controlled the ship girls, truck girls, and station girls of the 1950s and 1960s in three different ways: with the assistance of ship officers, the harbour police, and the station police; by issuing special orders; by means of patrolling and visiting these environments.

Some of the *ship girls* were arrested after officers on a ship alerted the police:

«A fight broke out between the men aboard; the captain contacted the harbour police who arrested O... She doesn't remember that she tried to board the ship again, but says it isn't impossible since her bra, pants, stockings, and hat were on the ship... The reason she undressed was that 'it was so hot on the ship'» (records 1949).

«The helmsman called the police... The crew couldn't get any work done as they were spending all their time with the girls on board» (records 1966).

«The ship's captain asked the police to fetch P. Conflicts had arisen as to whose girlfriend she really was» (records 1967).

«Q had functioned as 'entertainer' on board. The problem arose when the ship was to disembark and Q refused to leave. The helmsman contacted the police» (records 1969).

More common though are the instances when the harbour police, or patrolling vice police, intervened on their own: «R and S were arrested 2:30 am as they left a German ship»; «T was discovered in Kaisaniemi Park where she engaged in sexual relations with a foreign sailor»; «The two girls were observed in the Esplanade Park each arm in arm with a sailor» (records). Three Helsinki cafés, frequented by ship girls and other young prostitutes, were described in the police records as «a haven for foreigners and loose girls», «a gathering place for zoot suiters»; «a pit for semi-criminal juveniles» (records);

> «U's mother called the division and asked the vice police to arrest the girls. U, 16 years, spends all her time at café X and her mother has heard a lot of rumours about this place. U says she goes to X to meet her friends and to make 'new, exciting acquaintances'... She has been seen several times leaving the café with foreign sailors» (records 1961).

> «All of the arrested girls had arrived from (the city of) Turku that very same day and they found their way to café Y immediately. From there, their journey continued at midnight in a taxi to the West Harbour. At the harbour, there was only a Finnish ship with 'a bunch of drunk naked women on board'... The Turku girls then continued on to the Katajanokka Harbour» (records 1964).

The *truck girls* were the target of special control measures at the end of the 1950s. In the spring of 1958, the Ministry of Communications published a decree to transport companies forbidding long-distance lorry drivers from giving lifts to young girls:

> A recent reprehensible phenomenon in long-distance traffic has come to the attention of the authorities. It has been documented that some long-distance truck drivers give young, adventure-seeking girls lifts... sometimes escapees from reformatory schools for girls etc.,... and expose them to moral risks... Since long-distance trucks are intended only for the transport of goods, the Ministry of Communications decrees that such young girls may not be given rides in the vehicles. Violations of this decree may result in the forfeiture of the transport permit» (decree 1958 to transport companies).

In the police material, there is no indication that this prohibition led to the revocation of any transport permit. The Ministry's decree though seems (according to several newspaper interviews with representatives of the vice police during this period) to have created a more restrictive attitude towards hitchhikers on the part of transport companies. But how the prohibition affected individual truck drivers is unclear. The attitudes towards hitchhiking, a form of travel which became more common during the 1960s, were clearly ambivalent. On the one hand, the police stated in newspapers that hitchhiking created order and traffic safety problems; on the other hand, it was felt to be important not to discourage certain groups of hitchhikers, such as foreign tourists. According to the police, «female students» and «young women on vacation trips» could probably choose this cheap means of travel without «immoral intentions». It was merely a matter of them proving «that they had an entirely different goal than spending the night with the drivers» (records). Many young hitchhikers were unable to convince the police of this:

«V, 17 years, ran away from home seven days ago. She is unable to account for how she has supported herself... only says that she has hitchhiked with various truck drivers.» She was arrested at a trailer-truck station in Helsinki and was sent home to X, a small town in eastern Finland, after police interrogation (records 1959).

X, 15 years, was taken during a routine check of the trailer-trucks. She escaped from Y home for girls two days ago. She got a lift from a truck driver to Turku. From there she continued on to (the city of) Lahti and was now on her way to Helsinki. «X has no relatives or acquaintances in any of these cities» (records 1964).

The *station girls* were primarily controlled by the patrolling vice police in the central station area (secondly by means of station police intervention):

«The railway station was one of our usual spots (in the 1960s, MJ)... We patrolled there... We generally were on foot a lot of the time since we only had one car then... Day after day, month after month, we walked around that station. We learned to know them rather well, the young people who hung around there. We could spot newcomers immediately... The girls from the country hung around there... Kids from Helsinki too» (interview 1985 with vice police).

«We knew every nook and cranny, all the faces at the station. If a cousin from the country arrived, who walked pigeon-toed, with pants that were too short and thumbs in her pockets... who was offering herself, out of stupidity or poverty... we of course intervened and took care of this country cousin» (interview 1985 with vice police).

«You could go to the station if you wanted temporary companionship... Young, semi-criminal girls hung around there... They offered their services... and then a whole gang showed up who knew all the tricks. But the station was never a pure prostitution environment... not in the same way as the Esplanade (interview 1985 with vice police).

From Casual Visits on Ships to Life Style

The ship girls were arrested an average of 4.3 times and their contacts with the vice police stretched over an average period of three years. About half of the 189 ship girls were arrested only once by the Helsinki vice police, 22 per cent had two-three contacts with the vice police, and the rest had four or more arrests. The girls' first (and in many cases only) visit on a ship could be described as follows:

«Y, 24 years, claims that she and another girl met two Swedish sailors at a dance at X Hall last Saturday night... The next day they went to the movies with the sailors and after the movie went to the men's ship... Y says that neither she nor her girlfriend had sexual relations with the men. They were all in the same cabin the entire time. She admits that it was thoughtless of her to go to the ship, but she didn't realize it was forbidden to do so» (records 1951).

«Z, 16 years, says that she and a girlfriend visited Y Hall and there got to know two young Swedish men, who they then spent the evening with... Outside of Y, the men hailed a taxi who drove them to the harbour. The girls did not know that the men were sailors since neither of them speak Swedish. In the harbour, the men insisted that the girls come aboard so they could serve them coffee» (records 1962).

It is unclear whether the vice police actually suspected the girls involved in these types of sailor contacts for commercialized sex, despite the fact that they interrogated them in such detail about their «immoral intentions». The girls simply violated a norm prohibiting them from associating with sailors they did not know and, in particular, from visiting ships, since this opened up the opportunity for sexual contacts. The harbour and the ships were prohibited areas for unauthorized persons, and it was the job of the vice police to remove women found there. The Vagrancy Act was applied for purposes of prevention, regardless of whether the girls «habitually engaged in sexual relations for compensation» and, in fact, regardless of whether they had «engaged in sexual relations» at all.

In contrast, the girls described in the following passages are more in tune with the criteria for prostitution found in the Vagrancy Act:

A, 24 years, was arrested on a winter night in 1965 in the West Harbour, as she and two sailors were heading for a ship, «obviously for immoral purposes»... A had arrived in Helsinki four days earlier «to seek a job», but what she ended up doing was «seeking her way to the docks». According to the records, she had visited ships in (the cities of) Turku, Rauma, Pori, and Kotka. She claimed that she simply found sailors and ship life interesting and that she would like to seek work on a ship herself. - A month later, A was arrested again at the harbour. Her case was now judged to be so serious that she was sent to a workhouse (records 1965).

B was 16 when she was arrested for the first time. She was discovered in the harbour area and described in the records as «a sailors' broad who is used to hanging around the docks and visiting the ships, apparently for the purpose of earning money». In the interrogations it was learned that many sailors had B's telephone number and got in touch with her as soon as their ships arrived in port. B was arrested 11 times for visits on ships and was sent to the workhouse three times (records 1965).

The ship girls' encounters with seamen can be assessed according to the criteria for prostitution discussed in Chpt. 1: commercialism, promiscuity, non-selectivity, temporariness, and emotional indifference in the sex trade.

The degree of commercialism is unclear from several of the interrogation records. Most girls were offered something during their visits on board ships, but the refreshments or gifts (typically perfume or chocolate) were not perceived as «compensation» for their coming aboard. «Of course the sailors offered us something to eat or drink: coffee or alcohol; we were visitors in their 'home'», says C; «I received a bottle of perfume from X; he knows how expensive perfume is in our shops and he really wanted me to have it», says D in the records. It was relatively common for the sailors to provide the women with taxi money: «E claims that she never took money during her visits on ships... but that she sometimes received 15-20 marks in taxi money - 'it's not so strange that we got taxi money. They wanted us to get home in one piece'» (records).

«Promiscuity» and «non-selectivity» in the contacts with the sailors varied as well. Some of the ship girls seemed to have very limited sexual experience: «F cries and insists that she has only had sex with X, it was her first time, she says». Other women were more experienced: «G says she took care of the needs of four-five sailors while on board this ship» (records). Some of the ship girls were selective in their relationships: «A young good-looking Greek sailor is the only one that H wants to talk about». Yet others had «a broader repertoire»: J has many boyfriends: Italians, Swedes, Negroes and Whites» (records). The «temporariness» and «emotional indifference» of the sailor contacts also varied. The arrested women (both those with a single arrest and those with many) often explained their visits on ships in terms of a serious relationship with a particular sailor. In most cases, the vice police were quite sceptical about these relationships: «K claims to have a boyfriend on board; but she cannot remember his name»;

«Two marriage certificates were found among L's belongings, in different men's names. It is obvious that she hasn't even thought about getting married... She is only trying to fool the police and get aboard the ship» (records 1958).

«The informant has noticed that the ship girls increasingly talk about their 'fiancés'... This is because some of the ship girls have avoided being sent to the workhouse by telling this lie» (records 1953).

At times, the police were compelled to believe the women's stories, especially if the sailors attested to their truthfulness: «It does in fact seem to be the case that M, a vagrant well-known to this department, at a high age has married a sailor»; «N was arrested in (the city of) Hamina; X (a sailor) then came to the police station and verified that he and N were engaged. N was released immediately» (records). A characteristic of ship prostitution was that the girls' motives were seldom purely commercial. They visited ships because the seamen and life aboard interested them: «O freely admits that she finds foreign sailors sexually attractive». Or because there was nowhere else to go once the restaurants had closed: «P and Q did not know where to go. Better to spend the night at X's than out on the street, they reasoned». Or because they could get alcohol on board ship: «They stopped serving R alcohol at the restaurant, so she found her way to the harbour» (records). One woman who was working as a call-girl in 1985 described her earlier ship visits:

«I visited the ships a few times, together with a girlfriend... We were young, 15-16 years old. It was quite simply exciting to meet sailors... They were more interesting than the boys in our class... But, oh my God, it was not prostitution, I don't think. We didn't get paid, not like that... Yeah, they bought us alcohol and chocolate, but... we didn't get rich on that... I exchanged letters for many years with one of the boys on board» (interview 1985 with Tiina, 29 years).

A hotel prostitute tells the following about a girlfriend:

«My girlfriend took to sailors and ships like a kind of hobby... She had a Spanish boyfriend and an English boyfriend, and who knows what... She had snapshots of them and she received postcards and she always said that she would go and visit them... I don't think they gave her money, at least not in the beginning... It was pretty innocent... just romantic. They were cute boys in fact, and I thought about going with her sometime to the ships, but I never did... Then it changed. She also drank too much; I think that was the worst. Now I haven't seen her for a couple of years» (interview 1985 with Tanja, 22 years).

For some girls, contacts with seamen became a more or less permanent life style; according to the records, 19 of the 189 ship girls visited ships over a period of ten years or more:

S was 16 years when she was arrested for the first time in 1951, on board a ship. It was discovered that she had a venereal disease and she was sent to Kumpula Hospital. She was arrested 24 times for ship visits during the period 1951-67, with an interruption when she married and had children. S was divorced in 1966 and her children were in a children's home. She herself admitted that she spent all her time on ships and in «pubs of low repute». But she said that she grew up in these environments and had nowhere else to go (records 1951- 67).

From Hitchhiking to Promiscuity

The truck girls were arrested on an average of 4.8 times, and the time from the first to the last arrest stretched over a period of 2.6 years. Of the 89 truck girls, 42 per cent were arrested only once by the vice police, and 28 per cent were arrested two-three times. Thus, the truck girls resemble the ship girls in that the police-registered prostitution for most represented a short episode in their lives.

When interrogated by the police, the girls typically admitted to hitchhiking with trucks but seldom to having intercourse with the drivers. The police's suspicions were linked to two aspects of these hitchhiking escapades. The girls did not use the ride to get to the nearest town or the capital city, but instead followed the truck drivers without a definite destination. And the drivers apparently paid for the girls' food and overnight accommodations. According to the police, these cases did not involve hitchhiking for the purpose of cheap travel from one town to another, but rather derived from adventurousness and interest in truck drivers. Some of the records provide concrete evidence for the police's suspicions:

T, 16 years, was found «in the woods, having intercourse with a truck driver». She had escaped from a girls' home four days before, and since then had hitchhiked with trucks. T was arrested a total of four times 1960-64 (records 1960-64).

U, 14 years, embarked on a 12-day flight together with a classmate. «One day we were sitting at a café in our hometown and my girlfriend said she had decided not to go to school any more. I didn't want to either, so we left.» The girlfriends kept a diary throughout their hitchhiking travels (the diary was still in the police files). «As seen from the diary, the girls continuously hung around with boys during their trips», wrote the police. Neither U nor her girlfriend were arrested again by the Helsinki vice police (records 1971).

What is undecided in these cases is whether the sexual relations were «in exchange for» the trip, food, and overnight accommodations. The two schoolgirls above wrote in their diary that the whole hitchhiking excursion began with one of them «falling helplessly in love» with the young driver who later gave them a lift towards Helsinki. Half of the diary deals with this attachment and the other half with the girls' infatuation with two other men who gave them rides.

Mutual sexual interest between driver and hitchhiker though was not the general rule during such travels. Some police records contain information on rapes: «V tells how she was forced to have intercourse with both the driver and the shotgun driver.»; «X was discovered seriously chilled and dirty, with torn clothes; she says she had been raped in a truck» (records).

A minority of the girls systematically and over a long period of time hitchhiked and associated with trailer-truck drivers. Of the 89 girls, one-third had been arrested four or more times by the vice police. Two examples:

Y, unemployed and homeless 21-year old, was arrested in 1964. Y had been known to the vice police for a long time; she had been arrested several times previously for hitchhiking and for unauthorized presence at the railway and bus stations. She had recently served time in a workhouse and admitted that since her release, she «had been on a hitchhiking excursion, having had intercourse with about 30 men». She had not had «an opportunity to wash properly for two weeks» (records 1960-64).

Z was arrested a total of 13 times from 1956 to 1963 and was sent to the workhouse several times. One of her hitchhiking travels - in 1956 when she was 19 years old - is described as follows in the police records: «Z and her girlfriend hitchhiked towards Kuopio. The driver promised to hail a truck going in the opposite direction so that the girls could return. Z had intercourse with the driver... who gave her an orange... When the car that the girls were waiting for didn't come, they slept in a barn... Between Pieksämäki and Kuopio, the driver they then hitchhiked with stopped the truck and asked Z to have sex with him. She consented and followed him into a grove.» Z was arrested during a round-up together with four other hitchhiking girls (records 1956-63).

For this minority of truck girls, the excursions consisted of long trips without destination, during which they had sex with several different trailer-truck drivers. The hygienic conditions during the trips were often miserable: «The truck girls can be identified by their skin-tight pants and worn out leather jackets; the surest sign though is that the girls are dreadfully dirty... you can indeed often tell who they are by the smell» (records).

Obviously, not even this small group of «professionals» received money for their sexual services. At times, the drivers paid for food and overnight accommodations, but was this, from the girls' perspective, prostitution? The girls themselves explained their trips like this: «I hitchhike to get around; I have seen most of Finland»; «I couldn't stand it at home anymore, I had to get out... and I had no money»; «I don't really know why I hitchhike... It is exciting... When a huge freight truck brakes onto the side of the road, you don't know who is sitting in it»; «I have made many friends among the drivers, they are different from other people I know» (records). The girls did not hitchhike to earn money; they hitchhiked in order to travel, to be with the truck drivers, or to get away from their parents, school, or girls' home. But from the police's perspective, the truck girls - like the ship girls - were «young drifters», «girls who had gotten into trouble»; hitchhiking and sexual relationships with truck drivers were not acceptable behaviour for teenage girls. The girls were taken into custody in the hope that their escapes, hitchhiking excursions, and relations with the drivers would not develop into professional prostitution.

From Station Gang to Prostitution

The station girls were arrested an average of 3.3 times over a period of 1.9 years. Of the 159 station girls, 51 per cent were arrested only once by the vice police and 25 per cent were arrested two-three times. For the station girls as well, then, the police-registered prostitution was often a short-lived episode during one's youth.

A fair number of the girls appeared to be very innocent:

A was 16 years when she came into contact with the Helsinki vice police for the first and only time. She was arrested by the station police who told the vice police that «A is an unemployed person from another town who engages in sexual relations with strange men». A explained that she met a man at the station who promised her accommodations and that she spent the night with him at a mechanic's garage. «She had never before had sex with anyone». At five o'clock in the morning, A left the man and followed the train track towards the center of town, to the station where she was arrested. The vice police questioned her and made sure that she travelled home again. Thus ended A's trip to Helsinki which she financed by removing money from her brother's bankbook (records 1965).

Almost two-thirds of the station girls were domiciled in towns other than Helsinki; they were registered in the police records as «persons who are in Helsinki without a clear purpose» or «unemployed young people with no firm attachment in the capital city». The police tried to keep these visitors away from the station area, but the measures used were not always very effective:

B, 16 years, had twice been asked to leave the station. The police put her on a train to X (small town in the south). When the train pulled out from the platform, B jumped off and «returned to her hunting area» (records 1964).

C, 16 years, «had been observed at the station on 25 separate occasions and arrested on seven during 1969». The police once again put her on the Hämeenlinna train, but were informed that she did not turn up at home. The same evening, she was back «among the other rascals at the station» (records 1969).

D, 18 years, «lived» at the railway station. The police sent her to Hankoo where her parents lived. The district welfare board's representative refused to take her on as a client. «D's doings are no longer the concern of this municipality since she does not live here».

D returned to the station... Within one month, she was fined five times for unauthorized presence at the station, and two times for resisting the station police (records 1970-71).

According to the records, a small number of the girls were members of gangs:

E, 16 years, belonged to a «rascal gang» at the station... She was loud and irritating to the people around. She was «one of the worst young people in the station area». This time, some travellers asked the police to stop the girls (E and her girlfriends) from «wandering all around, yelling insults at people». E had also been seen making contact with strange men (records 1965).

In a couple of files, it was indicated that the station girls were used as «decoys»:

«F, 16 years, was observed together with three ruffians. She obviously functioned as the decoy... One of the ruffians went up and started talking with an older gentleman. F sneaked in between them... When the police came, the man said «where did the girl go in such a hurry?» (records 1954).

«G says that during the autumn, she spent her time around the railway station. She belongs to the 'station lice', a large gang of young boys and girls. Some of the lice are criminal. The girls promise to go with men for pay. As soon as they get the money, the boys come and take away both the girls and the money. Sometimes they hit the man, says G. The lice also sell alcohol at the station» (records 1960).

The central railway station was a gathering spot for young people, and as such, defined as a problem of public order. But was it a prostitution environment, in the strict sense of the word?: «H says that she has only had intercourse with X, her boyfriend who belongs to the same rowdy gang»; «J declares that she is not a challenge cup within the gang»; «K says that her contacts with men are pure theatre» (records). In some cases though, the police, or other outsiders, had kept track of the girls' doings over a protracted period of time: «The owner of a hot dog stand says that he has watched the girl for several weeks. She has left with at least eight different men»; «The stall salesman in the Kaisaniemi Park told us that L and her girlfriend have openly and shamelessly had intercourse with drunken men in the park, in the early morning hours» (records).

Information about the payment (in the form of money, alcohol, food) is only written down in a few files: «M admitted that she had gotten 15-20 marks some times for her services»; «N had intercourse with the man and got 30 marks. The boys in the gang got a bottle of spirits» (records).

It happened that the station girls eventually became «regular customers» of the vice police: 13 per cent of the 159 girls were arrested over a period of five years or more:

O, 16 years, was arrested in 1969 for the first time, followed by 32 arrests over nine years. The records also document 39 takings into custody for drunkenness. In the early 1970s, O spent her time at the station and in the nearby Kaisaniemi Park. Thereafter, she lived in Sweden and spent some time in Denmark. In 1975, she told the police that she always returns to the railway station since «after eight years, with short interruptions, she has most of her friends there» (records 1969-75).

Development of Prostitution Among Young Girls

The development in harbour prostitution is summarized by one of the vice police:

«The shipping traffic has changed... The ships spend one or two hours at port... Efficient working time, when all of the sailors have to remain in the harbour. Before, the ships were at dock for several days, even weeks... The men had free passes... and entertainment was brought on board. There was a fixed quota, a couple of dozen women, who waited in the harbour bars, the sailors' taverns... and they were picked up in taxis... Now it is only in Somppasaari, the harbour for timber, that the ships stay a little longer. It is primarily young girls, under-aged girls... who go there. There is no longer a market for professional ship girls, as there was in the 1950s and 1960s» (interview 1985 with vice police).

Changes in harbour prostitution can also be seen in the old sailors' taverns. Today, the clientele is very heterogeneous: ship girls, dock workers, sailors, and former sailors constitute only a small percentage. Here are some impressions from observations at these pubs in the 1980s:

«A dark cellar tavern. Can this restaurant even be called a sailors' tavern any longer? There is not much to remind one of sailors or ship life here. The clientele is very mixed. In one part of the pub, labourers, people who reside in the neighbourhood, and people who live in one of the nearby lodging-houses, and in the other part, university people. Some of the men are sailors or former ones. You don't see any sex commerce between sailors and harbour prostitutes. The only striking thing is the continuous use of the telephone: constantly, calls come in to the regular female and male customers. The phone is almost constantly occupied» (observations 1983, MJ).

Eventually, it became evident during these observation periods that some sort of prostitution was being conducted at the former sailors' taverns:

«About ten women, 30-45 years old... The women sit at their tables hour after hour. Then they leave as a group or with men. Presumably there is some kind of prostitution here... A conversation between two women: A says «we are just whores»; B answers, «we are not whores, we are rostitutes» (leaving out the first letter in this foreign word). Prostitution seems to follow its own logic. You come here to see people you know. Everyone is familiar with each other, the customers, the waitresses, the doormen. X (a waitress) is called Mom... We are the only ones not part of this community» (observations 1983, MJ).

«The pub fills many functions for these women... It is their home, all their most important social relationships seem to be linked to this place... We witness many scenes with friendship, infatuation, jealousy... When the occasion arises (if, for example, a sailor appears), the pub is also the women's workplace, where they can earn a little extra money... a supplement to their social security allowance» (observations 1983, MJ).

From the police material, I recognized some of these women as ship girls (some by name, others by photograph in the records). They had one or two decades' experience in harbour prostitution, but had not been arrested in recent years. Their present contact with sailors seemed sporadic and casual, and most of the paid, sexual encounters evidently took place between acquaintances or semi-acquaintances. In many cases, the women were in an extremely bad economic position, and financial «acts of friendship» (such as paid pub tabs) from male patrons were therefore considered a necessity. One of these women was depicted by the vice police along these lines:

«P, 42 years, belongs to the group of 'old' ship girls and vagrants, who have settled in at restaurant X. The women are more than at home at this pub. Some of them have for years used the pub's address as theirs, where sailors can send cards and letters. It might be a little scarce with the postal service these days. P has seen her better days and the sailors have forgotten her» (records 1979).

The former sailors' taverns do not attract new recruits to the harbour prostitution; one of the very few newcomers was described as follows:

Q, unemployed, homeless 20 year-old, was arrested in the harbour in 1983. It was registered in the records that she «had visited ships on a daily basis» and that she «had neglected to seek medical treatment for venereal disease and had infected at least ten men». Q claimed that she spent most nights with friends or on board ships, where she got food, alcohol, and taxi money: «When one ship left the harbour, I went over to the next one. If there was none, I waited at the railway station. Sometimes I spent the night on the street or in an all-night café». Q was arrested twice and was sent to treatment for her alcohol problems (records 1983).

Contacts with sailors are today managed by a small core group of girls who often have social problems: homelessness, unemployment, and alcohol problems. Many have experiences from prostitution abroad, especially as street-walkers in Sweden:

R, 18 years, was arrested for the first time in August 1981. She was without a home or work, and had previously been in Stockholm. She spent the summer in Finland during which time she «travelled around on different ships». R said: «I have never boarded a ship for the sake of money. To be able to drink alcohol, we girls visit the ships... I have not really prostituted myself here in Finland. The market in Sweden is much better» (records 1981).

In sum, the few ship girls of the 1980s fulfilled the Vagrancy Act's criteria for prostitution better than did the girls of prior decades; the occasional, innocent ship visits had gradually disappeared from the police material. What remained was a small group of girls who «habitually» boarded the ships. But, as the girl above remarked: «I have not really prostituted myself in Finland». The ship visits were not perceived as «real prostitution» even by these experienced girls.

Gone are also the truck girls of former decades: «I don't know where the truck girls vanished to», a former vice policeman says, «perhaps there are still girls who pay for their trips in natura, but I don't think it is as common as in the 1960s» (interview 1987). Indications of hitchhiking excursions with trucks are found in some of the women's files from the 1980s, but not of sexual relations between the hitchhikers and the drivers. The few women arrested for car-related prostitution had almost nothing in common with the truck girls of the 1960s:

S was 24 years old when arrested in 1985. She had been domiciled in Spain for many years where she worked as a model and street prostitute. She had hitchhiked around Europe and here in Finland: «I have had intercourse with the drivers, but I don't see that as payment for the trip... It was sex and nothing else. I have never asked for money. I spent the entire summer hitchhiking, drinking, and having sex. I have no idea how many men I have scalped... My ass is getting a little worn out, so it's time to go back to Spain» (records 1985).

Of the few women who were arrested for car-related prostitution after 1975, about half had experiences from prostitution abroad (cf. ship girls from the 1980s). These girls were older than their counterparts in the 1960s, and most were homeless, unemployed, and had alcohol problems. Generally, they had tried many different types of prostitution and they preferred to hitchhike in cars rather than in trailer-trucks. In recent police records then, there are no descriptions to be found of teenage girls standing by the road-side out of a sense of adventure and infatuation with truck drivers.

A similar development is evident for station prostitution. Two vice policemen assess the situation:

«No doubt, there is still prostitution in the station area. The railway station is and remains a gathering place for the elements of the night. But it is not the same as during the wild years» (interview 1985).

«Sure there are still some girls there. If there is a drunken man... who wants company... he can undoubtedly get it at the station. But he may have to wait for so long that he may just sober up and go home» (interview 1987).

The railway station is still defined as a problematic environment in many respects, but it is not depicted as a center for youth prostitution. Women who were arrested at the railway station during the 1980s differed in many ways from those arrested two decades earlier:

T was 25 years old when arrested for the first time 'round the station area. She had no permanent residence, was unemployed, and had recently served a prison sentence. She was registered in the records for «work-resistance, drunkenness, criminality, and sexual contacts for pay». She denied selling herself though: «Alcohol is my biggest problem; I am not a prostitute». She was arrested seven times by the vice police (records 1980-85).

Notes

1 See for example, Roby 1969, Rosenbleet & Pariente 1973, Jennings 1976, McLeod 1980, 1982.
2 See, for example, Partanen 1968; Haavio-Mannila & Snicker 1980.

5.

Newer Prostitution Environments

A substantial part of the prostitution arrests in the 1970s and 1980s (45 per cent and 57 per cent, respectively) was of women suspected of commercialized sex as part of their association with outdoor male drinking groups. Together with their male counterparts, these marginalized women constitute a quite visible - and, in many's eyes, disturbing - element in Helsinki's parks, public squares, and beaches. They are among the least exclusive and most despised prostitutes, whose desperate situation results in their sexual services not being highly sought after by men outside the drinking group.

Two vice policemen describe these women as follows:

«There is some prostitution, if you could even call it that, among alcoholic women too. They roam about with men in the parks and on the shores... and on the streets... They haven't worked in years... some wouldn't even be able to work. Wino ladies you could call them. But some are young, 20-30 years old. Many of them are petty criminals...» (interview 1985).

«These are women with alcohol problems... the alcohol problems determine their entire life style. They are in bad shape and their business doesn't go well. Perhaps one of the male drinking buddies will use them, but generally they are not even good enough for that. Some are helpless wrecks and are open and honest about their difficulties... often in order to get a bed in an institution so that they can rest» (interview 1985).

«Alcoholic women», «women who roam about with men», «wino ladies», «women in the parks», «women who live in vagrant hovels»: many of the homeless women I interviewed belonged or had previously belonged to these categories. Examples include: «I spend all my time in Rosen Park. I head out there first thing in the morning to meet my friends... there we keep at it all day, especially now when it's summer»; «I have lived with winos all my life... I learned to drink when I was 19 years old... and then it just kept going on... I walk along the shores as long as my legs hold me up»; «I can't sit here at the lodging-house all day. I go to the Bear Park... to see my buddies» (interviews).

5.1. Unemployed, Homeless Women With Alcohol Problems

These women's life style can best be sketched by use of three criteria: unemployment, homelessness, and alcohol problems. Of all 227 women in the police material who were suspected of prostitution in the male vagrant settings of the 1970s and 1980s, 98 per cent were registered as *unemployed* at one point or another during their career. For example:

«A maintains that after her latest stay at the workhouse, she tried to keep her job but her situation at present is impossible since she has no place to stay» (records 1975).

B straight out says that she has not looked nor intended to look for a job: «let them who invented workplaces work, and leave me alone» (records 1980).

C says: «I was accepted in April to a nine-week course for the long-term unemployed. It was supposed to prepare us for a return to working-life. I was there three weeks. Then my boyfriend stabbed me in the hand. I was put on sick leave and never returned to the course» (records 1984).

In many cases, protracted periods of unemployment are noted down: «D has not had a regular job since her divorce in 1975, only some temporary cleaning jobs» (records 1981); «E is celebrating her ten-year anniversary as lady of leisure»; «The arrestee has no real work experience whatsoever» (records).

Of the 227 women in the group, 74 per cent were registered as *homeless* (the category includes those «without permanent address or regular dwelling» and those living at overnight refuges) when arrested for the first time or later on. Homelessness was commented upon in the police records:

«F lives with a man in a tent on Lauttasaari Island. It is a regular two-man tent with two mattresses and a spirit-stove for heating the tent» (records 1973).

«G stays in a vagrant hovel, filthy and wretched... Her person is extremely dirty, and the floor is covered with empty bottles and other

rubbish, a thick layer of it. The place has not been cleaned for weeks
- and smells like it» (records 1973).

«H says that she lives in a tent at North Lake. The men provide food
by 'diving' into the dustbins in town, and the women cook something eatable from that. The men had also found some penicillin in
the garbage pails, which H used to cure her venereal disease» (records 1974).

These women typically alternated among different types of overnight
accommodations:

«I kept going on like that for several years. I had nowhere to go, so I
spent the night at hostels... if I had the money. Or I stayed with people I knew. For a while, I lived in a tent with my boyfriend... I spent
a couple of nights in Y park, where I used a particular stone as a pil-
low... always the same stone. Sometimes, the old bums stood around
and stared at me, a whole ring of old guys. 'Girl, you shouldn't lie
her', they would say» (interview 1988 with Karita, 29 years).

«They ask me how I have lived over the past few years. I don't
know how. I lived all over the place. Out in the woods, at friends' as
long as they would have me... In stairways... I waited until the newspaper boys came at about 3-4 am and then snuck in the stairway
with them... Then I would sleep for several hours before someone
called the police. Keep away from these stairs, the police would say,
you know how it is. People won't tolerate someone sleeping outside
their attic door» (interview 1988 with Marjatta, 58 years).

Many homeless women had experienced long periods of hidden homelessness before officially registered as lacking a permanent address.[1]
More than half of those interviewed related that they had «stayed with
friends» for shorter or longer periods before moving into the lodging-
house. This often meant that they lived with and kept house for various men - some also had sexual relations with the men. Two women
told:

«Before, lots of men needed housekeepers. I have lived with many...
But nowadays it is hard to find one. Some of my friends live in
municipal rental apartments where other people are not allowed to
stay, they say. And, anyway, heavy housework is too much for me
nowadays» (interview 1988 with Anneli, 58 years).

«I have kept house for men... all my life. I lived with X for many years. I left once in a while to do my own thing, but I always returned. He lived in a basement apartment and I just needed to knock on the window. Just come in, he would say, the door is open. I cleaned and washed clothes and cooked food. We slept in the double bed but we weren't a couple in that way... I was too old» (interview 1988 with Eine, 66 years).

What these «housekeepers» had in common was their very precarious housing situation. They were welcome as long as the men so wished: «After a while, he complained that I had been away too much... I was too high-strung, he would say»; «He found a younger woman»; «Suddenly, he claimed that I drank too much and that he could get evicted if he let me stay... Actually, he boozed a lot more than I did» (interviews).

Notations about *«alcohol problems»* at the time of the first arrest or later on were found for 91 per cent of the 227 women in the group, implying that the women had been taken into custody for drunkenness, that they had undergone treatment for alcohol problems, or that the records otherwise mentioned their «inebriation» or «alcoholism». Participation in drinking groups were noted as such: «J was found extremely drunk with ten men in the apartment»; «K was arrested together with four drunk men when the group tried to break into a summer cottage»; «L has spent the last two weeks out at the fort with a gang of male drinking buddies» (records).

In numerous records, the women themselves bring up their drinking problems: «M states that she is unable to function without alcohol, and that she drinks at least two bottles of wine a day»; «N maintains that she stopped drinking eight years ago but that she had a few drinking bouts last autumn. She says that she needs help in managing this» (records).

Typically, the marginalized women of the 1970s and 1980s had previously had a wide spectrum of contacts with social authorities. According to entries in the files, many agencies were anxious to refute the idea that these women fell under their jurisdiction:

«The county court has scrutinized the matter and rejected the proposal that O be sent to a workhouse. It maintains that O is instead in need of psychiatric care»... «O has been discharged from several different mental hospitals, since she is not considered to be mentally ill» (records 1972 and 1978).

«The arrestee was not sufficiently drunk to be put in a drying out cell. She was transported to a health center but no mental disease could be established» (records 1979).

«The ward received a letter from the workhouse where it was stated that P belongs in a mental hospital and not there... However, she has medical certificates showing that she is not in need of hospitalization... Nor will the mental hospital admit her. Out-patient care will not help in P's case» (records 1980).

Q came to the vice police and requested overnight accommodations. She said: «I was on furlough from the workhouse where I, at my own request, stayed on after the compulsory period ended. When I was to return, they told me I was no longer welcome there» (records 1982).

These poor and marginalized women were defined by various authorities as «hopeless» cases; the responsibility of many public agencies, yet bounced from place to place. One agency they repeatedly returned to was the vice police who arrested them, let them sober up, interrogated them, and released them to the parks again. The often recurring visits by a female vagrant resulted in a letter: «I want to thank you for the past year and for all the 'rewarding' visits. I hope we will see each other again in the new year and that I will be able to spend many memorable moments in your small, first-class hotel rooms. Best regards from a regular customer» (extract from letter 1971 to the vice police).

Marginalization - Prostitution

To what degree then did the vice police view these socially marginalized women as prostitutes, and to what degree did the women identify themselves as prostitutes? According to the files, about one-third of the suspects denied ever having engaged in «sexual relations for payment»:

Police: R is often absent from the shelter at which time she stays with different men. The staff at the shelter state that men often «place an order» for her by telephone. Irrefutably, she earns extra income by means of sexual contacts.

Woman: I have kept house for men... old men who can't manage on their own. In return, they provide me with a bed, food, and money... I deny having had sex for payment. Of course, I sleep with men from time to time, but they are younger than the old geezers I help out (records 1980).

Police: S is homeless and stays with her male acquaintances... all over town. She presumably earns some of her income in an immoral way.

Woman: I have never had casual sexual relations. I have gone steady with the same man for 3-4 years. We help each other out (records 1982).

Other women admitted having had sex «in exchange for» alcohol, food, and overnight stays, but never money:

Police: T hangs out with the Hakaniemi gang of vagrants. She is homeless and apparently sells herself for a place to sleep. T was arrested after having had intercourse with a man in the men's toilet at the social welfare building.

Woman: It just happened that this man and I had a sudden impulse to make love. So we went to the office building toilet. - I have never gotten rich off of men. It is only alcohol and accommodations, like at the hostel... that they pay for (records 1980).

Police: U is homeless and probably sells herself for spirits. She is suspected of commercial carnal knowledge, because when arrested, she had a paper with her from the out-patient clinic proving that she had had a check-up for venereal disease.

Woman: Sometimes I have had intercourse with men to get alcohol, meals... and a roof over my head. When you sit on a money-bag, you can always get booze. The men never give money nor do I ever ask for it (records 1984).

About one-fourth of the suspected women admitted during police interrogation to having had sexual relations «for payment in cash»:

Police: V has been in Helsinki for several months. She keeps to the railway station where she hunts men. V lives off of welfare assistance and her sexual relations.

Woman: Generally, I have picked up men in parks. My rate is modest, 20-30 marks, because my customers are not men of fortune and we often have to conduct the entire transaction outdoors. But I have never spent a single night in the open. I have always found a man who can offer me a place to sleep (records 1983).

Police: X was regularly employed until the summer of 1984. Now, she is homeless and sometimes lives with her sister, sometimes with men she picks up on the street. She was spotted at the Töölönranta Beach, apparently on the outlook for customers.

Woman: Over the past year, I have had seven male friends. Moreover, I have slept with others I succeeded in catching. Generally, the men have offered me alcohol and food, and money a couple of times. One time, 150 marks, and the other, 400 mk. Once I went to the social welfare office to get help, but couldn't hang around and wait for my turn (records 1985).

As a matter of fact, differentiating between these three types of responses (denying; admitting sexual relations for alcohol, food, accommodation; and admitting the exchange of money) was unimportant to the vice police, since the documented form of prostitution played no decisive role in their treatment of the women. The police apprehended the vagrants of the 1970s and 1980s, that is, unemployed, homeless persons with alcohol problems, and if the arrestees were women, they routinely investigated into possible prostitution. If the women were spared the label of commercialized sex, they were proceeded against on the basis of other vagrancy criteria.

However, the differences between the three response types mattered a lot for the women involved. Some were indignant over the mere suspicion of prostitution: «A drunk I am, a homeless wretch... but a whore I am not, cries Y... the interrogator asks her to calm down» (records):

«There I sat with X (name of vice police) who should know me by now. Dirty and miserable I was, had a black eye... and they had taken my handbag away from me... Work... nay, crazy... yes... an obnoxious boozer and so on. And then he suddenly started talking about professional carnal knowledge. I got so damn mad, you know... my sex life is nobody's business... I was just about to start screaming at him when I saw that he wasn't serious. He was smiling, the old fox» (interview 1988 with Lea, 42 years).

Other women draw a sharp distinction between intercourse in exchange for food, alcohol, and overnight accommodations, on the one hand, and intercourse for money, on the other. They also keenly distinguished having sex with «old acquaintances» from intercourse with unknown men:

«During the toughest years, there were a few times when I... went home with men to avoid sleeping outdoors. I remember once... I met a man at the Station Square. He invited me home. I was freezing. I had lost my winter boots and had to borrow a pair of shoes, thin summer shoes in the middle of winter, from my sister... He was nice, that man. He let me drink a little and we slept together... I stayed there for a few days» (interview 1988 with Anne, 34 years).

«I have never ever sold myself... no matter how miserable I might have been... I have lived at different men's places, but they have been... my boyfriends... even if I wasn't so fond of them all. I have taken care of them in many different ways... Why?... In order to be able to live there of course» (interview 1988 with Karita, 29 years).

«I have sometimes seduced a man to get a drink... or to be able to borrow money... from some guy in the gang that I had my eye on. He would probably have invited me up for a drink even if I hadn't slept with him... He knows that I will return the favour, when I have the money» (interview 1988 with Lea, 42 years).

A woman who «sells herself» for alcohol, food, or accommodations is not a prostitute, according to the interviewees, nor is a woman who «sells herself» to drinking buddies. Consequently, very few of the marginalized women, following their own evaluations, were «real prostitutes».

5.2. Call-Girls and Hotel Prostitutes in Earlier Decades

Two forms of prostitution primarily seen in the most recent police records are call-girl activities (that is, prostitution contacts mainly made by telephone with the women receiving their clients at home) and hotel prostitution. According to the records, these two forms of prostitution counted for less than ten per cent of the arrests until the end of the 1970s. In the 1980s, 18 per cent of the arrestees were registered as call-girls and 24 per cent as hotel prostitutes.

The few women classified as call-girls in earlier decades could, for example in the 1960s, be described in this way: «Several men have called the vice police and complained that Y keeps open house at home. One man reports that there is sometimes a line of men waiting on the stairs outside her door»; «Directly questioned, Z's girlfriend says that Z often brags about how much money she makes from receiving men in their joint apartment while the girlfriend is at work» (records). Sometimes, the call-girls conducted their activities in combination with or under the guise of other occupations: «A works as a 'travelling model' and 'representative'; under these designations she is sent for from other towns» (records):

«B is in the habit of receiving customers in her apartment on X-street, where she formally has a practice as a cosmetician... Finland's Association of Cosmeticians, though, has run ads disclaiming B's activities. The vice police have received at least ten telephone calls about B» (records 1960, 1965).

Some files contain information about the telephone girls' marketing techniques and rates:

«C has a reception on Y-street. In order to broaden her circle of clients, she has printed up 150 business cards, equipped with her photograph, and 20 business cards without a photograph. Her professional name is Mademoiselle R» (records 1966).

D received men in her home. Judging from the entries in her date book (which is still in the police files), she received three-five customers a month, and they paid her 10-100 marks each time. One customer apparently paid 265 marks but he stayed three nights and «stole the alarm clock when he left» (records 1973).

One factor that notably was of great significance for the proceedings against call-girls during the 1940s, 1950s, and 1960s was information provided by landladies/landlords and caretakers: «E returns to her rented room late at night and then sleeps until 11-12 in the mornings... Her telephone rings a lot. Those who call seem to be... educated gentlemen. I think they support her», claimed a landlady in 1957. Another reported in 1959: «I have suspected her for a long time and now this was confirmed... when my guests observed F on her way from the bathroom, in brassiere and slip at 4-5 o'clock in the afternoon. The door to her room stood open, and there was a half-naked man sitting inside». A third one declared in 1964: «G, who lives with us, has told me that she works in an architectural firm. I called her office and learned that she had not worked there for two years. But that doesn't stop her from having a lot of money...» (records).

However, the biggest category of informants consisted of neighbours to the call-girls: «H calls herself a masseuse and widow believe it or not... but she just whores around with men... in her apartment. I usually keep my door ajar... it irritates her... and I shout 'whore', 'whore'» (letter to vice police 1946). Sometimes the neighbours provided quite detailed descriptions about the women's ways of life. For example this gentleman: X, a retired man kept records of all traffic to and from a woman's apartment over several months during 1964. The documents he sent to the police revealed that he had stood out in the street for hours, day and night, jotting down when the lights went on and off in the apartment, how long the visitors stayed, where the woman went when she left the apartment, what she bought in the various shops, and even how and when she shook her rugs. «She came out to her balcony with her rugs; on this occasion, they were very dirty - clear evidence of her numerous guests» (records).

Frequently, the caretaker of the building, at the suggestion of the neighbours or on his own initiative, interfered in the activities: «J came home to her apartment with a man at about 11 pm. After 15 minutes, the caretaker entered the apartment using his own key, and informed them that it was forbidden to have guests in the house at this time of the day»; «The caretaker gave K a warning when she threw some paper slips out onto the stairwell; he picked up the notes and pieced together a letter where K had written that she is a 21-year old model with talents to satisfy all the needs an artist may have» (records).

In some cases, though, the cooperation between the police and landlords, neighbours, and caretakers failed, as in the instance cited below where the vice police tried to obtain information about a woman's life style:

«The owner of the building is a boozer who doesn't live there. The caretaker is also a drunk. One of the suspect's neighbours is a mentally ill man who does not dare open his door, and her other neighbour... doesn't want to get involved... The whole house leans 30 degrees towards the north and is soon going to be razed» (records 1961).

It was not always an easy task to function as a call-girl during these decades, nor as a hotel prostitute. The room-and-board regulations still dictated that unmarried persons of the opposite sex could not check into the same or adjoining rooms. The vice police's regular surveys at hotels and hostels revealed that the rules were often circumvented: «To get into the hotel, L registered as Mrs. X. She did this on the exhortation of Mr. X who presented her as his wife to the hotel staff» (records). At times, the women were informed on by the staff - «the receptionist called the station and said that M had entered the hotel again and gone around knocking on doors» (records) - or by other persons:

«Now it was about time that the police tried to return Miss N to the straight and narrow. She is only 21 years old... and lives a life like Satin-Sara in Helsinki. She travels around with different gentlemen, stays at the finest hotels, and says herself: 'She who whores for gentlemen doesn't show up in the vice police records'. In her tax returns, she claims to support herself as a laundress. But it is a lucky and rare laundress who has such long, well-manicured nails» (letter 1954 to vice police).

The police even went so far as to register themselves at the hotels in order to discover illicit sexual affairs. Below are two quotations from reports by policemen who lived next door to prostitutes at hotels:

«O has a regular room here... On 6/8/52, the following occurs: at 10:30 am, she has a visit from a middle-aged man. He stays a half hour and the couple apparently has intercourse - it is possible to hear her bed squeaking through the walls... At 5:30 pm, a young man comes for a visit, and the squeaky bed is again heard. All day, O moves around freely in the kitchen and elsewhere. It is evident that the staff is aware of her activities» (records 1952).

«P has a stack of business cards, from innumerable leading men. She does not wish to discuss this any further... In her handbag is also found a reply to an ad, signed 'an unhappy certified engineer'... Furthermore, she uses birth control despite the fact she has been sterilized and cannot become pregnant... She claims to have the birth control so that her boyfriend cannot infect her with venereal diseases» (records 1966).

 ## 5.3. Call-Girls and Hotel Prostitutes in the 1980s

Investigations and Arrests

During the 1980s, the vice police arrested a total of 64 call-girls and hotel prostitutes. These can be classified into three groups: women who solely worked as call-girls (24), women who solely worked as hotel prostitutes (17), and women who shifted between these two types of commercial sex (23).

Some of the call-girls and hotel prostitutes had been detected through «police surveillance and investigations». The methods used by the police were described by two interviewed women:

«The first time I was arrested, they had called me. It was the vice police pretending to be customers. We even agreed to meet. It was on a Saturday night and I sat here with a girlfriend. We were having a good time and had drunk a little... They said there were four of them and insisted on our coming over. We were to meet them outside the hotel. I went along with it and told them, that even if there were ten of them, we would fix them all... We never went out there. If we had, we would have been nabbed for sure... I was arrested the next morning» (interview 1985 with Leena, 38 years).

«I have the constant feeling that someone is watching me. Even though I live a straight life now... It upsets me that they monitor everything I do... A couple of weeks ago, I was eating out with an old friend who had also been interrogated... Can you imagine, that a policeman was sitting there at the restaurant, watching us and taking notes» (interview 1985 with Sirkka, 32 years).

The investigatory methods used by the vice police, albeit correctly or erroneously described, were a source of considerable concern for many of the women I interviewed. Some of them felt downright persecuted. «The girls are of the opinion that we snoop around too much», a vice policemen stated; «they see policemen everywhere, even where there are none» (interview with vice police).

To a considerable extent, police control of call-girls and hotel prostitutes was based on a «snow-ball method», whereby the police investigated girlfriends incidentally mentioned by the interrogated women: «You have to be a little sceptical. But if a name pops up during interrogation in a convincing manner, then we start slowly by checking into what that girl is up to... and then we call her in for inquiry» (interview with vice police).

Sometimes the police also inquired after the names of customers to question them as well and have them witness against the prostitutes. To the question of how these customers were selected, a vice police responded: «We usually pick out four or five different types from different occupations to see what the circle of customers looks like. We try to bring in both small and big fish». Naturally, the customers were seldom interested in being questioned: «Maybe if there were a tunnel under the bay that they could crawl through... They do not want to be seen at the entrance to the vice police. They do not view themselves as clients of the vice police» (interview with vice police).

In addition, according to the police, it was difficult to convince the women to submit the names of customers. Sometimes, the prostitutes' address or telephone books were confiscated: «There were some John Smiths, made-up names. There could be a hundred names in the girls' card index. Once I tried to go through such a card index, and only a handful of those men were listed under their correct names. These are cautious men, most are married...» (interview with vice police).

How the prostitutes were arrested is only briefly described in the files: «Q was picked up in a hotel room, naked, with a customer»; «R was arrested at home, dressed in her bathrobe and refusing to open the door. When we threatened to fetch the caretaker, though, she did what we said» (records). As a counterbalance to these short and matter-of-fact notations, we have the prostitutes' own descriptions of the arrests. For many, the first confrontation was humiliating and unforgettable:

«The police came to our home, all of a sudden. My husband and children were at home. And four people stormed in. First, they yelled through the mailbox: Open the door! What did the neighbours

think... The police have a gruff tone, they are used to handling criminals... I stood there about to cry... I am accustomed to associating
with people of class. Many of my customers are real gentlemen.
From having been a queen, I was suddenly dragged down into the
mud... And my husband later said:'What did I tell you, I have been
waiting for this to happen'» (interview 1985 with Sonja, 40 years).

«It started out with me contacting the police myself. I had problems
with a man who sent me the most shameful pictures and repeatedly
called me... Before that, I had never even heard of the vice police...
But now I asked for help. After that they interrogated me. They
came to my home to get me... They didn't explain much... I had a
dog at that time and couldn't leave it alone, so the dog was taken to
the animal clinic...» (interview 1985 with Sirkka, 32 years).

«It was about 9:30 pm. and I was watching TV. The doorbell rang
and I let a man in... I thought he was a customer. He started asking
me all sorts of questions and I thought he was the most curious customer I had ever had. I tried to change the subject but he kept return-
ing to the same discussion... At last he said: 'wow, now you have
been too naive; its going to end badly for you'... Then off to the
clink. I took my hairbrush, my toothbrush, and a litre juice with me -
I asked whether I'd have to stay over night... Then I threw in a tran-
quillizer to be able to sleep» (interview with Eeva, 27 years).

According to the women, the police showed very little discretion;
sometimes they asked the caretaker for help to enter the building or
they permitted neighbours, family members, or colleagues to watch the
entire course of events:

«I worked in a hospital then. The vice police came to get me there...
That was a hard blow for me. I changed workplace soon thereafter»
(interview 1985 with Marita, 30 years).

«They came to get me at my parents' home... My boyfriend followed along in the police car... I kept asking 'what have I done'. I
couldn't imagine - everything had been so innocent. And my boyfriend asked, 'What has this young woman done, can you tell us?'...
'It will dawn upon you once we get to the police station' they said»
(interview 1985 with Helena, 26 years).

Many women asked why the police had not simply telephoned them
and requested they come in for questioning: «Of course I would have

shown up at the appointed time if I had just been given the chance. I'd rather do that than to have them come charging in here with a great hullabaloo» (interview). But it was only in the most innocent of cases that the police used such a procedure:

«The vice police called and said that two men had reported my girlfriend and me after we had spent the night in a hotel with them. I went to the police and discussed the matter with them. They were very tactful and said that they would forgive me this time, and that they would not write down my name anywhere. But, they said, if you show up here again, your name will be entered into the journal once and for always» (interview 1985 with Annikki, 28 years).

Police Interrogation and Detention

Some of the women were lucky enough to be questioned immediately upon arrival at the station, and if found innocent were allowed to leave after only a couple of hours. Others were detained for several days: «Generally, we try to question them straight away in the morning, if they have been arrested the night before... But some remain here up to three days. And when we had those big complicated messes to deal with, the women could be detained for five days or more. One sat here for a couple of weeks, but she was also suspected of other crimes» (interview with vice police).

According to the women's own statements, they were given little information about what they were suspected of, how and when they were to be interrogated, and which rights they had as suspects. One of the interviewed women expressed that she had never even heard of the Vagrancy Act, and that she did not understand what the word vagrancy meant (Finnish was not her mother tongue). Another related that the police briefly explained the contents of the law, but she could not understand how her situation fit in: «They babbled on somewhat about the Vagrancy Act and I asked how in hell I could be a vagrant when I have an apartment and a job... I don't roam around... That has nothing to do with this, they said. Right now it is a question of your immoral habits» (interview).

Nor have the women been clear about when they were called in as witnesses (on suspicion of procurement) and when they were suspected of prostitution themselves:

«You are the principal villain in this drama, they said to me... What a drama, I thought... When I finally realized what the whole thing was about, I felt like laughing... I don't remember how long they kept me there at the police station, it might have been 17 days... And it finally turned out that I was called in as a witness... Most witnesses must be treated a little.... more civilly? But they explained practically nothing. Just into the 'slammer' at night and new questioning the next morning» (interview 1985 with Helena, 26 years).

Similarly unclear is the distinction between witness and suspect in the police records, as many women have played a double role in the interrogations. They were simultaneously questioned as suspects of prostitution and as witnesses in investigations of procuring activities.

The women's uncertainty was also related to the fact that the content of the Vagrancy Act was to some degree a blend of treatment and punishment. Some women operated under the assumption that prostitution was not criminalized, and they were amazed to be treated by the police «like criminals»: «There I sat with a number badge on my lap and was photographed. I thought, oh God, how did I end up here» (interview). Others assumed that prostitution was illegal and protested when I as interviewer claimed that the Vagrancy Act was seen as a law specifying «treatment/care» measures: «Care... what do you mean by that? Care, I don't need any care. I have not requested any social services... Prostitution is forbidden in Finland - the police have told me that» (interview).

Asked to describe the police's attitudes and behaviour towards them during interrogations, two women responded: «Don't lie, don't lie, don't lie, they say.... So you have to be on your toes. They can ask you the same question 20 times... By the end, you are prepared to admit to all of the child murders in all of Finland. But it is not enough... into the slammer to think for ten minutes, and then out again» (interview);

«Why do you just sit there and grin, they said. I always smile, I answered. I usually smile to my customers. We can well understand that you smile to your customers, they said, but there's nothing to grin at here. I meant my customers at the café where I work, but the police wanted to talk about the men who visited me at home. I have never called them 'customers' and since that day, I've hated the word customer and will never use it again» (interview 1985 with Anja, 32 years).

Worse than the interrogation though was the detention: «The questioning isn't so bad, but to be shut up in a cell for hours can be awful», as one of the vice police expressed it. One woman gave the following description of the days she spent in jail:

«First, they took my shoelaces and the belt from my pants. I said to the female guard that 'for hell's sake, I am too fleshy to be able to hang myself with those shoelaces'. Then I had to wait three hours before I could go to the toilet. I didn't get to shower... When the next shift of guards came on duty, I screamed: 'I won't get into that dog-house until I've been able to shower'. I asked for something to read; it's impossible to sleep in the slammer. They gave me a book entitled Alcoholics Anonymous. Can you imagine how it feels, sitting there, completely alone, not hearing any sound from anywhere, and with such a book dropping through the slot... Learn something, they said. They assumed I was an alcoholic! I was there three days and that's too much, you know, to be in the joint and alone... And what horrible thing had I done. I was there as a witness. In the first interrogation, they accused me of procuring. But I don't know who they accused me of coupling with whom?» (interview 1985 with Tuija, 22 years).

A long sojourn with the police also complicated these women's ties to their surroundings:

«They arrested me on a Saturday afternoon... And on Monday morning the interrogation started. I called my job and arranged for a few days off. I was lucky to have a few vacation days saved up - otherwise, I probably would have been fired... I forced myself to say something about 'private matters' on the phone and asked if I could be excused for a few days. I didn't know how long the police would keep me» (interview 1985 with Sirkka, 32 years).

Often, the stay in jail ended as abruptly as it had begun: «Suddenly, they just came and said that I could go. They gave me no advance warning. They gave me my things and all I could do was leave» (interview). The period following police questioning could be very difficult: «As long as I was in custody, the whole thing seemed unreal. But afterwards... the whole week was a nightmare. I couldn't sleep at night. I was so afraid of what was going to happen next» (interview).

Acquiring a Clientele

Call-girl activities largely involved two basic forms of mediation: advertisements in newspapers, and personal communications (from prostitute to prostitute and customer to customer). The advertisements were either submitted to the daily press or to men's magazines. In the newspaper ads a cover-up vocabulary was used, where the concept of «prostitution» was substituted with terms such as «coffee drinking», «afternoon coffee», «coffee time», and so on, since the biggest news-

paper, the *Helsingin Sanomat*, did not accept explicit prostitution ads. The wording of the ads could be: «young woman seeks coffee companionship»; «secretaries invite bosses for afternoon coffee»; «temperamental Little Red wants to meet well-to-do men». Or when men were advertising: «reliable well-to-do man without place to drink coffee»; «older man seeks secret companionship during daytime»; «company boss who often visits Helsinki wishes to be invited for coffee».[2]
A woman described her first advertisement:

«It was my girlfriend's idea. She said that she would put in an ad in the *Helsingin Sanomat*. Something about afternoon coffee - everyone understood what that meant, she said. So we wrote an ad together. We both sat with our drinks and wrote... Something about a blond and a brunette... We weren't serious, we just wanted to see how many responses we would get to such an idiotic advertisement» (interview 1985 with Eija, 33 years).

The response to the ads was often great, according to police interrogations and interviews: «We advertised regularly in *Ratto* (a men's magazine) and *Helsingin Sanomat*. We got about 70-80 responses each time»; «I had an ad in *HS*. I got at least 100 responses»; «'Two cute girls looking for male companionship day and night', we wrote in the ad. And day and night we received guests. We got tons of answers» (interviews). This necessitated a certain selection: «You could say that about half of the letters were strange or sick and they ended up directly in the wastepaper basket»; «I always check the man's telephone number to see whether it is an unlisted number or where it is from»; «If the man wrote 'we can meet outside of the Post Office at such-and-such a time - I'll have a newspaper under my arm', then I wouldn't meet him. But if he gave his name, address, and telephone number, then....»; «Of course you choose the best: company managers, doctors, and others who seem to be well-off and reliable» (interviews).
   During the process of establishing a call-girl clientele, «man-to-man mediation» played an important role, that is, one customer shared a woman's address/telephone number with others. Typically the women first acquired a few reliable customers by means of advertisements and then received male friends of the original clientele. This method was based on the assumption that regular customers do not send other than reliable men to their «hostesses» - an agreement that sometimes failed. One customer was quoted in the police records as saying: «I was sitting in a nightclub and was rather drunk. I was playing the rather important businessman that evening. Somehow I started discussing the affairs of womenfolk with the man next to me and I ended up giving him S's

telephone number» (records). This type of dissemination of information was very unpopular among the prostitutes. Naturally, they wanted to have control over who knew about their activities: «My first customer asked me if he could give my telephone number to some acquaintances; you can give it to some, I answered, but just remember, they have to give your name when they call»; «First I met a man, and then his friends called, and the circle got larger and larger. By last spring, I had had enough. I felt like I was going crazy. The phone never stopped ringing. I changed number» (interview).

Another important channel for establishing a call-girl clientele was the exchange of customers by the women. Some men told the police how they had preferred to vary their women or to meet two at a time, and the prostitutes often cooperated: «I usually send my customers to her and she sends hers to me; the men like it this way»; «I gave her the phone number to one of my best regular customers, and he ended up a regular customer of hers as well... At the end, though, I got really jealous, when it turned out that he had bought her a stereo, too» (interviews).

One occupational group that was often mentioned in the files as a channel of mediation for call-girl activities was taxi-drivers: «According to one man, who wishes to remain anonymous, the arrestee has an agreement with the taxi drivers in this part of the city, so that they steer customers to her» (records). Another occupational group named in the records was that of hotel and restaurant porters. Prostitutes were sometimes called by a porter who told them that some spendthrift men were in the nightclub, but too few interested girls, or they learned through rumours that «someone at Hotel X or Restaurant Y was selling their telephone numbers». A third group mentioned in the records was car dealers. One woman said during interrogation: «I have heard that if you buy a Mercedes, you get a list of names of prostitutes from some car dealers. One of my customers who bought such a car found a list 'left' in the back seat. My name was on the list». A man told the police: «I know many car dealers from the countryside. Time and again they ask for telephone numbers of prostitutes. I have given T's number to three dealers. But I haven't gotten any remuneration for this.»

Becoming a Regular Customer in the Bar

A hotel might serve as a meeting place for prostitutes and their customers in two different ways. The meeting could be agreed on beforehand, with the prostitute visiting the hotel room, sent for by a particular customer: «I have met the foreign gentlemen listed in my datebook when they are in Finland on business trips... They usually inform me by letter when they will be coming to Helsinki and at which hotel they will be staying. Then I spend three-four days with them at the hotel». The other, and more frequent type of prostitution in the hotel milieu was when the contacts were first established at the bar in the nightclub: «Those women sit there in a row at the bar in a ranking order, pecking order, so that the best women have the best places, and the others compete for the other seats» (interview with vice police). The hotel prostitutes themselves said: «We seldom go directly up to a table where there are men sitting. The customers can come and fetch us at the bar»; «For a long time, we have had our special corner at the bar where we sat rather close together so that we could see and hear all the transactions that were made»; «It was good times when there were dozens of girls who hung out at the bar; but on an average night, there were only about ten of us» (interviews).

If a newcomer, a woman on her own, came and sat at the bar of these hotels, the interviewed women assumed that she was interested in sex commerce: «Of course she could be a tourist or someone attending a conference... But most often she is there to make contacts» (interview). A newcomer told:

«I was alone in town and started going to nightclubs. I went out to dance, but the other girls at the bar thought that I was out for the same reason as them. The staff did too... Even though I always came and always left alone... Of course I knew that some of the girls took money... And there was a man one night who hung around me for hours. I am not the type of woman you think I am, I said to him. But then it happened anyway. I went with him, maybe because he was so goodlooking. He said, come and see where I live... And did he ever pay! 1 000 marks» (interview 1985 with Irina, 28 years).

Another related:

«I went to Hotel X a few times with a girlfriend. We liked to dance and we really had fun... The men sometimes bought us drinks and food. It is expensive at the night-club, and eventually one thing led to another. I started going there alone... got to know the other girls. A couple of times I went up to someone's hotel room. And then there was a man who paid me. Why not, I thought. He was rolling in money» (interview 1985 with Tanja, 22 years).

One of the more experienced bar prostitutes described the hotel bar as a theatre stage where she and her girlfriends played the lead roles. The men and the other women in the restaurant were spectators who watched the prostitutes and appraised their clothes and demeanour. «We often had on the most expensive and best looking clothes in the whole restaurant», said one woman. Another said: «We were a close-knit team. We swept in like we owned the place and the other women in the restaurant paled in comparison» (interviews).

The most active hotel prostitutes visited the hotel bar four or five evenings a week. For some, the bar became a type of second home. They said they found it impossible to sit calmly at home when they knew that their girlfriends «and who knows what good business» awaited them. In these cases, life might become a long series of bar evenings and nights at the same hotel, or at many different ones. «One night we were in Helsinki, the next night in another town», said one woman; «the police question you about what you did that and that evening. How am I supposed to remember dates, when even the years all run together» (interview).

The bargirls were unanimous that it was the customers who made contact with them, and not vice versa. One prostitute I interviewed said ironically: «Of course it is the man who makes the first move. It is not suitable in our society for a woman to chase a man». And another: «You don't just rush up to the men and pull them by their ties. Neither the customers nor the personnel would accept us if we behaved too conspicuously» (interviews). But how did the men know that this was to be a commercial meeting? «They fumble about and make a few suggestions. They have to be a little careful. They might have been mistaken»; «Actually, I am rather shy. You can't see that I am one of them. I bring up the question of money at a rather late stage». Some prostitutes, especially experienced ones, said that customers always seem to be sure about themselves in this regard: «When they see a woman sitting alone at the bar, beautifully dressed, with carefully applied makeup and well-coiffed hair, then they can assume she is for sale»;

«They guess right enough. I just sit there looking around, catch sight of a man and look at him straight in the eyes. He looks back. I smile. It's always me who smiles first. I haven't needed to explain myself for years. Men only need to see my gaze and my smile, and then they know... I have simply a rather intense stare» (interview 1985 with Sonja, 40 years).

To the question of when and how the payment was discussed, some women responded: «I can't be bothered anymore to chatter on and on about everything. I get to the point immediately, that it all depends on how much he is willing to pay»; «Many men scrutinize you from top to toe, then they move closer and say, you are pretty, how much do you want?»; «They ask me for a price and I say 1 000 marks. A few try to bargain, but they seldom succeed» (interviews). Men who tried to bargain and women who agreed to lower their price were viewed with the greatest of contempt: «I know that there are girls at the restaurants who sell themselves cheap. I have also been offered different prices... But then I tell the rams my rate and they shake in their pants» (records).

When the parties had agreed to a price, they often went to a room at the same hotel or a nearby one. The hotel setting was, according to the women, safer than a residence. Consequently, they unwillingly went home with customers, and then only after making sure that one of their girlfriends knew when, how, and where they went. In general, the prostitutes remained with their customers between 30 and 60 minutes, sometimes they stayed over night: «It is only when you are very inexperienced or fancy a particular man that you spend the night with him»; «Men often want a whole night. They may even pay for it. But in the end, they usually prefer sleeping alone, after they've gotten what they want». The latter woman defined a successful evening in the hotel bar as one where «you get your first customer after about 15-20 minutes, take care of him for a half hour, return to the bar and find a similarly easily cared-for customer. After that, you can go home with a good conscience and wake up the next morning feeling good about life» (interviews).

An especially active hotel life was recounted by this woman:

«Over the past year, I have not had an apartment. I haven't needed one either, since I have lived with men at different hotels... I usually meet the men in the hotel restaurant... They often have a hotel room where I can spend the night and then rest the next day, after they leave. So I find myself a new man in the bar who pays for one or two nights... And in this way it just keeps rolling along. Sometimes I pay for a night myself... I'm familiar with almost all of the hotels in Helsinki» (records 1980).

When asked if the hotel staff knew about what was going on, the vice police answered: «They are 100 per cent informed. After a week of working at such a place, you start recognizing the women». The interviewed women were of the same opinion: «Of course they knew what we were doing. They could see who we came and left with»; «We could carry on exactly like we wanted to. Oh, the girls are at work again, the staff would say. Where's your punch-clock card? We could run back and forth between the hotel rooms and the bar without them raising an eyebrow» (interview). A sure method at many hotels was to pay to get past the doorman. «At first I had problems... I didn't know the porters and I didn't know that I was supposed to slip them a fifty to get by and then do as I please» (records).

«Entertaining» at Company Parties

The vice police were very interested in whether the women had been hired to attend private business gatherings, since arranging prostitutes for such events could be interpreted as procurement under the penal law. This type of mediation appeared to be quite widespread: more than half of the arrested women (among both call-girls and hotel prostitutes) told the police that they had been invited to such gatherings, and all of the women I interviewed had at some time received such invitations - although not all accepted.

These gatherings took many forms. They could be planned for Finnish men or for foreigners, whereby representatives of a local firm made the arrangements with the prostitutes. For instance, the police records contain these entries: about a businessman in Helsinki who wanted to surprise his French colleague on a visit in town, by inviting a prostitute; about a representative for a Turku company with the task of arranging «female companionship» for some visiting Germans; about a large Helsinki company who invited prostitutes to a dinner with Russian guests, and so on. At times, the arrangements involved only a couple of men, a company president and a bank director, for example; at other times they could be large meetings or dinners with dozens or hundreds of participants. Some of the arrangements were planned at the top levels within industry and public administration; others were, according to the women, «common small-time Christmas parties».

The gatherings might be one-time events where a company brought in a woman for a special guest, but they could also be recurring occasions for which a company contracted with particular women to be on call. One woman told the police that over a long period of time, she visited a specific company once a week and «entertained» five-six men per visit. Two others related:

«I was called by a man unknown to me, who said that one of my acquaintances had given him my name. He asked me to come to X-town. I accepted but said I wanted to be paid up front. The next day, a car came and picked me up. The driver gave me money and an airline ticket and drove me to the airport. At the X airport, I was picked up by another car who drove me to a hotel, where a room had been reserved for me. First, it was dinner for the men and I waited in my room. When they moved into the nightclub, one came to get me and pointed out which of the guests I was to entertain» (records 1982).

«Once I was in Y-town with a girlfriend. A building contractor called me. He was our guide and drove us to a summer cottage. There were two men in the cottage, one was a colleague of the contractor and the other worked in one of the government departments. We both took care of the government man; it was for his sake that we had been invited there. I got the impression that they wanted to soften him up before he made some important decision» (records 1982).

The guests at these gatherings were not always aware that they were conversing with prostitutes:

«Last spring, I invited bank director X to dinner at a hotel. As a surprise, I brought a prostitute with me to the hotel. I treated the bank director to food and drink and then all three of us took a sauna together. The woman slept with him, but he didn't know that I had brought her for that purpose. He thought she was my partner and that he had succeeded in seducing her during the evening» (records 1982).

I asked the women if it was common for the customers not to know what was going on and they said that it varied greatly. At certain discreet events, the prostitutes performed incognito; at «wilder» parties, everyone was clear about why the women had been invited. In the interviews, the women talked proudly about events where no one dealt openly with money, and about arrangements to which they were picked up by chauffeurs who drove them to lofty dinners attended by «the high-ups in society». During the dinner, the prostitute would serve as a table companion for a particular man with whom she later went to bed. The transaction was conducted smoothly and as far as possible made to look like a non-commercial encounter. Less popular were events attended by «small-time pen-pushers and ordinary labourers», where the women were «treated as prostitutes and compelled to take several customers per evening». The worst thing about this type of party was that the men got so intoxicated that «they start talking dirty... and many are unable to have sex». Nor were sauna evenings popular among the women: «After you spend hours on your hair and make-up, no one wants to spoil it all with the steam in the sauna», as one woman said. Another preferred not to see her customers in a sauna: «They sit there, fat and flabby, all lined up in a row. That sight really kills any romantic illusions» (interviews).

Associating With Other Prostitutes

Characteristic of the call-girl activities and hotel prostitution was that the women involved often knew each other. This can be seen from the following sociogram, based on the names of 47 prostitutes mentioned during interrogations, when the police asked the arrestees to list their girlfriends and other acquaintances within the commercial sex sphere.

Fig 5. Sociogram showing prostitutes who (according to the police records) know each other.

a → b a gives b's name
a ← b b gives a's name
a ↔ b a gives b's name and b gives a's name

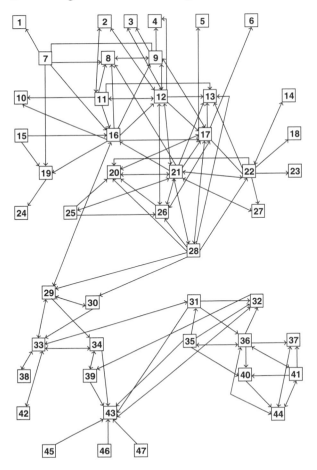

The sociogram shows that the arrested women made up a rather tight contact network. This may be a sign that the prostitution milieus in Helsinki are relatively small and closed social systems consisting of girlfriends and girlfriends' girlfriends. On the other hand, it could also indicate that the police, by means of their snow-ball method, only reached certain rings of prostitutes, whereas other groups of women were never subjected to police control.

The sociogram divides the women into two groups: the upper half shows call-girls and some women who fluctuated between call-girl activities and hotel prostitution, and the lower half contains only hotel prostitutes. It appears that these two groups did not associate with each other to any great extent, and that contacts among call-girls were tighter than among hotel prostitutes. Generally, the women closest to the center of the sociogram were those with the most extensive clientele. There are 12 prostitutes in the sociogram who had one single contact-link to the milieu. These were often women who entered the sex trade through a (often centrally located) girlfriend: «I was on a trip with a girlfriend when she told me that she let men pay for sex with her. She said that she also had customers for me. I agreed since I owed her money for the ticket»; «She was a sort of idol for me, my girlfriend. She was an intelligent business woman who earned lots of money. She was no whore, just a successful woman» (records).

If the hotel prostitutes did not know each other beforehand, they soon got acquainted at the bar - or in the women's restroom: «We met in the ladies' room... We still haven't exchanged phone numbers, she said to me. She had often seen me with different men and guessed what I was doing in the bar»; «We had sort of watched each other for a while when we met in the ladies' room. We talked a long time about men, love, everything... So you are available for service, she said before we parted» (records). However, it was not easy for all new women to gain entry: «We didn't want just anybody to join the gang. If a new girl came, we scrutinized her from head to toe. If she was too unassuming, she didn't have a chance»; «The poor newcomers. We appraised their appearance, clothes, jewelry... We found out what languages they spoke and what rates they intended to charge... But eventually, they all melted into the group» (interviews). At times, the women learned to know each other in the hotel rooms, when the customers had invited several prostitutes up at the same time: «I went with the men to their suite where I slept with them. I was drunk and actually don't remember anything except that I met X that time, who then became my girlfriend. She was with some men in the other room of the suite» (records).

Many women are quoted in the police records as saying that they learned about each other through advertisements. Keeping abreast of what is said in prostitution ads was a natural part of many call-girls' activities, and they sometimes answered other women's ads. Lesbian relationships among prostitutes are mentioned in about a dozen records, but it is not always easy to determine whether it is a question of homosexuality or whether lesbian shows were performed for the sake of customers. Compare, for example: «I answered an advertisement in *Ratto* (a men's magazine), where a woman sought another woman. We started meeting and after a short time, she took me on a hotel visit where we both had sexual relations with the same man»; «A customer told me about X. He claimed that she was also interested in other women. I got in touch with her, since I really longed for a girlfriend. But I soon understood that she had other plans. She wanted a co-worker» (records). The boundaries between lesbian relationships and lesbian performances seemed to be vague; what started out as a mutual sexual interest could gradually be diluted into a show for customers, and vice versa; what originated as lesbian scenes might with time develop into a genuine lesbian relationship. «After all those customers, I was incapable of having any further sexual relations with men. I became more and more interested in women», a prostitute is quoted in the police records.

The sense of community among the prostitutes was sometimes hard-pressed by conflicts involving «informing the police on a girlfriend», «a good regular customer going over from one prostitute to another», «one prostitute giving the telephone number of another to an undesirable customer», and so on. Two women said: «I never want to listen to that old gossiping hag again. She called me and said she was going to tell my mother that I am a whore»; «You haven't interviewed X I hope. You can't trust her. She has convinced one of my customers that I have gonorrhea» (interviews).

Conflicts among the women sometimes stemmed from competition, especially between different groups of prostitutes. An example from hotel bars was the rivalry between Finnish women and the small group of foreign women. The irritation was mutual. The Finnish women said that their foreign counterparts were «alcoholics», that they «threw themselves at the customers and practically forced them to go with them», and that they «lowered the standards» by often being willing to grant the customers a discount. The foreign women in turn thought the Finns «lacked style», that they «dressed much too simply», and that they «shouted and fought at the hotel» jeopardizing the presence of all prostitutes there.

A Finnish woman stated:

«There was rivalry between us and the foreigners. We competed in clothes - they had to be more and more exclusive and more expensive... We went to the hairdresser practically every day. Spent more and more money on these things. Incredible sums when you think back on it. But the more expensive we looked, the more money we got out of the men too. They didn't want just cheap old geese» (interview with Tuija, 22 years).

A foreign woman countered:

«There was some sort of envy then. We spent more and more money on our appearance. We had new clothes nearly every night. The Finnish girls didn't like that... They saw that the men preferred to look at us. And suddenly we felt we were too many girls in the bar. They badmouthed us and we them» (interview 1985 with Irina, 28 years).

Competition also arose between the regular prostitutes and the women who occasionally frequented the bar. The prostitutes referred to the latter as «clandestine-whores», meaning women who sold themselves now and then but were not identified as prostitutes by the personnel or the police: «They were amateurs and we despised them. They were so cautious, such cowards... And didn't dare acknowledge that they took money»; «The clandestine-whores, they were office clerks who came to the bar two-three times a week, stood there and looked down their nose at us. And the next day you heard from a customer that the small-time whores had sold themselves for 500 marks» (interviews).

Professionalism in the Sex Trade

Most of the call-girls and hotel prostitutes who were arrested in the 1980s were only arrested once by the vice police (47 of 64). Professionalism in call-girl activities and hotel prostitution can be related to the five criteria listed previously: commerciality; promiscuity; non-selectivity; temporariness; and emotional indifference in the customer relations.

The commercial dimension is clear in most cases; according to police records and personal interviews, all of the call-girls and hotel prostitutes have had sexual relations for remuneration. Women who received customers at home claimed to earn about 200 - 500 marks[3] per customer, while hotel prostitutes typically reported a higher rate, 500 - 1 000 marks per customer. Of course, this information may be unreliable; in order to tone down the commerciality of their activities, the women might have understated their rates. Prostitution money is «black income», and many women feared retaliation by the tax authorities. (One woman I interviewed actually had to pay back tax arrears on her income earned from prostitution.) On the other hand, prostitution rates are a source of a certain pride, so that the women - especially in my interviews - could be disposed to exaggerate their rates somewhat. Perhaps they quoted a standard rate, without considering that they may occasionally have to go down in price.

The promiscuity in the sex trade, the number of customers received, varied considerably. For example, in the interviews, one woman admitted to two customers only, another stated that she had received about one customer per month over the past two years, and a third that she «entertained» five-six customers per day. The average number of customers was about four per week, with a general tendency for the hotel prostitutes to have somewhat fewer customers than the call-girls.

The third criterion, «non-selectivity» was fulfilled in very different ways too. All of the interviewed women claimed to choose their customers, and this selectivity was not only part of some basic safety precautions. Two call-girls said: «If my girlfriend sends a customer to me, she knows he has to be reliable... and nice, sympatico... and clean»; «A couple of times I had really unpleasant men look me up... Smug types who talked a lot of bullshit... I see to it that they never come again and I warn my girlfriends about them» (interviews).

To the question of how they choose their customers, the hotel prostitutes responded: «Customers must look good and they can't be too drunk»; «I don't go with any common labourers»; «I don't want a man who is sweaty, bald, and smells bad, even if he was a bigger boss than the rest»; «I look at his appearance. The man doesn't have to be handsome, but he must look rich. I look at his watch, his shirt, his suit - which preferably is tailor-made - I smell his aftershave lotion» (interviews). However, these prostitutes admitted that not all customers lived up to their ideal: «You make mistakes sometimes... You don't always have time to scrutinize them very carefully» (interview).

Several hotel prostitutes told about incidents where men had gone from woman to woman in the bar with the necessary money in their fists and tried to get someone to go with them. The girlfriends in unison refused to sell themselves to these men who were assessed as «repulsive», «pushy», «primitive», «crude», or «unreliable». There were legends about men who offered 4 - 5 000 marks to prostitutes but who were categorically refused by every woman they approached. When these men had been labelled as undesirable, the front against them might be rather united, at least as long as there were other customers in the bar to choose from.

One of the rejected customers told the police: «I tried in vain to make contact with her, but she wouldn't dance with me or let me sit down beside her. I just didn't make the mark that time. But I got her telephone number, called her and said, now my beauty, shall we pick up where we left off last time» (records). Other files, as well as interviews, document that rejected customers might feel deeply offended. A «whore» is a woman up for sale to anyone, in their eyes; to be unable to buy one is both confusing and provoking. The police records contain statements by hotel employees about frustrated prostitution customers leaving the hotel in a fury or behaving so badly that they have been asked to leave.

The fourth traditional criterion for prostitution, that the clientele is to be temporary and anonymous, was not particularly applicable to the hotel prostitutes and call-girls either. The commercial contacts were, especially among the telephone girls, built on a system of «regulars»: «Believe it or not, my business is limited to about six or seven men who visit me regularly»; «Now I never have to be nervous when the doorbell rings. I know all my customers and feel safe with them»; «I know exactly which days they call. I sit and wait and while away the time by planning how I will spend the money» (interviews). As regards the length of these relationships, the women stated: «Some of these men were among those who answered my first advertisement... That's about five or six years ago»; «I have some men who always come to the same hotel when they visit Helsinki... I have known one of them for four years now» (interviews).

Women with many regular customers often denied to the police and in the interviews that what they did was prostitution in any real sense: «I have almost stopped with my business. Nowadays only old acquaintances come to me. You should have interviewed me three years ago» (interview). Regular customers were no longer «customers», according to these women; they were «friends», «visitors» or «acquaintances». One visitor paid the woman's rent, another her telephone bills, a third gave her money for clothes and jewelry, and a fourth took her to restaurants. This was not prostitution, and even less so, vagrancy, but «a question of private relationships with which the police have no business interfering».

Emotional indifference (the fifth criterion for prostitution) was also not very applicable to the customer relations of the call-girls and hotel prostitutes. Some of the women talked about friendships: «When you meet a man regularly over five years' time, you can no longer call it a distant, business relationship»; «These are my friends. They call me at Christmas and on my birthday and sometimes just to talk about anything, big or small»; «I can always call them if I have problems with money, the apartment, the car... or the police» (interviews). These women said that their regular customers were the only people with whom they could discuss the difficulties of prostitution. The women did not deny that the remuneration aspect was clearly part of their friendships, but they emphasized that the compensation was given discreetly and naturally: «My friends know what I want. They pay much more than I would ever have the heart to ask for» (interview).

Some relationships, regular or non-regular, were described as love affairs: «I have often fallen in love with my customers, especially when I was just starting out... Then you don't sleep with them for the money's sake. The money is an extra gift»; «Sure I have been infatuated with customers. Why wouldn't I have been?... But if I am in love, the issue of money becomes a little unclear, and that's not good» (interviews). Several women though stated that love and prostitution are a bad combination: «It is difficult to have a love affair based on a paid-for sexual contact. Jealousy and blame enter the scene - from the man's side. It is probably best for a customer to remain a customer» (interview). Half of those interviewed said they had been sexually interested in some customers:

«Fond of, well... It can be a type of person that makes me feel a certain way... Like that man I told you about. He came to me a few times and something happened between us.... Something like what you asked about... We have a stronger relationship... a sexual relationship... It is not only for the money. It is something else. And the last time he visited me, he said: 'You are my type of woman... you are a woman that'... And I sensed something in him and he sensed something in me... So it wasn't for the pay. We make love, fully and completely, holding nothing back... But he is an exception, this man» (interview 1983 with Laura, 48 years).

Other women expressed: «I have at times felt that this is a man I like, a man who is good in bed»; «There is something sexually exciting in the anonymity. He doesn't know me, I don't know him. Maybe we will never see each other again»; «I think that I am a warmer type than many other prostitutes. A whore who enjoys herself, a man will never forget her» (interviews).

Information of this type of course is to be regarded with scepticism. In all likelihood, some prostitutes romanticized their contacts with customers in order - for themselves, for the police, and for me - to legitimize their participation in commercialized sex, and perhaps to shield themselves from the condemnation or pity they expected from the police or from me as an interviewer. They gladly described wealthy and prominent persons who visited them and became regular customers. The crude economic side of prostitution was softened by romance, excitement, and flirtation: «It is like a work of art, the entire interaction. Perhaps only prostitutes are treated with respect nowadays»; «I have met innumerable interesting men. Refined men, old-fashioned men. Men who I never would have met if I didn't have my business» (interviews).

It is possible that these prostitutes played a role that they were unable to shed during the interviews, the role of «the warm and understanding woman», «the hostess», «the courtesan». Some of them conceded that they do play roles with customers, but that they tried to be honest during the interview. «I don't look or act like a whore when I walk down the street or sit here and talk to you. But I am completely different when I receive customers», said one woman. «You have to be so bloody neat, polite, and careful. My real temperament would send these gentlemen right through the roof», said another.

With these reservations, though, I believed the prostitutes when they described their customer relations as warm and committed. Some had difficulty distinguishing between commercial and non-commercial contacts:

«Boyfriends? I have already told you about them... They are in fact my boyfriends (the regular customers she described, MJ). But I have of course had lovers who were not the paying sort.... Paying and paying for that matter... Sometimes they paid my restaurant tabs, tickets to the movies... And sometimes I paid. All my boyfriends have not paid of course. Once I kept company with a real down-and-out type... And on top of that, he was miserly... So I had to pay then... And X, the one coming here tonight... I am in fact in love with him. He doesn't pay me, well a few times he has paid, but...(interview 1985 with Sonja, 40 years)

All contacts with customers though were not characterized by friendship, love, and sexuality. Some women pointed out that the term revulsion is the only accurate one to describe a prostitution contact: «I could never get involved with a customer. All of my feelings are blocked by disgust, distaste for this strange man in bed with me»; «I try to think of something else. Plan what I am going to do with the money»; «He will never be able to reach me, I think to myself. It is like the condom guarantees that he will never touch me». Three women said that their customers were forbidden to kiss them: «I absolutely do not want to kiss customers, and actually they don't want to kiss me either» (interviews).

An important aspiration in this type of prostitution encounter was to get the sexual act over as quickly as possible. «A good customer is a fast customer», as many women proclaimed, or «an experienced customer understands that time is money for us». He finishes within a half hour without the woman needing to look at her watch. The prostitutes found customers (non-regular customers) who tried to stretch out their time, or talked or asked too much, distasteful: «You are Matti and I am Eeva, more we don't need to know about each other, I say»; «They can talk about themselves, if it doesn't take too much time. But I don't want to tell them anything about my life» (interviews). The women were critical of men who were too inquisitive, men who went on and on about their wives and children, and men who «after the business is done, start reading poetry aloud, instead of pulling up their pants and getting the hell out of here» (interview).

Asked about whether contacts with customers had changed their view of men, their attitudes toward men, some prostitutes replied: «I have seen many men in situations that make it impossible for me ever to take men seriously again. Perhaps you could say that I have contempt for them»; «I watch TV and see some high-and-mighty minister from a government department and laugh aloud when I picture what he looked like crawling towards me with his black whip» (interviews). The women's contempt was particularly strong for customers with «special requests»: «If a person is crazy enough to want to pay me to piss on him, then he is welcome to do so»; «If he wants to be whipped, the disgusting old coot, then I might as well be the one holding the whip» (interviews).

In summary, the call-girls and hotel prostitutes of the 1980s did fulfil the criteria for prostitution in the Vagrancy Act to a greater degree than did the prostitutes described in the earlier sections. The clearest commercialized relations in prostitution registered by the police in Helsinki are thus found in the most private and exclusive milieus. However, not even for these forms of prostitution do we find uniform and consistent commerciality. According to the police records and my interviews, some call-girls and hotel prostitutes have a relatively limited experience with customers - others have worked as prostitutes over many years. Some women's activities seem to be concentrated to a few selected regular customers, while others are less selective. And finally, some women claim to be emotionally involved with their customers - others clearly disassociate themselves from them.

Notes

1 Järvinen 1988.
2 For an analysis of the prostitution ads in the Helsingin Sanomat, see Varsa 1986.
3 Using today's exchange rate 1 000 Finnish marks equal 225 U.S. dollars.

6.

Amateurs and Professionals

The prostitutes of Helsinki do not constitute a homogeneous, easily definable category. The arrested women have displayed greatly varying degrees of professionalism: some have met both criteria for prostitution in the Vagrancy Act (sexual relations for payment and habitualness of these relations), others have met the first criterion but not the second, and still others do not seem to have met either one. In this chapter, the amateurism versus professionalism issue among Helsinki's prostitutes is analyzed from four perspectives: «prostitution as social relations»; «prostitution as identity»; «prostitution as occupational ideology»; and «prostitution as subculture».

6.1. Prostitution as Social Relations

Paid Relations as Seen by the Women

As shown in the two preceding chapters, a considerable part of the sexual relations described does not fulfil the traditional criteria used to define prostitution (commercialism, promiscuity, non-selectivity, temporariness, and emotional indifference). However, applying these criteria, the arrested women can be divided into three main groups: amateurs, semi-professionals, and professional prostitutes.

Amateurs in commercialized sex are women who are suspected of sexual relations for payment, but do not fulfil the other criteria. For instance, among the young prostitutes arrested in the 1960s, there were many amateurs. The ship, truck, and station girls were accused of taking payment for sex, but, according to the records, seldom in the form of money. Their sexual relations were not numerous and the girls were typically selective about their partners. Their liaisons with sailors and truck drivers were the result of infatuation and sexual interest, and the men were referred to as boyfriends, fiancés, or lovers.

Amateurs are also found among the marginalized women (homeless, unemployed women with alcohol problems) of the 1970s and 1980s, some of whom had sexual relations with men in exchange for food, alcohol, and accommodations. The records do not always indicate the extent of the women's activities, but in most cases the clientele seems to have been very limited. The women themselves did not portray their sexual relations as casual or indifferent, but rather told of male friends or old acquaintances helping them out and providing them with alcohol or a roof over their head for the night.

The question of whether the «payment» received was to be considered as downright compensation or not, was commented upon by an ex-ship girl: «The most expensive thing I ever received was a transistor radio... but payment... no, I wasn't together with X to get a radio (laugh). I liked him. He was the love of my life... at that time» (interview). A homeless woman said: «You can't call it compensation, I'm no paid woman... I got to live with him because I had nowhere else to go... I cooked and cleaned... and he demanded nothing more from me. I slept with him because I wanted to» (interviews). In general, the amateurs did not engage in sexual relations in order to earn money. Some of them did profit economically from their male acquaintances, but this gain was described as a «natural part» of and not the reason for the social/sexual relationship.

The *semi-professionals* differ from the amateurs in that they clearly admitted to having had «sexual relations for compensation» and often with more than one man. However, they did not meet the other criteria for prostitution (non-selectivity, casualness, and emotional indifference in their sexual liaisons). Among restaurant prostitutes in the 1940s and 1950s, for instance, the payment criterion was frequently fulfilled: men paid for meals, alcohol and taxis, and the link between the sexual contact and the remuneration was unambiguous. Furthermore, these women were registered for «negotiations with several men», for «having a large number of sexual relations» or «having a different escort every evening». But the women in question did not always view these relationships as prostitution, nor their partners as customers. They left with men «because they wanted to themselves», «because the guys interested them», or «because the men were boyfriends or old acquaintances» (records).

Semi-professional women are also found among the call-girls and hotel prostitutes who were arrested for sexual relations for payment, but not fulfilling a) the Vagrancy Act's prerequisite that the prostitution develop into a life style, or b) the criteria of promiscuity, non-selectivity, temporariness, and anonymity. For example, a call-girl who, judging from both records and interviews, had commercial sexual relations with only three men - can this be called «prostitution as life style»? Or another call-girl who claimed to have «only one lover, a foreign wealthy man, an old friend who means a lot to her and who assists her economically» - can such a long-term and apparently affectionate affair be called professional prostitution? Or an ex-hotel prostitute who admitted to having «a very active sex life, sometimes with men who pay», but who claimed never to sleep with men who did not attract her - is mutual sexual attraction to be defined as professional prostitution? The answer to these questions depends of course on the weight given to the various criteria of prostitution.

Finally, *professional prostitutes* are women whose sexual relations for payment can be characterized as casual, non-selective, and non-committal. Professionals are found in all prostitution settings: on the streets and in restaurants during the 1940s and 1950s; among the young ship, truck, and station girls of the 1960s; among the marginalized women as well as call-girls and hotel prostitutes in more recent years. In general, prostitutes of the 1980s meet the prerequisites of commercialized sex to a higher degree than did their counterparts in former decades. By the end of the period under study, the police had lost interest in the young amateurs of prostitution and had started focusing all their resources on controlling the very core of the professional sex commerce.

What distinguishes professional prostitution in Helsinki, however, is the apparent retention of certain mitigating, amateurish features. In comparison with career descriptions found in the research literature, the women in this study come out looking more like casual prostitutes than professional ones. The principle of maximizing gain while minimizing effort - characteristic of professional, sexual transactions - cannot even be applied to the most active prostitutes in Helsinki. According to the police records and interviews, the majority had few and sporadic contacts with customers, and they invested considerable time as well as affection in the relationships. With a few exceptions, participation in commercialized sex did not attain the status of a systematic profession that structured the women's life and identity.

Paid Relations as Seen by the Men

The incomplete commerciality of the Helsinki prostitution has been illustrated in another study as well. Hannele Varsa (1986) conducted telephone interviews with 30 men who responded to ads from prostitutes in the *Helsingin Sanomat*, the largest morning daily. The object of the study was not to illuminate the issue of professionalism - amateurism. But some general information on this theme is discernible from the responses obtained.

A minority of the men had a decidedly business-like attitude towards prostitution: they viewed buying sex as a smart and non-committal transaction, which they neither wanted nor expected to develop into a more complicated relationship: «It is... a matter-of-fact affair, pure sex... no strings attached»; «When you pay for the services, everything is understood. These women don't start tieing you down» (interviews with customers, Varsa 1986). For these men, liaisons with prostitutes were clearly distinct from other social/sexual relationships: «It makes no difference if he (the customer) is married, newly engaged, or whatsoever. Buying sex... is a casual adventure... it doesn't affect a marriage or other established partner relations at all» (interviews with customer, ibid.).

Nevertheless, most of the men had very ambivalent attitudes towards the commercial terms of the contacts. Though prepared to barter for the sexual services rendered, they did not totally rule out the possibility of mutual, more committed attachments:

«When it's only a matter of money, it doesn't mean much to either party. But if the man pays, and everything goes well, and feelings get involved - as they so often do with people - then it's totally OK. We help each other» (interview with porter, «over 50 years of age», ibid.).

«Maybe many of the men (who respond to prostitution ads) and the girls as well (who place the ads, MJ) expect something different... The girls are looking for their dream prince... They think they can find him this way, that they can find the needle in the hay stack. Both the women and the men believe they can find something better. They despair, but keep on looking anyway. It's not merely a question of quickies» (interview with physician, «over 40 years of age», ibid.).

The men professed that this «compassionate something» - «something different», «something better» - was difficult to find in a prostitution liaison, but they did not consider it impossible. The distinction between prostitution and other social/sexual relationships was not absolute, and some men did contact prostitutes in the hope of finding «a girlfriend, a partner, a friend».

Half of the men had gone to prostitutes abroad, and these customers described the commercial sex settings in other countries as more open

and accessible than those in Helsinki. However, they generally preferred Finnish prostitutes, as paid sex abroad was «overly business-like
and mechanical»:

> «In Germany, it's nothing more than 'put your money on the table'.
> Two minutes and the money on the table... You take, and you ask
> nothing. You don't really enjoy yourself there. Ten or fifteen min-
> utes, and if you go overtime, you have to pay for every motion of the
> hand... Everything costs. It has no resemblance to normal sex in any
> respect... The TV is on, the woman is knitting a wool sweater during
> the act, and with that, it's over. That's the way it always is in Ger-
> many» (interview with self-employed businessman, 37 years, ibid.).

The rules of the prostitution game were clear-cut abroad, and the customers expected nothing more than what they paid for. In Helsinki, on
the other hand, they could seek out «students who are earning extra income for a while and who are not professional», «likeable girls»,
«smart women who know when it's time to stop, before prostitution takes its toll». What remains unanswered in the study, however, is the degree to which the customers had actually indulged in this kind of amateurish contact. Had they found compassion, caring, and affection in
prostitution, or was this merely something they - like customers in other countries[1] - dreamed about and hoped for? Whatever the answer, it
is clear that even from the customers' perspective, prostitution in Helsinki is unsystematic, with ambiguous rules and vague boundaries between commercial and non-commercial relationships.

Prostitutes and Procurers

In the research literature, pimps and other procurers are important components of the world of professional commercialized sex. Pimps influence women's careers as prostitutes, reinforce women's identities as
prostitutes, and contribute to the creation of commercial sex subcultures.[2]

Throughout the period under study, the vice (and criminal) police in
Helsinki processed procuring under Section 20:8 of the Penal Code.
From 1945 to 1986, only 49 cases of procuring were entered into the
police journals. More than half of these persons were arrested during
the 1980s, corresponding with the fact that procuring in Helsinki has
generally been linked to call-girl activities and hotel prostitution. The
number of cases of procuring becomes negligible when compared to
the more than 5 000 women arrested on suspicion of prostitution (1945-
1986). It is unlikely that all these women - amateurs, semi-professionals,

and professionals alike - would have operated totally free of procurers. The number of such cases in Helsinki is also low compared to other Nordic countries.[3]

Using the five traditional criteria for prostitution, the registered cases of procuring in Helsinki can be seen as ranging from selective and long-term friendships to more commercial, casual, and anonymous arrangements - with the former type being the most common.

Girlfriends - Proprietresses

Of all persons registered for procuring, 27 per cent were women, typically prostitutes working in cooperation with their colleagues. Some were call-girls who helped out their girlfriends: «I was suspected of procuring because I let my girlfriend live in my apartment while I was in Spain. She took care of some of my customers» (interview). Other women presented customers to their girlfriends: «I lived with X at that time. Once I heard her say to one of her acquaintances on the telephone: 'I have a pretty young girl here that I'm sure you haven't met yet'. According to the police, that was supposed to be procuring (laugh)» (interview). One woman told the police: «Y asked me to come along and help entertain a group of Arabs, who were going to be in Finland for one month... They had offered her a 'per-night' arrangement, 200 Finnish marks for each night» (records). The women themselves had a hard time conceiving of this as procuring: «It was totally crazy... procuring... I didn't get a dime from her or from anyone else... she was my best friend. Of course I introduced her to people I knew» (interview). «She didn't come to me and ask me to join up... I went to her myself, since I had a lot of debts...» (records).

According to the police, these types of cooperation had existed for decades, but it was not until the 1980s that they had started pursuing them. Due to insufficient evidence, however, most investigations did not lead to prosecution. But the investigations did serve to frighten many of the prostitutes and arouse uncertainty as to where the line was to be drawn between friendship and procuring: «We found out then... that we were souteneurs, the whole lot of us... Since then I haven't dared invite any of my girlfriends home»; «Now that the law is going to be changed (repeal of the Vagrancy Act), the police can't interfere with what I do... But one cop warned me about associating with other paid women» (interviews).

Only three of the arrested prostitutes had conducted their procuring function more systematically. For instance: A, 32 years old when arrested in 1982... had worked as a prostitute for seven years and eventually started specializing in sado-masochism. She hired about a dozen female assistants who received customers in her apartment while she showed pornographic films or participated in lesbian scenes. A was described by witnesses as «a cold businesswoman», who was never «turned on by her customers», and who did not even want to know their names - she referred to them as Slave 1, Slave 2, Slave 3, and so on. The police estimated that A earned a great deal of money from these activities, and invested it in two apartments in Helsinki which she moved back and forth between so as «not to disturb the neighbours». She received a six-month conditional sentence (records).

Another, more professional, female procurer was B, 44 years old, «student and free-lance artist», who was arrested in 1985 on the basis of several denunciations. Since 1976, B had run a contact club which mediated more than 2 000 visitors to at least 15 prostitutes. Through newspaper ads, B came in contact with interested men who received the telephone numbers of prostitutes after paying a certain sum to B. She did not admit having knowingly mediated prostitution liaisons: «Women who resort to contact clubs are looking for long-term relationships - men are seeking adventure. What could I do about this difference? Some of the women whose names I gave out might have been adventuresome, yes. But prostitutes, no...» (interview). According to the police records, there is no doubt that the women and men involved knew that prostitution was being mediated. One of the women reported: «I called the club and the proprietress asked me if she could give my number to men who wanted love for payment. If any quick-witted gentlemen should inquire, you could give it to them, I replied» (records). Correspondingly, a man related: «I called the club and said I was looking for prostitutes. I paid 300 marks and the next week I got three names and telephone numbers» (records). The club proprietress was sentenced to a two-month conditional sentence and a fine of 80 000 marks to be paid to the public treasury coffer.

Friends - Proprietors

Only three of the 36 men arrested for procuring could be called «live-in pimps», that is, men who lived with a single prostitute and shared finances with her. This small number of pimp-partners was unexpected[4] Among all of the women arrested for prostitution during the years 1945-86, at least 12 per cent (according to the records) had been living with men at the time of at least one of their arrests. Some of the women lived with their male partner, and others were registered as living with «male acquaintances», sometimes older retired men for whom they kept house.

Some of these men seemed to be genuinely unaware of the women's commercial sexual activities. One interviewed woman explained: «My husband works in another city and only comes home on weekends... He knows that I see other men... They write letters to me sometimes...but he doesn't open my mail. If he found out about the money, he would divorce me on the spot» (interview). Other men knew what was going on but, according to the women, were not involved: «At first my husband thought I was going out with my girlfriends... just normal stuff... but soon he caught on... I had money... He wanted a divorce... but we kept living together for a few years, him doing his thing, and me doing mine» (interview).

However, the police were not always convinced of the men's innocence. One woman is quoted in the records as saying: «I have lived with an older man for many years... and he doesn't charge me anything to live there. He doesn't know that I sometimes receive men at home while he is at work». The man in question reported: «She lives with me and takes care of the home and household. We are not in a steady relationship... so she can of course have boyfriends if she wants. But she is not allowed to invite them over to our place (records). One vice policeman commented upon the man's ignorance: «It's impossible for him not to know that his apartment is one of the most well-known spots for customers in that part of town... But we don't know whether he is operating as souteneur or not» (interview with vice police).

These types of relationships were rarely investigated by the police in any great detail, although some of the men were described as «sly types skirting around on the brink of illegality» (interview with vice police). As long as the men merely provided the women with an apartment (cf., the law's criterion «maintain a house for the pursuit of illicit fornication») and did not demonstrably procure customers for them or receive direct income from the liaisons, the police did not pursue the cases.

Only nine men were sentenced both for providing apartments and receiving income from prostitution. One was C, 70 years old in 1951, who on two occasions had prostitutes living with him. One of the women, 22 years old, told the police that at restaurant Y she had become acquainted with «an old man who suggested that she start living off of men and at the same time proposed marriage to her». The woman moved in with C, and he began acquiring customers for her with the help of coachmen and taxi drivers. He served the customers to snaps and watched through a hole drilled in the wall when she had intercourse with the men. She had to turn over most of her earnings to C, and the records indicate that he had earned 4 - 5 000 Finnish marks from this operation. He was sentenced for procuring, illegal sales of alcohol, and possession of a firearm to one year and three months in the house of correction (records 1952).

Another example was D, a 44 year-old entrepreneur, arrested in 1982 for having allowed prostitutes receive customers on his firm's premises. D came in contact with the prostitutes by answering their ads. One woman related: «D suggested I meet my customers in his apartment for 50 marks per customer... In the beginning, he kept watch on the stairway and counted the customers...» The police records show that D earned at least 40 000 marks from this arrangement. He received a one year conditional sentence (records 1982).

Acquaintances - Intermediaries

A slightly different type of male souteneur operated within hotel prostitution (23 per cent). In these cases as well, the relationship souteneur-prostitute can be placed along a continuum from relatively innocent friendships/acquaintanceships to commercial relationships. To give one example from the former category: a hotel prostitute accused her former associate, E, a 50 year-old author, of having induced her to enter into prostitution, in order to use her experiences for his books. During the interrogations, it became clear that underlying the charge was jealousy, since the prostitute and the author shared the same boyfriend. The case was dropped due to «insufficient evidence» (records 1982).

Another instance was F, a 40 year-old accountant, arrested in 1969 for maintaining a standing hotel-room reservation in his name and letting the room to prostitutes he knew. The police records revealed though that F had initially booked the room in order to «drink on credit» in the hotel-bar (which he could do only as a hotel guest) and to have a place to meet women himself - he lived with his elderly mother and was not allowed to have female visitors at home. It was unclear whether F had actually made any money from these procuring activities. He received a three-month conditional sentence (records 1969).

A more systematic procurer was G, a 36 year-old director of a company, who was arrested in 1985 for sponsoring «sauna parties» on his company's premises for dozens of hotel prostitutes, company customers, and other business associates, over a two or three-year period. The prostitutes denied that G had in any way exploited them. Quite the contrary, he had been a faithful friend and a good employer, who discreetly paid them about 1 000 marks per customer. G claimed that he had not made any direct profit on the transactions (records 1985), and one of the prostitutes I interviewed agreed: «G is a good friend of mine. He helped me and I helped him. Why should the police interfere in this... as if he had hurt me or anyone else?» (interview).

While there were exceptions, the main impression one receives of both male and female souteneurs is that their operations were seldom purely commercial. The registered procuring was neither extensive nor organized, and to a large extent was a matter of friendship and cooperation rather than economic or emotional exploitation. The direct economic gain was difficult to establish in most cases, and the suspects and witnesses (the prostitutes) alike repudiated claims that these were cases of «real pimping».

Nevertheless, some men in the police material attempted to set up pimping operations based on foreign models. One of them was H, an unemployed 23 year-old who decided to try his luck as souteneur after reading a book about prostitution. H and his girlfriend went to Stockholm to find prostitutes, and, inspired by the book, they rented a big car in order to impress the women. X, a Swedish woman recruited, «had gotten the impression that a big organization was behind the whole deal». H installed two prostitutes in an apartment in Helsinki and procured customers for them. After a few weeks, the police intervened and charged him with procuring (and theft). H received a 14-month conditional sentence (records, 1975).

From the procurers' point of view, the problem in most cases seemed to lie in not having successfully created - or sustained - a bond of dependence between themselves and the prostitutes. An exploitative, commercial pimp-relationship is only possible if the prostitutes are emotionally/sexually involved with the souteneur. If no such bond exists, the women work with the pimp only if the arrangement is mutually advantageous. As one woman put it, «I had no apartment and accepted his invitation to move in here. Eventually, though, he got to be a drag. He started watching me and accusing me of withholding money from him. So I packed my bags and left» (records). Another woman said: «He was supposed to get customers for me, deliver me to them, and so on... He was a weird little man... We tried this for a while, but I soon realized that I could manage a lot better on my own» (interview).

Obviously, «successful» pimping operations presuppose a tradition that is non-existent in Finland. In fact, there was a deep-seated belief among the interviewees that Finnish prostitutes do not allow themselves to be exploited by souteneurs. One vice policeman said: «Finnish prostitutes don't want any souteneurs. They're proud of their status as self-employed enterprisers». Another stated: «I would like to see the man that could put these girls in their place... (laugh)... Some of them are really strong and smart... and wouldn't waste their money on men» (interviews). The prostitutes I talked with agreed that souteneurs were unusual in Helsinki: «Souteneurs are something you only read about. Other countries have them... but we don't»; «I have never heard of anything like that here in Helsinki». Both of these women were themselves interrogated in cases of suspected procuring (cases B, the proprietress

of the contact club, and G, the businessman who arranged «sauna parties» on his company's premises), but they did not regard B or G as
souteneurs. «If they are not souteneurs, are they procurers?», I asked
these women, in an attempt to capture nuances of the words. One of the
women responded: «I guess this is procuring (case B) if the police say
so, but the club proprietress didn't force me to be there. I was the one
who contacted her». The other woman said: «No, this (G) was never
procuring. We were working associates. I made this clear to the police
and I say it to you» (interviews).

When asked what «real souteneuring or procuring» was - «something you find in other countries but not here» - the prostitutes were
very unsure: «Don't ask me. It (procuring) is an odd word»; «It's when
an old man sells young girls... like at the railway station»; «If a woman
sells herself... and then gives all her money to her man, who just lies
around the house all day»; «I once saw a film where a man forced some
girls onto the street... He must have been a souteneur» (interviews).
According to the women, procuring/souteneuring entailed an exploitative, unequal, and perhaps involuntary relationship, where a man (not a
woman) had one or more prostitutes working for him. Their descriptions clearly reflected the traditional image of a male pimp engaging in
exploitation, polygamy, and violence. Since these elements were missing from their own lives, the mediating operations in Helsinki were
repeatedly described in terms of friendship and cooperation - and not
procuring.

6.2. Prostitution as Identity

Customer Relationships and Identity

As shown, a majority of the women arrested did not accept the label of
prostitute. This can be seen in the interviews as well, when the women
were asked to define the terms «a prostitute», «a paid woman», «a
whore». According to the homeless women interviewed, a whore was a
promiscuous woman who slept with many different men - whether or
not she got paid was irrelevant: «A whore, that's easy, 'coz I share a
room with one (at the shelter, MJ). It is a woman who has slept with all
the men in X-Park» (interview). The word «whore» also implied a general insult against «aggressive» or «troublesome» women: «Whore,
I've been called that many times. If you are too out-spoken... then you
are called a whore. 'Keep your mouth shut, whore!'» (interview). The
concepts of prostitute and paid woman were less familiar to the women
at the shelter: «I'm not a prostitute. I don't know any paid women... I
wonder if there are any prostitutes at all in Helsinki»; «A paid woman...

If you want to talk to those women, then you'll have to go to the... fancy hotels» (interviews). In these more «fancy» milieus, the women I talked with defined the concepts of prostitute and paid women as follows: «A prostitute is a wretched type, who goes out in all types of weather... and has sex with anyone who will have her»; «A prostitute... that's a woman who has to sell herself to avoid starving or freezing to death... no, who starves to death these days?... a paid woman, it's the same thing as a prostitute, huh?»; «A prostitute has a lot of customers, five-six a day, and her telephone rings all the time... the men come and go... at arranged times» (interviews with hotel prostitutes).

Thus, their image of a prostitute closely resembled the traditional one of a woman with many casual, anonymous sexual relations, an image that their own experiences did not reflect. Although some did admit to having had «paid-for sexual relations», they fended off the charge of prostitute by use of three basic arguments.

The first argument addressed the voluntariness of their participation in prostitution: «I am not a prostitute. It was my choice to start a business, and no one forced me» (interview). Since participation was voluntary, they believed it possible to pull out whenever they wished: «I don't have to keep doing this... I could stop tomorrow... or in a month... I don't plan to keep going until the day I retire» (interview).

The second argument concerned power (or at least the absence of submission): «I have been paid yes, but I still don't feel like a prostitute... 'coz I'm the one who dominates, I'm the strong one... Not physically, but mentally... I conquer men, if I want to... It would be different if I was ugly or something like that» (interview). As some women stated, though, the power aspect of commercial sex is complicated. Taking everything into consideration, prostitutes as a group are in a weaker social position than their customers in terms of economic resources, social status, societal influence, and respect. But within the individual prostitution liaison, these women truly felt in command: «As time goes by, you get rather sure of yourself... you learn a whole lot about people... feel a little sorry for these men... I mean... they might be very nervous, and you have to... take care of them»; «At my house, I am the one who decides... I decide who gets to come here and how long they get to stay. I am rather dominant, which many men like... It's like raising kids (laugh); it's firmness that counts» (interviews).

The third argument the women used to differentiate themselves from the label of prostitution was in regard to selectivity. «I decide myself who gets to come here» was a recurring theme in the interviews and police records, and there is much to indicate that this was indeed the case. Many call-girls who advertized in newspapers described how they chose «the best customers» from among the many respondents. Correspondingly, many customers revealed to Hannele Varsa (1986) in interviews that they had repeatedly answered ads without success: «I have answered before, but it hasn't often worked. One time out of ten, maybe... the woman calls back»; «You usually don't hear anything, don't even get a telephone call. They get so many answers...» (interviews);

> «The women choose. They are the ones who rule in this matter. I think the reason they don't contact me is that I am too old. They probably get hundreds of responses, and they choose the best. As I said, I am 57 years old... They don't call me back» (interview with man with a master's degree, Varsa 1986).

Some customers thus felt that prostitution contacts were conducted on the women's terms, and that it was the men, and not the prostitutes, who «put themselves up for appraisal». The customers also knew, from their own and others' experiences, that it was rather futile to place ads themselves: «A good friend of mine put an ad in the paper and he got a few responses»; «I have tried to place ads, but it only ended up in misunderstandings. Maybe I didn't really know myself what I wanted... anyway, many of the women who answered thought I was looking for a more permanent relationship» (ibid.).

Not only were the prostitution contacts made «on the women's terms», according to both customers and prostitutes, but they were also sustained on their terms. Since it was difficult to come into contact with new prostitutes, many men wished to become a prostitute's regular customer. Thus, they had to «act properly»: the women did not accept troublesome, unpleasant, or violent clients. In many respects, the prostitutes were in fact in charge; they were the ones who «determined the rules of the game». In this position, they could easily fend off any self-image of «a real prostitute», or, (in their own words) «a wretched type», «a woman having sex with anyone who will have her», and so on.

Control Measures and Identity

The link between official measures taken against commercialized sex and the women's identity as prostitutes is naturally not easy to determine. When asked to judge the effects of the anti-vagrancy measures (warnings, supervision, institutionalization), a vice policeman commented on one aspect as follows:

> «It used to be that supervision had a certain function... it became a fixed point in the vagrants' lives, their regular appointments to meet

someone... someone who asked how it was going, whether you had got work... or an apartment. Nowadays, it makes no difference, especially for... the ladies of the night. Reporting to a probation officer doesn't do anything to improve them. They just get... hurt... 'I'm no vagrant, I shouldn't be on probation'» (interview 1985 with vice police).

One social worker, with vagrants on probation, stated:

«The impact of supervision... it is hard to say anything sensible about that... Especially when prostitutes are involved... Prostitution has always been difficult to talk about... We practically avoid bringing it up... It doesn't feel right to moralize about such things. So you mostly talk about finances and ask whether the client has looked for a job. I don't think supervision has any effect on these women... except that they are ashamed about having to show up here... and we think it is embarrassing to have them come. They prefer to come in the evening when it is dark, so that no one will see them coming in» (interview 1985 with probation officer).

The call-girls and hotel prostitutes described supervision as follows: «Once when I reported to my probation officer, he admitted that the whole thing was idiotic... I have a job and I study as well. I showed him my work voucher and he told me I didn't have to report to him anymore. 'We have enough to do as it is', he said»; «It was rather a farce to go to the social welfare office to get my warning. A very young man was supposed to warn me, and he was shaking like a leaf, poor kid... I wasn't quite like all the other vagrants he had seen» (interviews).

Institutional care was not given high marks either. One probation officer said:

«Institutionalization, I wouldn't brag about it. Earlier, the women saw it as a higher place of learning. They came back and boasted about all the screwing techniques they had learned there. They worked in the greenhouse and their conversations must have made the tomatoes blush... It's the same thing today. It is always the toughest cases that are sent to the institutions» (interview 1985 with probation officer).

The director of one such institution reported:

«In the past, the vagrant women were difficult cases... They were not motivated and didn't want to do anything to better their lot...

They had not asked to be sent here and they played tough, with frequent escape attempts. They were seen as hopeless cases, 'vagrant' - that's the worst thing you can call a human being. It is offensive... And the treatment results were in accordance with this... Today this place is a therapeutic institution and our clients come here voluntarily... everyone except the vagrants. There are not many of them but... it is not easy to help someone who doesn't want to be helped» (interview 1985 with director).

The call-girls and hotel prostitutes generally considered institutionalization as something that had nothing to do with them: «I know that prostitutes used to be sent to the workhouse or to prison, but that doesn't happen anymore, does it?»; «I have no alcohol problem, so they can't lock me up»; «The vice police told me about the institution, that you can be sent there. But I'm not that bad off» (interviews).

Some of the women reacted to the anti-vagrancy measures with agitation and defiance. They regarded official intervention as illegitimate because a) they defined themselves as prostitutes but rejected the vagrancy control; or b) they admitted to being vagrants but maintained that they were falsely accused of prostitution; or c) they did not regard themselves as belonging to either category. Whether they had a subjective identity as prostitutes or vagrants (or rather as homeless alcoholics) or neither, they obstinately resisted any further labelling:

«You ought to interview J; she is incredible. Her file has to be 12 inches thick. We arrested her time after time... we gave her warnings, put her under supervision, institutionalized her. But she was proud... held her head high... never mind that she was old and a drunk... I am no vagrant, she would say, I am the most popular whore in Helsinki. And so what are you, little boys? Yeah, what was I compared to her (laugh)?» (interview 1987 with former vice policeman).

Other women reacted to the interventions by changing their life styles: «I got scared, of course. It was so unpleasant... the police interrogation... After that, I took a long break, and isolated myself for a while»; «I got more careful... no new customers, only old acquaintances»; «I in fact gave up the life... almost completely... I looked for a job. The police said I had to» (interviews).

Sometimes the police measures were described as extremely humiliating and stigmatizing. One women who refused to meet me explained: «No, I don't want to be interviewed. Those police interrogations broke me... I don't dare go out anymore. I can't go to the store; I think everyone's staring at me. 'Look, she's been arrested by the vice police'» (telephone conversation 1985). Feelings of being vulnerable and exposed were especially common among those women who had attended procuring trials. Two women summoned as witnesses recalled:

«Then there was the trial... The courtroom was full. The press was there... The judge read from the interrogation file, word for word... I got to hear how many men I had had sex with, and what I had done with them... There was this awful silence, everyone was listening... I got sweaty all over; everything sounded so horrible» (interview 1985 with Helena, 26 years).

«So we witnesses snuck in. They looked at us like you'd think we were rats. Repulsed. 'Here come the whores, that's how they look... One, two, three, four whores. That's bad. Think that people pay good money for sex with them'... And then when I testified, they didn't believe me; that was clear... A whore can never be trusted. I have never felt so worthless» (interview 1985 with Anja, 32 years).

The most frightening factor in the courtroom was the press:

«I couldn't sleep the whole night before. At five o'clock in the morning, I got up and wrote down what I was going to say in court, and what I was going to say to the press. I decided to beg the press in the courtroom not to describe me in a way that everyone could guess who I was. I didn't want to lose my job. Or ruin my daughter's life. She doesn't know anything about all this» (interview 1985 with Anja, 32 years).

Many of the women had bitter experience of articles in both the serious and less serious press:

«All of the newspapers covered it (a procuring case), giving our names and everything... with only slight changes... and our occupations. My co-workers read the newspapers at the office. They talked about it all the time. Maybe they suspected something, but no one said anything» (interview 1985 with Marita, 30 years).

«The whole story was run by the afternoon papers, with big headlines and with our names... All of my relatives bought these newspapers. My mother read it all but never said a word about it. Not a word» (interview 1985 with Helena, 26 years).

All of the prostitutes I interviewed had persons close to them - parents, siblings, children, and so on - who knew nothing about their commercial sexual relations. As one call-girl said: «Are you crazy?... My parents don't know anything... My father has a high position in the social services administration, and I am real afraid he'll find out. Do you know where the vice police send their reports?» (interview). Another told me during an interview at her house: «If my boyfriend comes home, I'll tell him you are conducting a Gallup poll... and you should then start asking questions about toothpaste. Then he won't suspect anything.» Still another introduced me to her teenage daughter as «a colleague of mine. We clean in the same department store and are planning the Christmas party». She said to me afterwards that «it's awful to lie to her, but I have to. After meeting her, maybe you can understand?»

Thus, many prostitutes lived a double-life, out of regard for those in their surroundings as well as for their own sakes. This type of existence was difficult; the more people who knew about their commercial activities, the greater the risk that these women would be forced to admit to themselves, and to those close to them, that, at least in the eyes of society, a person who gets paid for sex is a prostitute.

Prostitution as Occupational Ideology

«Society Needs Prostitution»

There are many statements in the police records and interviews that indicate the existence of a professional ideology among the prostitutes of Helsinki. First, call-girls and hotel prostitutes often professed that prostitution fulfils an important social function. The great demand for their services - typically measured by the amount of answers to their ads - was seen as proof of the necessity of commercial sex.

The most common explanation offered for this indispensability was the customers' sexually frustrating marriages: «Most of my customers are married... But there must be something wrong with their wives... Maybe a lot of women aren't very interested in sex»; «Men get bored after long years of marriage... the same bathrobe, the same curlers, no make-up... Who would get turned on by that?» (interviews). Another repeatedly stated explanation was the customers loneliness: «Many are businessmen, married or unmarried, who get lonely in their dreary hotel rooms... they want company, someone to talk to. It's as simple as that»; «Some are lonely... they don't have time or can't get a girlfriend or wife... they want company, they want to discuss things and hear my opinions» (interviews). A further notion was that men are attracted to prostitution because of the excitement: «It is forbidden, sinful, exciting... The forbidden is always interesting»; «They do it on the sly... no one knows about it, not family nor relatives... No one gets to know... it is exciting» (records). Finally, many prostitutes said their customers come to them because of their «special desires»: «Some want to be whipped, others want to dress up... it can turn into pure clownery at times»; «They wanted me to dress up... in black underwear and boots ...and I was supposed to show porno films, but I never did... maybe that's why I never became popular (laugh)» (interviews).

It was also alleged during interviews that prostitution is necessary because men's and women's sexual appetites are different: «Men are polygamous... a woman can be married to the same man for 30 years without cheating on him, but a man can't be faithful that long»; «Men's sexual needs are so great, that they need this type of care... we ought to have brothels... and then you'd see a drop in the number of rapes and sex murders» (interviews).

Generally, the women saw prostitution as «a safe and comfortable type of liaison», whether the man was only after sex or whether he wanted sex plus other social contact: «Why should men go to restaurants night after night, dancing with women, buying them drinks... and then getting the brush-off, when they can just call one of us?» (interview). The women further claimed that prostitution generally represented no serious threat to a customer's marriage: «It is better for the men to come to us than to have affairs... which could lead to divorce» (records). However, this rule of thumb did not unconditionally apply to long-term and affectionate liaisons: «If the man falls in love and starts spending all his time here, then that's not so great for his family» (interview).

Most prostitutes worked under the assumption that commercialized sex provided their customers with the sexual satisfaction, excitement, and social contact they were seeking: «Yeah, a lot come back again, so I think they're satisfied»; «Gradually you learn what each one wants: one wants consolation, another wants admiration... still another wants straight sex... one only wants to talk... they all get what they want...» (interviews). Admittedly though, some customers leave disappointed: «Perhaps the hardest customers are those who don't know what they seek... some are really looking for a girlfriend, and if you're not interested, well then...» (interview). «Not all of them leave happy. Some of them look like they're thinking, 'why did I come here when I have a bitch like her at home'»; «Sometimes I can really be hard and cold, if I don't like the guy... so of course he's not so happy either...» (records).

Above all, the interviewed women saw prostitution as «a service»: «Sometimes I refer to myself as a therapist... I help men... but it's not just for the money... sometimes I feel like big mamma to whom all the boys can come and cry their hearts out» (interview). Nevertheless, prostitution is not a service without its drawbacks: «We are needed, but people have no respect for us... and I guess we don't have much respect for ourselves either»:

«Prostitution... it's unreal. You live a life... like a movie star... men worship you and you get money. And I don't think it's so bad... if the men are willing to pay. I'm not hurting anyone... maybe I'm even helping some... At the same time, I know it is forbidden, forbidden. I'm a worthless human being because I am a paid woman» (interview 1985 with Sonja, 40 years old).

«Prostitution is Like Other Human Relationships»

An important defence strategy adopted by the prostitutes was to normalize their paid sexual relations. The women emphasized that their own involvement in prostitution was not of a purely commercial nature, but rather resembled «normal» sexual relationships. Some compared their own behaviour with that of their girlfriends who were not prostitutes: «I am soiled... I am a whore... but, for God's sake, aren't my girlfriends whores too. They go to restaurants... bring home different men, have sex with them and kick them out in the morning» (interview). Others used the term «clandestine-whores» to describe «round-heeled» women who did not take payment for their «services»: «They don't dare take money. They give themselves for nothing, even though foreign men take it for granted that they have to pay. And that just wins them the contempt of these foreigners - worthless women who give it away for free» (interview). One prostitute compared her earlier sex life with her commercialized relations of today: «I have always expected the man to pay something... he had to pass some kind of test before he could have me... Nowadays I just do it more systematically... first the money, and then the sex» (records). Another compared her previous commercial sex with her life today as a «kept woman»: «I hope the police are satisfied now. I don't go to nightclubs any more and only one man supports me... But, come on, isn't it really the same thing» (interview).

Comparisons with other typically female occupations were also made: «Stewardesses... there's a lot of prostitution in that job as well... those women walk around smiling... and the men sit along long rows and drool»; «I could just as well have been the private secretary to a president of some company... and taken care of him in all conceivable ways... then at least I'd have a respectable job» (interviews).

«Prostitution Ought to be Regulated»

Although the women stressed that prostitution is indispensable and that it mirrors other heterosexual relationships, they still found it necessary for society to control, or regulate, prostitution. Though they supported the repeal of the obsolete Vagrancy Act, they thought that «a new law ought to be passed in its place», that «the police ought to have some power to intervene in prostitution», and that «it would be wrong to let it run loose» (interviews).

Nowhere are the women's ambivalent attitudes towards prostitution more visible than in these responses. The interviewees strongly defended their own activities but still criticized «prostitution in general» and «commercial sex in its most professional form»: «The police ought to concentrate on the professional whores, those who earn big money»; «The police better keep a close eye on the prostitution here so that it doesn't develop... like it has in many other countries»; «Let's just hope we don't get street prostitution now (after the repeal of the Vagrancy Act)... and all the crime that comes with it» (interviews).

Controlling or regulating prostitution was seen as a very difficult task, however: «The vice police have a hopeless job... they won't eradicate prostitution... prostitution has always been around»; «It is amazing that society can afford it... to pay police to sit and watch us for hours on end, days on end... and what do they have to show for it?» (interviews).

The prostitutes of Helsinki seemed to articulate an occupational ideology similar to that described in studies from other countries. The most startling aspect of this ideology, however, is the degree to which it coincides with the traditional, functionalist view of prostitution as discussed in Chpt. 1.1. To repeat, prostitution is necessary, in order to address the differences in male and female sexuality, to remedy social isolation, and even to prevent criminality. In this perspective, prostitution is imperishable and thus ought to be accepted, even though the disruptive factors that follow in its wake must be restricted.

The prostitutes' ideology is not a new or deviant one, which is diametrically opposed to traditional values. On the contrary, it is a direct reflection of the societal view of prostitution, embracing a sexual ideology of ancient standing. The women do find an inherent paradox, though: commercial sex is accepted as a necessary evil, but prostitutes are condemned. To deal with this double standard, they shield themselves from the label of prostitute. They struggle to retain their self-image as normal women who in «a typically female fashion» use their bodies to attain economic benefits.

6.4. Prostitution as Subculture

Prostitution networks are often described as subcultures, as organized social systems with identifiable norms and activities (see Chpt. 1.3.). The prostitution environments analyzed in this study, however, deviate in many crucial respects from the most common descriptions found in the literature. The prostitution known to the Helsinki police was not organized around extensive and systematic networks of procuring. Judging from both police documents and interviews, it was operated almost exclusively by the individual prostitutes. The few profiteers known to the police have not played a decisive role in the city's prostitution as a whole, nor has their presence led to the creation of clearly delimited subcultures.

The women arrested, on the other hand - be it call-girls, hotel prostitutes, or other prostitutes - often knew one another. Ship girls knew other ship girls, marginalized women knew others like themselves, and so on. The social networks within the milieus were loosely structured sets of acquaintances consisting of small circles of girlfriends who were important to each other in terms of cooperation, loyalty, and the dispersal of information. In this limited sense, Helsinki prostitution was structured and dominated by women.

The circles of prostitutes, however, were not women-determined social systems or «subcultures» in the traditional sense. The prostitutes belonged more to «dual worlds» than to a «subculture sustained by commercialized sex» (see Chpt. 1.3.). Their social contacts were not limited to other prostitutes, customers, and procurers, and they had no pronounced identities as prostitutes - quite the reverse. A majority operated in the gray zone between reciprocal sexual relations and commercialized sex and not in clearly defined markets which were in opposition to conventional sexual relations. The prostitutes' occupational ideology was not a deviant one, nor was it an ideology of women preparing to combat the masculine values of society. Moreover, any notion of power - or solidarity - among women within prostitution has its definite limitations. The ambivalent attitudes found among them towards being prostitutes, and the substantial gaps between the status of women operating in different milieus, make extensive cooperation inconceivable. Loyalty is a luxury affordable only among the closest of friends.

Notes

1 See, for example, Prieur & Taksdal.
2 McLeod 1982; Miller 1986; Romenesko & Miller 1989.
3 Månsson 1981; Høigård & Finstad 1986.
4 Cf., for example, police documents from Oslo 1968-1982, where nearly half of the arrested souteneurs were the prostitutes' «nearest and dearest», Høigård & Finstad 1986.

7.

Controlling Prostitution – Controlling Women

Conclusions

The basic assumption in this study has been that the concept of prostitution is a social construction whose contents and meaning vary from setting to setting. The line of demarcation separating prostitution liaisons from reciprocal sexual relations is determined by a process of social definition. In a feminist perspective, the concept of prostitution is directly related to the gender system in a given society. The supply side of commercial sex reflects the traditional role assigned to women, and the demand side reflects a typical male role.

Another underlying assumption has been that through the regulation of prostitution, society has forced a distinction between prostitution and non-prostitution or, more accurately, between prostitutes and other women. This prototyping of «normal» women and prostitutes symbolizes a very decisive moral division in patriarchal societies. Of all conceivable classifications applied to women, the designation «a prostitute» has the most degrading connotations.

In this closing chapter, the study will be summarized in terms of the four themes set out in the beginning: the nature of the control of prostitution; the relativity of commercialized sex; the degree of its professionalism - amateurism; and the control of prostitution as an overall control of women.

Firstly, it seems adequate to use a functionalist model to describe the policy for controlling prostitution in Helsinki. In all key respects, the concrete steps taken to curtail the socially disruptive aspects of commercial sex have represented a male control of female behaviour. Prostitution has been assessed as a public health problem, but the «preventive examinations», specified in the Vagrancy Act, were exclusively intended for prostitutes, not for customers. Alternatively, commercialized sex has been viewed as a social policy problem, but here again, only prostitutes were subjected to the «educational and supportive measures» called for by the Vagrancy Act. Further, commercial sex has been defined as a public order problem, but the policy adopted for combatting the disorder and criminality accompanying prostitution has never targeted customers. Finally, prostitution has been viewed as a youth problem, but the measures adopted to combat it were only directed at the young girls selling sexual services, while the customers were ignored. It is also noteworthy that only female prostitutes have been registered, although the Vagrancy Act was intended to control male prostitution as well. This gender specificity is demonstrated in the nation-wide register on vagrants: of the 1 556 male vagrants remaining in the files in 1983, only two had entries about prostitution. The corresponding proportion among female vagrants was 84 per cent of 1 332. These figures could hardly reflect the actual gender distribution within commercial sex: male homosexual prostitution must be of greater dimensions than indicated here.

Secondly, prostitution, and the anti-vagrancy measures implemented, have taken very different forms in the various settings and decades under study. The prostitution dealt with by the Helsinki police has not been static or uniform. The social relations within prostitution, the detained women's identity as prostitutes, the interaction between the controllers and the controlled, have all varied. The changes in the settings described can be summarized in the following trends. The first tendency within registered prostitution is towards an increased concentration. The large number of young ship, truck, and station girls of the 1960s has been replaced by a small group of harbour and station prostitutes with serious social problems. Restaurant prostitution, once spread over a large number of establishments of varying types and price classes, has become limited to a few night-clubs and former sailor taverns. Another discernible trend is an increased professionalism in the registered prostitution settings. The young amateurs who hitchhiked, associated with sailors, and developed crushes on truck drivers, have been replaced by call-girls and hotel prostitutes, who at least periodically pursue prostitution as an occupation. Simultaneously, a change can be noted, concerning status differentiation. The social gap between call-girls and hotel prostitutes, and the other large group - the homeless, unemployed, low-status women with alcohol problems - is great. The difficult to classify middle category of street, restaurant, and harbour prostitutes has almost entirely disappeared.

Thirdly, regardless of these changes, it is revealed that police-registered prostitution in Helsinki - including the most professional forms - has many amateurish features. As seen in both police records and personal interviews, call-girl activities and hotel prostitution have not been particularly systematic or extensive, nor have the women viewed themselves as professional prostitutes. Commercial sex in Helsinki has not been organized but instead administered nearly exclusively by the individual prostitutes.

The Vagrancy Act provided the vice police with broad powers to establish the boundaries between commercial and non-commercial sexual behaviour. In many respects, these distinctions have been made arbitrarily. Particularly in earlier decades, some of the detained women did not fulfil the criteria for prostitution found in the Vagrancy Act, nor the criteria set out in theoretical discourse. The police largely used the Act to prevent ship visits, hitchhiking, and patronage of the railway station and restaurants from developing into commercialized sex. Participation in prostitution was limited for most of the women: ship visits, hitchhiking, and hanging around restaurants belonged to a specific phase of their lives. Nevertheless, the records also contain data about a group who worked as prostitutes over extensive periods of time. These women were often burdened with social problems such as unemployment, homelessness, and alcoholism. Typically, as the extent of their social problems grew, so declined the degree of professionalism in their prostitution. Participation in commercial sex was related to a process of social marginalization in these cases, but, according to the records, it was seldom the most important factor in the process.

The control of prostitution in Helsinki has had two major acknowledged objectives, that of combatting the visible and socially disruptive features of commercialized sex, and that of hindering detained amateurs from becoming professionals. Nonetheless, the control measures have had other functions than those formulated in the law texts and circulars. These functions can be summarized in four themes, always implicit, but seldom articulated: the issues of women's sexuality, female drinking, family life, and poverty.

7.1. Prostitution and Female Sexuality

The street prostitutes of earlier years obviously violated important norms by «wandering back and forth on the streets», «behaving provocatively», «responding to strangers in the streets», or «accompanying men to hostels». Unescorted women at the restaurants were condemned for «arriving alone, yet leaving with men», «making eyes or toasting with all the men in the restaurant». The young amateurs of the 1960s were registered for «visiting ships», «having many boyfriends, Italians and Swedes, Blacks and Whites», or «having many truckdrivers as friends». Finally, the socially marginalized prostitutes were registered for «being picked up drunk together with ten men», or «living at several places around town, with male acquaintances».

The focus in these records is on behaviour related to female sexuality, female promiscuity, or at least the invitation by women to sexual relations. The street-walkers legitimized their evening and night-time strolls by claiming to have been to the movies or visiting relatives. Unescorted women were only able to patronize restaurants if they chose the right type of establishment, at the right time of day, and for the explicit purpose of eating. Preferably, the young amateurs were not to hitchhike, but if they did, it should be for the sole purpose of getting from one place to another and not for meeting men.

Naturally, the arrested women's behaviour can be interpreted as a sign of prostitution. Some of them acted «provocatively» in the streets, in restaurants, and on ships and were in fact offering their body for sale. Remarkably, however, the forms of behaviour described here were in and of themselves sufficient grounds for intervention by the authorities. Women moving around in these settings, without acceptable reasons, at the wrong time of day, and without appropriate male companionship, risked being labelled as prostitutes, regardless of whether their intention was to engage in commercial sex or not. The restaurants, the harbours, the railway station, and the streets at night, all constituted male territory. The women discovered by the police in these settings were compelled to motivate their presence and prove their «respectability». If they failed in this, their motives were defined as sexual and the women themselves were identified as prostitutes. The public control of prostitution thus sharply curtailed women's social and sexual freedom of movement.

Right up to the 1960s, there apparently existed a normative «map» denominating which domains should be regarded as male and female, respectively. The female sphere was quite narrow compared to that of men, and primarily linked to private life and to certain sectors of working life. Controlling female sexuality was a fundamental instrument for preserving these gender specific spheres. The prescribed combination of female sexuality, monogamy, and privacy has traditionally been a cornerstone of the patriarchal sexual order. Women crossing over into male territory, and - according to the observers - publicly demonstrating their sexuality, were therefore defined as «abnormal». Their sexuality was no longer private, and thus, they were public women; they belonged to all men; they were prostitutes.

7.2. Prostitution and Female Drinking

The «unescorted» women of earlier decades violated social norms by «ordering too many or too strong drinks» at the restaurants, «drinking alcohol in doorways», or «appearing in public while intoxicated». The teenage prostitutes aroused suspicion if they «allowed themselves to be served alcohol while on board ships» or «emptied bottles with the boys in the station gang». The marginalized female vagrants in their turn, caught the attention of the surroundings and of the police for «wandering around with male alcoholics» or «being boisterous with other drunkards in the park».

That the use of alcohol is interpreted as a sign of faulty sexual morality is clearly revealed in the police records. Drinking and intoxication among young ship, truck, and station girls were often used as evidence of prostitution. Since the girls violated the norms for female sobriety, they were also supposed to break another rule, namely, that of sexual inaccessibility. The analogy between drinking and low sexual standards was applied to adult women as well. The marginalized vagrants of the parks, the beaches, and the public squares were taken into custody and registered for «refusal to work, a shiftless life, inebriation, and possible prostitution». The vice police did not consider these women to be professional prostitutes as much as potential prostitutes. Drunkenness and social marginalization were assumed to bring about a deterioration of their sexual standards, or at least an impairment of the women's ability to defend themselves against male sexual encroachments. Women who had sunk so low as to associate with alcoholic bums must also be deficient in their sexual morals.

In this manner, the controlling of prostitution implied a sexualization of women's drinking habits and alcohol problems. Instead of viewing female problem drinkers as in want of treatment, they were labelled as prostitutes, compelled to undergo examinations for venereal disease, and subjected to the control measures set out in the Vagrancy Act. This process of definition was, indeed, confusing to many female vagrants, who had resigned themselves to being homeless alcoholics, but not to being prostitutes.

7.3. Prostitution and Family Life

The measures taken to control prostitution were not only used as a means for controlling women's sexuality and use of alcohol, but also as a form of family control. The amateurs and semi-professional women broke - or revolted against - the basic gender roles in society. These were women who out of defiance, lack of judgment, or indifference engaged in behaviour reserved for men. They patronized restaurants, drank alcohol, and engaged in sexual liaisons with strange men, and were therefore seen as «drifting». But these women were shiftless in another sense as well; they had drifted out from the direct control of the patriarchal family.

The majority of the arrestees were young women who had recently left or were in the process of leaving their original families and who had not yet formed their own nuclear family. The records reveal that many ship, truck, and station girls were facing various types of family problems. Some came from families that had been separated by divorce or death, and others found themselves in direct conflict with their parents. At least for the time being, these girls were beyond the control of their original family and were therefore seen as a risk group with regard to sexual morality. Their «unmanageableness» and their revolt against their parents were sufficient grounds for official intervention, since running away from home and loitering in suspect places could end in prostitution. The responsibility of the police was to take the girls into custody and to return them to their parents or deliver them to the child welfare authorities for further disposition. In many cases, the police obviously considered the girls' family situation to be the primary problem, but were powerless to help them. The girls were charged for «ship and station visits, hitchhiking, promiscuity, and possible prostitution». Thus, yet another social phenomenon - that of family problems and conflicts with parents - was sexualized and registered as prostitution.

Not infrequently, the adult prostitutes had conflict-filled marital relationships in their past. The police records and interview responses reveal numerous incidents of woman battering, jealousy, and alcohol problems. Especially in earlier decades, arrests for prostitution were often made while the women were in the process of breaking out of these problematic relationships. In certain cases, the husbands had implored the police to deal with their «unfaithful», «promiscuous», or «immoral» wives, which the police proceeded to do - the women were detained and registered under the vagrancy provisions. It is perhaps these cases that most clearly exemplify the notion of prostitution control as male control of female behaviour. The husbands named in the police records were not «live-in pimps» - on the contrary, they cooperated with the police in controlling the women.

However, the anti-vagrancy measures were primarily applied to single women, that is, women not committed to one man. When the restaurant prostitutes were apprehended by the police, they had to prove that they had come to the restaurant in appropriate male company - with a husband, fiancé, or male family member - and that they had not made new acquaintances while at the restaurant. When the ship girls were arrested, they often tried to convince the police that they were formally engaged with a particular sailor on board. Likewise, when the marginalized women were found with a group of male vagrants, they needed to prove that they had a steady, male partner in the group, in order to prevent «possible prostitution» from being entered into their files.

The control measures were not only implemented in cases of «unaccompanied» women, «rebellious» daughters and «unfaithful» wives, but also in cases of «unsuitable» mothers. Most of the women who had given birth to children did not have custody of them. That the roles of mother and of prostitute - whether amateur, semi-professional, or professional - were often defined as incompatible is evident from the records. Entries about children who had been adopted or taken into custody were used as definitive proof of the women's asocial nature and societal marginalization. Women who had relinquished their children were seen as hopeless losers and shiftless vagrants; and, inversely, women who had been detained for prostitution were automaticly expected to be bad mothers.

Young girls running away from their parents, adult women leaving their husbands and abandoning their children all violated social norms for how normal daughters, wives, and mothers are to behave. If they, moreover, were registered for using/abusing alcohol and for openly flaunting their sexual liaisons, their status as vagrants was settled.

7.4. Prostitution and Poverty

Finally, the control of prostitution has served to regulate the poverty of women. Perhaps the most distinguishing feature of the control measures described here is the fact that all social problems not directly assignable to other control systems have been relegated to the provisions of the Vagrancy Act.

Indigence was a common feature for most of the women arrested. This is clearly seen in their position on the labour market. Typically, they worked or had previously worked at low-waged female occupations: as maids, nursemaids, salesgirls in shops or cafés, factory workers, restaurant employees, or cleaners. Extremely few had the education or working experience that might have given them well paying jobs. Furthermore, engaging in amateur and semi-professional prostitution seems to have done little to improve their economic situation. According to the records, their monthly income from prostitution was generally lower than that required by the minimum-wage standards. Exceptions to this rule were found among some of the most professional call-girls and hotel prostitutes. At least periodically, some seemed to enjoy rather high earnings from commercialized sex - but earnings that presupposed extensive expenditures.

Resourcelessness was also manifest in the women's status on the housing market. Not infrequently, the prostitutes used their parents' address as their own, although they had not lived there for years. At the time of registration, they were living as lodgers, in some cases in the homes of single, elderly men. A minority of the women (mainly call-girls and hotel prostitutes) had their own rental apartments. Significantly enough, one third of the prostitutes were at some time during their careers as vagrants registered as homeless, that is, they were living at public lodging-houses or reported no address at all.

Some of the women arrested under the provisions of the Vagrancy Act had been defined by all relevant social authorities as «hopeless cases». Not only did their records contain entries for unemployment, homelessness, and alcohol problems, but also for criminality and psychiatric disorders. Despite this fact, the health services had forsaken them («ambulatory treatment forms are no longer of help in A`s case»), as had the mental hospitals («no mental disturbance has been established in B's case»), alcohol- treatment facilities («the examined woman cannot be diagnosed as an alcoholic»), and sometimes even the overnight shelters («the detainee has violated shelter rules and is no longer welcome here»). But there was no release from the jurisdiction of the vagrancy provisions. The vice police was the agency assigned to take care of the poorest women in the welfare society. The 1936 Vagrancy Act scooped up all the «hopeless cases» - both women and men - which had fallen through all other safety nets: «We have taken care of these people... but there wasn't much we could do for them... other than give them a roof over their heads for the night. I wonder who is going to take care of them after the Vagrancy Act is repealed» (interview 1986 with vice police).

With the repeal of the Vagrancy Act at the end of 1986 disappeared an important instrument of control with regard to female drinking, family disorders, and poverty. These problems are now to be handled by other social agencies who are, or at least ought to be, better equipped for the task than were the vice police. An old tradition of public control, observation, and disciplinary measures against behaviour designated as prostitution has been broken. The limited market for commercialized sex in Helsinki and the predomination of non-public forms of prostitution are probably to some degree consequences of the strict control policy. The objective of this policy was to force prostitution into as discreet forms as possible, and in terms of this goal, it has been successful. However, the price paid for this success has been high. The vagrancy regulations not only legitimated extensive interventions into the lives of individual prostitutes, but they also affected the lives of all women.

The vagrancy provisions were part of a control tradition where prostitutes were viewed as «social deviants». The feminist perspective, however, challenges this tradition. If prostitution is seen to reflect the central gender structure and sexual ideology of a society, it can hardly be analyzed in terms of social deviance. Prostitution is not a marginal phenomenon on the far fringes of society nor populated exclusively by «deviant» individuals. It represents no real violation of the norms and values of a patriarchal, male-dominated society. The feminist goal of eliminating prostitution is impossible to combine with a functionalist regulatory policy. A policy based on the assumption that commercial sex is a necessary evil involves at worst a direct legitimation of prostitution, and at best a countermeasure to the social disruption caused by prostitution, but not to prostitution itself.

The repeal of the old vagrancy legislation was a welcome change. However, the resulting development for prostitution in Finland may not be particularly appealing. With the removal of the vagrancy provisions, the police lost their primary mechanism for intervening in the sphere of commercialized sex and this at a point in time when attention had begun to be focused on the professional core of prostitution. During the 1980s, the police had a good grasp of a rather broad spectrum of commercial sex environments, including those which enjoy a high social status. Today, the police have less information about prostitution than at any other point in the post-war period. With the escalating European integration and a general internationalization, it is very difficult to prophesy the development of Finnish prostitution. Will the general limitedness of prostitution, backed up by a relatively well developed gender equality, stand the test of internationalization? Or will the small and amateurish prostitution scenes in Helsinki give way to the wholly commercial, systematic, and flagrant forms of commercialized sex known from many other Western countries?

Note
1 Varsa & Heinonen 1984.

References

Anderson, Eric. 1974. Prostitution and Social Justice: Chicago, 1910-15. Social Service Review, Vol. 48, pp. 203- 228.

Armstrong, Edward G. 1978. Massage Parlors and Their Customers. Archives of Sexual Behavior, Vol. 7, pp. 117-125.

Armstrong, Gail. 1977. Females under the Law - "Protected" but Unequal. Crime & Delinquency, Vol. 27, pp. 109-122.

Arnold, Katherine. 1977. The Introduction of Poses to a Peruvian Brothel and Changing Images of Male and Female, in Blacking, J. (ed.): The Anthropology of the Body. Academic Press, London, pp. 179-197.

Barry, Kathleen. 1981. The Underground Economic System of Pimping. Journal of International Affairs, Vol. 81, pp. 117- 127.

Barry, Kathleen. 1984. Female Sexual Slavery. New York University Press, New York.

Becker, Howard S. 1973. Outsiders. Studies in the Sociology of Deviance. Free Press, New York.

Becker, Howard S. 1974. Labelling Theory Reconsidered, in Rock. P. & M.McIntosh (eds.): Deviance and Social Control. Tavistock, London, pp. 41-46.

Benjamin, Harry. 1961. Prostitution, in Ellis, A. & Abarbanel, A. (eds.): The Encyclopedia of Sexual Behavior. Hawthorn Books, New York, pp. 869-882.

Benjamin, Harry & Albert Ellis. 1954. An Objective Examination of Prostitution. International Journal of Sexology, Vol.8, pp. 100-105.

Benjamin, Harry & R. E. L. Masters, (eds.) 1964. Prostitution and Morality. Julian Press, New York.

Binderman, Murray B., Dennis Wepman & Ronald B. Newman. 1975. A Portrait of "The Life". Urban Life, Vol. 4, pp. 213- 225.

Boldt, Jean. 1897. Prostitutionens reglementering och läkaresällskapet. J. C. Frenckell & Son, Helsingfors.

Boles, Jacqueline & Charlotte Tatro. 1978. Legal and Extra- Legal Methods of Controlling Female Prostitution: A Cross- Cultural Comparison. International Journal of Comparative and Applied Criminal Justice, Vol. 2, pp. 71-85.

Borelli, Siegfried & Willy Starck. 1957. Die Prostitution als Psycholog-ishes Problem. Springer-Verlag, Berlin.

Borg, Arne m.fl. 1981. Prostitution. Beskrivning, analys, förslag till åtgär-der. Liber Förlag, Stockholm.

Boyer, Debra & Jennifer James. 1979. Juvenile Prostitution, in Griffiths, C. T. & M. Nance (eds.): The Female Offender. A Publication of the Crim-inology Research Centre, Simon Fraser University, pp. 99-118.

Bracey, Dorothy H. 1983. The Juvenile Prostitute: Victim and Offender, Victimology, Vol. 8, pp. 151-160.

Brake, Mike. 1980. The Sociology of Youth Culture and Youth Subcul-tures. Sex and Drugs and Rock'n'Roll? Routledge & Kegan Paul, Lon-don.

Bristow, Edward J. 1982. Prostitution and Prejudice. The Jewish Fight against White Slavery 1870-1939. Clarendon Press, Oxford.

Brundage, James A. 1976. Prostitution in the Medieval Canon Law, Signs, Vol. 1, pp. 825-845.

Brundage: James A. 1987. Law, Sex, and Christian Society in Medieval Europe. The University of Chicago Press, Chicago.

Bryan, James H. 1965. Apprenticeships in Prostitution, Social Problems, Vol. 12, pp. 287-297.

Bryan, James H. 1966. Occupational Ideologies and Individual Attitudes of Call Girls, Social Problems, Vol. 13, pp. 441- 450.

Bryant, Clifton D. & C. Eddie Palmer. 1975. Massage Parlors and "Hand Whores". Some Sociological Observations, Journal of Sex Research, Vol. 11, pp. 227-241.

Bryant, Marshall A. 1977. Prostitution and the Criminal Justice System, Journal of Police Science and Administration, Vol. 5, pp. 379-389.

Bullough, Vern & Bonnie L. Bullough. 1964. The History of Prostitution. University Books, New York.

Butler, Anne M. 1985. Daughters of Joy, Sisters of Misery. Prostitutes in the American West 1865-90. University of Illinois Press, Urbana.

Böök, Einar. 1936. Den nya lagen om lösdrivare och dess förhistoria, So-cial Tidskrift, Vol. 30, pp. 615-630.

Campbell, Anne. 1987. Self Definition by Rejection: The Case of Gang Girls, Social Problems, Vol. 34, pp. 451-466.

Caplan, Gerald, M. 1984. The Facts of Life about Teenage Prostitution, Crime & Delinquency, Vol. 30, pp. 69-74.

Caplan, Pat (ed.). 1987. The Construction of Sexuality. Tavistock, London.

Carmichael, Kay. 1982. A City and Its Prostitutes, New Society, Vol. 59, pp. 53-55.

Cavan, Sherri. 1970. B-Girls and Prostitutes, in Douglas, J. D. (ed.): Obser-vations of Deviance. Random House, New York, pp. 55-85

Chesney-Lind, Meda. 1977. Judical Paternalism and the Female Status Of-fender. Training Women to Know Their Place, Crime and Delinquency, Vol. 23, pp. 121-130.

Chesney-Lind, Meda. 1979. Re-Discovering Lilith: Misgony and the "New" Female Criminal, in Griffiths, C. T. & M. Nance (ed.): The Fe-male Offender. A Publication of the Criminology Research Centre, Simon Fraser University, pp. 1-35.

Chesney-Lind, Meda. 1989. Girls' Crime and Woman's Place: Toward a Feminist Model of Female Delinquency, Crime & Delinquency, Vol. 35, pp. 5-29.

Choisy, Maryse. 1961. Psychoanalysis of the Prostitute. Philosophical Library, New York.

Clarce, John, Stuart Hall, Tony Jefferson & Brian Roberts. 1976. Subcultures, Cultures and Class, in Hall, S. & T. Jefferson (eds.): Resistance through Rituals. Youth Subcultures in Post-War Britain. Hutchinson & Co, London, pp. 9-74.

Clinard, Marshall B. 1968. Sociology of Deviant Behavior. Holt, Rinehart and Winston, New York.

Cohen, Bernard. 1980. Deviant Street Networks: Prostitution in New York. Lexington Books, Lexington.

Cohen, Stanley. 1980. Folk Devils and Moral Panics. The Creation of the Mods and Rockers. Martin Robertson, Oxford.

Cohen, Stanley (ed.). 1982. Images of Deviance. Pengvin Books, Middlesex.

Coleman, Kate. 1973. The Real Thing. Carnal Knowledge: A Portrait of Four Hookers, in Csicsery, G. (ed.): The Sex Industry. New American Library, New York, pp. 1-21.

Connelly, Mark Thomas. 1980. The Response to Prostitution in the Progressive Era. The University of North Carolina Press, Chapel Hill.

Corbin, Alain. 1987. Commercial Sexuality in Nineteenth- Century France: A System of Images and Regulations, in Gallagher, C. & T. Laqueur (eds.): The Making of the Modern Body. Sexuality and Society in the Nineteenth Century. University of California Press, Berkeley, pp. 209-219.

Corrigan, Paul. 1979. Schooling the Smash Street Kids. Macmillan Press, London.

Coveney, Lal, Margaret Jackson, Sheila Jeffreys, Leslie Kay & Pat Kahony. 1984. The Sexuality Papers. Male Sexuality and the Social Control of Women. Hutchinson, London.

Cowan, Rex. 1956. The Female Prostitute, Criminal Law Review, Vol. 29, pp. 611-615.

Coward, Rosalind. 1983. Patriarchal Precedents. Sexuality and Social Relations. Routledge & Kegan Paul, London.

Datesman, Susan K. & Frank R. Scarpitti. 1977. Unequal Protection for Males and Females in the Juvenile Court, in Ferdinand, T. N. (ed.): Juvenile Delinquency. Little Brother Grows Up. Sage Research Progress in Criminology, Beverly Hills, pp. 59-76.

Davis, Kingsley. 1937. The Sociology of Prostitution. American Sociological Review, Vol. 11, pp. 744-755.

Davis, Nanette J. 1971. The Prostitute: Developing a Deviant Identity, in Henslin, J. H. (ed.): Studies in the Sociology of Sex. Appleton Century Crafts, New York, pp. 297-322.

Dinnerstein, Dorothy. 1976. The Mermaid and the Minotaur. Sexual Arrangements and Human Malaise. Harper & Row Publ., New York.

Dominelli, Lena. 1986. The Power of the Powerless: Prostitution and the Reinforcement of Submissive Femininity, Sociological Review, Vol. 34, pp. 65-92.

Douglas, Jack D. 1977. Shame and Deceit in Creative Deviance, in Sagarin, E. (ed.): Deviance and Social Change. Sage Publications, Beverly Hills, pp. 59-86.
Drake, Sunniva. 1983. Besiktningskvinnorna i Helsingfors 1867 och 1877. Pro-gradu avhandling i Finlands och Skandinaviens historia, Helsingfors universitet.
Dworkin, Andrea. 1987. Intercourse. Secker & Warburg, London.
Edwards, Susan. 1981. Female Sexuality & the Law. Martin Robertson, Oxford.
Eisenbach-Stangl, Irmgaard. 1983. Lust-Laster und Laster- Lust von Ehrlosen und Ehrbaren Frauen. Kriminalsoziologische Bibliographie, Vol. 10, pp. 107-126.
Ellis, Albert. 1959. Why Married Men Visit Prostitutes. Sexology, Vol. 25, pp. 344-349.
Ericsson, Lars. O. 1980. Charges against Prostitution: An Attempt at a Philosophical Assessment, Ethics, Vol. 90, pp. 335-366.
Esselstyn, T.C. 1968. Prostitution in the United States. The Annals of the American Academy, Vol. 376, pp. 123-135
Evans, Richard J. 1976. Prostitution, State and Society in Imperial Germany, Past and Present, Vol. 70, pp. 106-129.
Exner, John E., Joyce Wylie, Antonnia Leura & Tracey Parrill. 1977. Some Psychological Characteristics of Prostitutes, Journal of Personality Assessment, Vol. 41, pp. 475-485.
Feinman, Clarice. 1979. Sex Role Stereotypes and Justice for Women, Crime and Delinquency, Vol. 25, pp. 87-94.
Finnegan, Frances. 1979. Poverty and Prostitution. A study of Victorian Prostitutes in York. Cambridge University Press, London.
Finstad, Liv, Lita Fougner & Vivi-Lill Holter. 1981. Oslo- prosjektet. Rapport fra to års forsøksvirksomhet blant barne- og ungdomsprostituerte i Oslo 1979-1981. Stencil, Barnevernskontoret i Oslo.
Finstad, Liv, Lita Fougner & Vivi-Lill Holter. 1982. Prostitusjon i Oslo. Pax Forlag, Oslo.
Finstad, Liv & Hanna Olsson 1983: Skandinavisk prostitusjonsforskning. I. Høigård, C. & A. Snare (red.): Kvinners skyld. En nordisk antologi i kriminologi. Pax Forlag, Oslo, pp. 131-175.
Foltz, Tanice G. 1980. The Process of Becoming a Prostitute: A Comparison between Lower-Class and Middle-Class Girls, in Kelly, D. H. (ed.): Criminal Behavior. Readings in Criminology. St. Martins Press, New York, pp. 255-262.
Fredriksson, Torsten & Britt-Inger Lind. 1980. Kärlek för pengar. En bok om prostitutionsprojektet i Malmö 1976-80. Ordfronts Förlag, Stockholm.
Gagnon, John. 1968. Prostitution, in International Encyclopedia of the Social Sciences, Vol. 12, pp. 592-598.
Gagnon, John. 1977. Human Sexualities. Scott, Foresman and Company, Illinois.
Gallo, Maria Teresa de & Heli Alzate. 1976. Brothel Prostitution in Colombia, Archives of Sexual Behavior, Vol. 5, pp. 1-7.

Geis, Gilbert. 1972. Not The Law's Business? An Examination of Homo-sexuality, Abortion, Prostitution, Narcotics and Gambling in the United States. Center for Studies of Crime and Delinquency, Rockville.

Gelsthorpe, Loraine. 1986. Towards a Sceptical Look at Sexism, International Journal of the Sociology of Law, Vol. 14, pp. 125-152.

George, B. J. 1965. Prostitution, in Slovenko, R. (ed.): Sexual Behavior and the Law. C. C. Thomas, Springfield 1965, pp. 645-669.

Gibbens, T. C. N. 1957. Juvenile Prostitution, British Journal of Delinquency, Vol. 8, pp. 3-12.

Gibbens, T. C. N. 1963. Men and Prostitutes, New Society, Vol. 40, pp. 6-9.

Gibbens, T. C. N. 1971. Female Offenders, British Journal of Hospital Medicine, Vol. 32, pp. 279-286.

Gibbens, T. C. N. & M. Silberman. 1960. The Clients of Prostitutes, British Journal of Venereal Diseases, Vol. 30, pp. 113-117.

Gibson, Mary. 1980. The State and Prostitution: Prohibition, Regulation, or Decriminalization? In Inciardi, J. A. & C. E. Faupel (eds.): History and Crime. Implications for Criminal Justice Policy. Sage Publications, Beverly Hills, pp. 193- 208.

Gill, Owen. 1977. Luke Street. Housing Policy, Conflict and the Creation of the Delinquent Area. Macmillan Press, London.

Girtler, Roland. 1983. Frankisten, Teilhaber und Burenhäutlstrizzis: Stellung und Funktion des Zuhälters im Wiener Milieu, Kriminalsoziologische Bibliographie, Volume 10, pp. 1-16.

Golowin-Salonen, Ulla-Britt. 1974. Kvinnliga lösdrivare och alkoholmissbrukare i Åbo. Meddelanden från Statsvetenskapliga fakulteten vid Åbo Akademi, Serie B:37, Åbo.

Goode, Erich. 1978. Deviant Behavior. An Interactionist Approach. Prentice-Hall, New Jersey.

Gornick, Vivian. 1971. Woman as Outsider, in Gornick, V. & B. Moran (eds.): Women in Sexist Society. Basic Books, New York, pp. 76-89.

Gray, Diana. 1973. Turning-Out: A Study of Teenage Prostitution, Urban Life and Culture, Vol. 4, pp. 401-425.

Greenwald, Harold. 1970. The Elegant Prostitute. A Social and Psychoanalythic Study. Walker and Company, New York.

Greenwood, Victoria & Jock Young. 1980. Ghettos of Freedom, in National Deviance Conference (ed.): Critical Criminology. Macmillan Press, London, pp. 149-174.

Grönholm, Pertti & Seppo Laine. 1976. Tutkimus prostitutiivisesta käyttäytymisestä ja siihen liittyvistä tekijöistä. Sosiologian pro-gradu ja laudatur-työ, Turun Yliopisto.

Haavio-Mannila, Elina & Raija Snicker. 1980. Päivätanssit. WSOY, Juva.

Hall, Stuart & Tony Jefferson (eds.). 1976. Resistance through Rituals. Youth Subcultures in Post-War Britain. Hutchinson & Co, London.

Hall, Susan. 1974. Gentleman of Leisure: A Year in the Life of a Pimp. Quadrangle/The New York Times Book Company, New York.

Harrison, Paul. 1975. The New Red Light Districts, New Society, Vol. 53, pp. 69-72.

Haug, Frigga and others. 1987. Female Sexualization. A Collective Work on Memory. Verso, London.

Hawkins, Keith. 1981. The Interpretation of Evil in Criminal Settings, in Ross, H. L. (ed.): Law and Deviance. Sage Publications, Beverly Hills, pp. 99-126.

Hawkins, Richard & Gary Tiedeman. 1975. The Creation of Deviance. Interpersonal and Organizational Determinants. Charles E. Merrill Publishing Company, Columbus.

Heikel, Rosina. 1888. Uttalande i prostitutionsfrågan vid läkaresällskapets sammanträde den 21 April 1888. J.C.Frenckell & Son, Helsingfors.

Henriques, Fernando. 1963. Prostitution in Europe and the New World. Volume 2. Macgibbon & Kee, London.

Heyl, Barbara Sherman. 1977. The Madam as Teacher: The Training of House Prostitutes, Social Problems, Vol. 24, pp. 548-555.

Heyl, Barbara Sherman. 1979. The Madam as Entrepreneur. Career Management in House Prostitution. Transaction Books, New Brunswick, New Jersey.

Hirschi, Travis. 1962. The Professional Prostitute, Berkeley Journal of Sociology, Vol. 7, pp. 33-49.

Hollender, Marc H. 1961. Prostitution, the Body and Human Relatedness, International Journal of Psychoanalysis, Vol. 42, pp. 404-413.

Holmes, Kay Ann. 1972. Reflections by Gaslight: Prostitution in Another Age, Issues in Criminology, Vol. 7, pp. 83-101.

Hong, Lawrence K. & Robert W. Duff. 1976. Gentlemen's Social Club: Revival of Taxi-Dancing in Los Angeles, Journal of Popular Culture, Vol. 9, pp. 827-832.

Hong, Lawrence K. & Robert W. Duff. 1977. Becoming a Taxi- Dancer. The Significance of Neutralization in a Semi-Deviant Occupation, Sociology of Work and Occupations, Vol. 4, pp. 327-342.

Hudson, Annie. 1988. Boys will be Boys: Masculinism and the Juvenile Justice System, Critical Social Policy, Vol. 7, pp. 31-48.

Huttunen, Oiva. 1926. Förslaget till lag om lösdrivare. Social Tidskrift, Vol. 20, pp. 612-623.

Härö, A. S. 1961. Prostituution epidemiologiasta Helsingissä 1945-57, Duodecim, Vol. 77, pp. 1-24.

Härö, A. S. & O. Kilpiö. 1961. Venereal Diseases among Prostitutes in Helsinki 1945-57, Acta Dermato-Venereologica, Vol. 41, pp. 309-319.

Härö, A. S. & Ulla Siivola. 1965. Irtolaismaisen elämäntavan vuoksi huolletut alle 19 vuotiaat tytöt Helsingissä v. 1956- 62, Sosiaalilääketieteellinen Aikakauslehti, Vol. 4, pp. 35- 41.

Høigård, Cecilie. 1985. Halliker - finnes de? Materialisten, Vol. 13, pp. 108-141.

Høigård, Cecilie & Liv Finstad. 1986. Bakgater. Om prostitusjon, penger og kjærlighet. Pax Forlag, Oslo.

Jackman, Norman R., Richard O'Toole & Gilbert Geis. 1967. The Self-Image of the Prostitute, in Gagnon, J. H. & W. Simon (eds.): Sexual Deviance. Harper & Row, New York, pp. 132-146.

Jackson, Margaret. 1984. Sexology and the Social Construction of Male Sexuality, in Coveney, L. et al. (eds): The Sexuality Papers. Male Sexuality and the Social Control of Women. Hutchinson, London, pp. 45-68.

Jackson, Margaret. 1987. "Facts of life" or the Erotization of Women's Oppression, in Caplan, P. (ed.): The Cultural Construction of Sexuality. Tavistock, London, pp. 52-81.

James, Jennifer. 1977. Ethnography and Social Problems, in Weppner, R. S. (ed.): Street Ethnography. Selected Studies of Crime and Drug Use in Natural Settings. Sage Publications. Beverly Hills, pp. 179-200.

James, Jennifer & Jane Meyerding. 1977. Early Sexual Experience and Prostitution, American Journal of Psychiatry, Vol. 134, pp. 1381-1385.

James, Jennifer & Nanette J. Davis. 1982. Contingencies in Female Sexual Role Deviance: The Case of Prostitution, Human Organization, Vol. 41, pp. 345-350.

James, Lionel. 1973. On the Game, New Society, Vol. 50, pp. 24-28.

Janus, Mark-David, Barbara Scanton & Virginia Price. 1984. Youth Prostitution, in Burgess, A. W. & M. L. Clark (eds.): Child Pornography and Sex Rings. Lexington Books, Lexington, pp. 127-146.

Janus, Sam, Barbara Bess & Carol Saltus. 1978. A Sexual Profile of Men in Power. Warner Books, New York.

Jennings, M. Anne. 1976. The Victim as Criminal: A Consideration of California's Prostitution Law, California Law Review, Vol. 64, pp. 1235-1284.

Jokivartio, Erkki. 1946. Tutkimus Ilmajoen työlaitoksella v. 1941 hoidetusta 100 irtolaisnaisesta, Huoltaja, Vol. 34, pp. 311-318.

Jonsson, Gustav. 1977. Flickor på glid. En studie i kvinnoförtryck. Tiden Folksam, Borås.

Järvinen, Margaretha. 1984. Prostitutionen i Finland - accepterad eller fördömd? Sosiologia, Vol. 21, pp. 226-236.

Järvinen, Margaretha. 1986. Restaurangen - en plats för kvinnor? In Järvinen, M. & A. Snare (eds.): Kvinnor, alkohol och behandling, NAD-publikation 13, Göteborg, pp. 62-78.

Järvinen, Margaretha. 1987. Fallna kvinnor och hållna kvinnor. Polisen och prostitutionen i Helsingfors åren 1965, 1975 och 1980-85. Publikationer från Institutet för kvinnoforskning vid Åbo Akademi, nr 2. Åbo.

Järvinen, Margaretha. 1988. Kvinnorna på härbärget, Sosiaalinen Aikakauskirja, Vol. 82, pp. 37-41.

Järvinen, Margaretha & Kerstin Stenius. 1985. "En karl lyder mycket bättre": Restaurangkontrollen och kvinnan, Alkoholpolitik, Vol. 2, pp. 46-50.

Karch, Cecilia A. & G. H. S. Dann. 1981. Close Encounters of the Third World, Human Relations, Vol. 34, pp. 249-268.

Karras, Ruth Mazo. 1989. The Regulation of Brothels in Later Medieval England, Signs, Vol. 14, pp. 399-433.

Kemp, Tage. 1936. Prostitution: An Investigation of Its Causes, Especially With Regard to Hereditary Factors. Munksgaard, Copenhagen.

Khalaf, Samir. 1965. Prostitution in a Changing Society. A Sociological Survey of Legal Prostitution in Beirut. Khayats, Beirut.

Khalaf, Samir. 1967. Correlates of Prostitution: A Comparative View of some Popular Errors and Misconceptions, Sociologia Internationalis, Vol. 5, pp. 110-122.

Kinsey, Alfred C., Wardell B. Pomeroy & Clyde E. Martin. 1948. Sexual Behavior in the Human Male. W. B. Saunders Company, Philadelphia.
Kirkendall, Lester A. 1960. Circumstances Associated With Teenage Boys' Use of Prostitution, Marriage and Family Living, Vol. 22, pp. 145-149.
Kitsuse, J. 1968. Societal Reaction to Deviant Behavior, in Rubington, E. & M. Weinberg (eds.): Deviance: The Interactionist Perspective. MacMillan, New York, pp. 15-24.
Kleinman, L. 1973. Sex Parlor. Signet Books, New York.
Koivusaari, Maila. 1958. Vuosina 1945-1947 työlaitoksissa hoidettujen Helsingin naispuolisten irtolaisten myöhempi sosiaalinen sopeutuminen. Tutkielma Yhteiskunnallisen Korkeakoulun sosiaalihuoltajatutkintoa varten, Helsinki.
Kon, Igor S. 1987. A Sociocultural Approach, in Geer, J. H. & W. T. O'Donohue (eds.): Theories of Human Sexuality. Plenum Press, New York, pp. 257-286.
Kölli, Tuija. 1982. "Prostitutsioonikysymys". Pro-gradu tutkielma, Suomen ja Skandinavian historia, Helsingin yliopisto.
La Fontaine, Jean S. 1974. The Free Women of Kinshasa: Prostitution in a City in Zaire, in Davis, J. (ed.): Choice and Change. Essays in Honour of Lucy Mair. University of London, pp. 89-113.
Lanu, Reijo. 1970. Työlaitokset rangaistus- ja hoitolaitoksina. Sosiaali- ja terveysministeriö. Sosiaalipoliittinen tutkimusosasto. 5. Helsinki.
Larsson, Stig. 1983. Könshandeln. Om prostituerades villkor. Skeab Förlag, Stockholm.
Laws, Judith Long. 1979. The Second X. Sex Role and Social Role. Elsevier, New York.
Lemert, Edwin M. 1951. Social Pathology. A Systematic Approach to the Theory of Sociopathic Behavior. McGraw-Hill, New York.
Lemert, Edwin M. 1972. Human Deviance, Social Problems and Social Control. Prentice Hall, Englewood Cliffs, New Jersey.
Lerner, Gerda. 1986. The Creation of Patriarchy. Oxford University Press, Oxford.
Lubove, Roy. 1962. The Progressives and the Prostitute, The Historian, Vol. 24, pp. 308-330.
Lukkariniemi, Marja. 1980. Irtolainen vai alkoholisti. Sosiaalipolitiikan pro-gradu tutkielma, Helsingin Yliopisto.
Mackey, Thomas C. 1987. Red Lights Out. A Legal History of Prostitution, Disorderly Houses and Vice Districts 1870- 1917. Garland Publishing, New York.
MacKinnon, Catharine. 1987. Feminism Unmodified. Discourses on Life and Law. Harward University Press, Cambridge.
MacKinnon, Catharine. 1989. Sexuality, Pornography, and Method: "Pleasure under Patriarchy", Ethics, Vol. 99, pp. 315-346.
MacMillan, Jackie. 1976. Rape and Prostitution, Victimology, Vol. 1, pp. 414-420.
MacNamara, Donal E. J. & Edward Sagarin. 1977. Sex, Crime, and the Law. The Free Press, New York.

Maerow, Arnold, S. 1965. Prostitution: A Survey and Review of 20 Cases, Psychiatric Quarterly, Vol. 39, pp. 675-701.

Martinussen, Willy. 1969. Prostitusjon i Norge. Levevei eller levevis, Tidsskrift for samfunnsforskning, Vol. 10, pp. 134-160.

Matthews, Roger. 1986. Beyond Wolfenden? Prostitution, Politics and the Law, in Matthews, R. & J. Young (eds.): Confronting Crime. Sage Publications, Bevery Hills, pp. 188- 212.

Matza, David. 1969. Becoming Deviant. Prentice-Hall, Englewood Cliffs, New Jersey.

McCombs, Nancy. 1986. Earth Spirit, Victim or Whore? The Prostitute in German Literature 1880-1925. Peter Lang, New York.

McHugh, Paul. 1980. Prostitution and Victorian Social Reform. Croom Helm, London.

McLeod, Eileen. 1980. Man-Made Laws for Men? The Street Prostitutes' Campaign against Control, in Hutter, B. & G. Williams (eds.): Controlling Women. The Normal and the Deviant. Croom Helm, London, pp. 61-78.

McLeod, Eileen. 1982. Women Working: Prostitution Now. Croom Helm, London.

McLeod, Eileen. 1983. A Fresh Approach? A Critique of the Criminal Law Revision Committee's Working Paper on Offences Relating to Prostitution and Allied Offences, Journal of Law and Society, Vol. 10, pp. 271-279.

McRobbie, Angela & Jenny Garber. 1976. Girls and Subcultures, in Hall, S. & T. Jefferson (ed.): Resistance through Rituals. Youth Subcultures in Post-War Britain. Hutchinson & Co, London, pp. 209-222.

Melby, Kari. 1980. Prostitusjon og kontroll, in Gotaas, A-M. et al. (eds.): Det kriminelle kjønn - Om barnefødsel i dølgsmål, abort og prostitusjon. Pax forlag, Oslo, pp. 81- 128.

Merry, Sally Engle. 1980. Manipulating Anonymity: Streetwalkers' Strategies for Safety in the City, Ethnos, Vol. 45, pp. 157-175.

Messerschmidt, James. 1987. Feminism, Criminology and the Rise of the Female Sex "Delinquent", 1880-1930, Contemporary Crises, Vol. 11, pp. 243-263.

Miller, Eleanor. 1986. Street Woman. Temple University Press. Philadelphia.

Miller, Gale. 1978. Odd Jobs. The World of Deviant Work. Prentice Hall, Englewood Cliffs, New Jersey.

Millet, Kate. 1976. The Prostitution Papers. "A Quartet for Female Vote". Ballantine Books, New York.

Milner, Christina & Richard Milner. 1972. Black Players. Little, Brown & Company, Boston.

Musheno, Michael & Kathryn Seeley. 1987. Prostitution Policy and the Women's Movement. Historical Analysis of Feminist Thought and Organization, Contemporary Crises, Vol. 10, pp. 237-255.

Månsson, Sven-Axel. 1981. Könshandelns främjare och profitörer. Om förhållandet mellan hallick och prostituerad. Doxa, Karlshamn.

Månsson, Sven-Axel. 1988. The Man in Sexual Commerce. Meddelanden från Socialhögskolan 1988:2, Lunds universitet.

Månsson, Sven-Axel & Annulla Linders. 1984. Sexualitet utan ansikte. Könsköparna. Carlssons, Malmö.

Mäkinen, Tuija. 1979. Suljettujen laitosten laitospopulaatioiden kehitys. Oikeuspoliittisen tutkimuslaitoksen julkaisuja 31, Helsinki.

Nelson, Nici. 1987. "Selling her Kiosk": Kikuyu Notions of Sexuality and Sex for Sale in Mathare Valley, Kenya, in Caplan, P. (ed.): The Cultural Construction of Sexuality. Tavistock, London, pp. 217-239.

Nissi, Maisa. 1965. Irtolaishuollon toimenpiteet ja niiden tehokkuudesta. Sosiaalipolitiikan pro-gradu tutkielma. Yhteiskunnallinen Korkeakoulu, Tampere.

Nygård, Toivo. 1985. Irtolaisuus ja sen kontrolli 1800-luvun alun Suomessa. Studia Historica Jyväskyläensia 31, Jyväskylän Yliopisto.

Olsson, Hanna. 1985. Kvinnosyn, sexualitet och makt - en ny syn på prostitutionsfrågan, Socialmedicinsk tidskrift, Vol. 22, pp. 373-379.

Ortner, Sherry B. & Harriet Whitehead (eds.). 1981. Sexual Meanings. The Cultural Construction of Gender and Sexuality. Cambridge University Press, Cambridge.

Otis, Leah, Lydia. 1985. Prostitution in Medieval Society. The History of an Urban Institution in Languedoc. University of Chicago Press, Chicago.

Paasio, Anneli. 1956. Irtolaisten ja elatus- tai korvausvelvollisten asosiaalisen käyttäytymisen syistä lähinnä Länsi-Suomen työlaitoksen hoidokkiaineksen pohjalta. Moniste.

Partanen, Juha. 1969. Ravintolatutkimus 1968. Alkoholipoliittisen tutkimuslaitoksen tutkimusseloste 41, Helsinki.

Pateman, Carole. 1983. Defending Prostitution: Charges against Ericsson, Ethics, Vol. 99, pp. 561-565.

Pateman, Carole. 1988. The Sexual Contract. Polity Press, Oxford.

Pearsall, Ronald. 1972. The Worm in the Bud. The World of Victorian Sexuality. Penguin Books, Harmondsworth, Middlesex.

Pearson, Michael. 1972. The Age of Consent. Victorian Prostitution and its Enemies. David & Charles Newton Abbot, Plymouth.

Peiss, Kathy. 1984. "Charity Girls" and City Pleasures: Historical Notes on Working-Class Sexuality, 1880-1920, in Snitow, A. et al. (eds.): Desire. The Politics of Sexuality. Virago Press, London, pp. 127-139.

Penttilä, Marjatta. 1965. Länsi-Suomen työlaitoksessa v.1964 hoidetut irtolaisnaiset. Sosiaalihuoltajatutkinnon laitoshuollonlinjan tutkielma. Yhteiskunnallinen korkeakoulu, Tampere.

Perry, Mary Elisabeth. 1978. "Lost Women" in Early Modern Seville: The Politics of Prostitution, Feminist Studies, Vol. 6, pp. 195-214.

Pippingsköld, J. 1888. Om prostitution, dess begrepp, orsaker, förebyggande och öfvervakning. Andragande vid Finska Läkaresällskapets diskussion härom den 21 April 1888. J. C. Frenckell & Son, Helsingfors.

Pippingsköld, J. 1890. Uttalande i frågan om prostitutionens hygieniska behandling. Finska Läkaresällskapets handlingar, band 32, J. C. Freckell & Son, Helsingfors.

Plummer, Kenneth. 1975. Sexual Stigma: An Interactionist Account. Routledge & Kegan Paul, London.

Potterat, John J., Lynanne Philips, Richard B. Rothenberg & William W. Darrow. 1985. On Becoming a Prostitute: An Exploratory Case-Comparison Study, Journal of Sex Research, Vol. 21, pp. 329-335.

Powell, Rachel & John Clarce. 1976. A Note on Marginality, in Hall, S. & T. Jefferson (eds.): Resistance through Rituals. Youth Subcultures in Post-War Britain. Hutchinson & Co, London, pp. 223-230.

Prieur, Annick & Arnhild Taksdal. 1989. Å sette pris på kvinner. Menn som kjøper sex. Pax Forlag, Oslo.

Prus, Robert & Styllianoss Irini. 1980. Hookers, Rounders and Desk Clerks. The Social Organization of the Hotel Community. Gage Publishing, Toronto.

Pätiälä, Risto & Helena Mäkikylä. 1948. Sukupuolitaudit, tuberkuloosi- ja mielisairaudet Helsingin irtolaisaineksessa vuosina 1937-46, Huoltaja, Vol.36, pp. 372-378.

Pönkä, Antti. 1984. Prostituution vaikutuksesta sukupuolitautien esiintyvyyteen Helsingissä. Sosiaali- ja terveysministeriö. Tutkimusosasto. SVT XXXII:97, Helsinki.

Rasmussen, Paul K. & Lauren L. Kuhn. 1977. The New Masseuse, in Warren, C. (ed.): Sexuality, Encounters, Identities, and Relationships. Sage, Beverly Hills, pp. 53-79.

Rauhala, Urho. 1984. Huoltopoliisin tietoon tullut prostituutio Helsingissä. Sosiaali- ja terveysministeriö. Tutkimusosasto. SVT XXXII:97, Helsinki.

Reckless, Walter C. 1973. The Crime Problem. Appleton Century Crafts, New York.

Reiman, Jeffrey H. 1979. Prostitution, Addiction and the Ideology of Liberalism, Contemporary Crises, Vol. 3, pp. 53- 68.

Reynolds, Helen. 1986. The Economics of Prostitution. Charles C. Thomas Publisher, Springfield.

Riegel, Robert E. 1968. Changing American Attitudes Toward Prostitution (1800-1920), Journal of the History of Ideas, Vol. 29, pp. 437-453.

Roby, Pamela A. 1969. Politics and Criminal Law: Revision of the New York State Penal Law on Prostitution, Social Problems, Vol. 17, pp. 83-109.

Roebuck, Julian & Patrick McNamara. 1973. Ficheras and Free- lancers: Prostitution in a Mexican Border City, Archives of Sexual Behavior, Vol. 2, pp. 231-244.

Rolph, C. H. (ed.). 1955. Women of the Streets. A Sociological Study of the Common Prostitute. Secker & Warburg, London.

Romenesko, Kim & Eleanor M. Miller. 1989. The Second Step in Double Jeopardy: Appropriating the Labor of Female Street Hustlers, Crime & Delinquency, Vol. 35, pp. 109-135.

Rosen, Ruth. 1982. The Lost Sisterhood. Prostitution in America 1900-1918. The John Hopkins University Press, Baltimore.

Rosenbleet, Charles & Barbara J. Pariente. 1973. The Prostitute and the Criminal Law, American Criminal Law Review, Vol. 11, pp. 373-427.

Rosenblum, Karen E. 1975. Female Deviance and the Female Sex Role: A Preliminary Investigation, British Journal of Sociology, Vol. 26, pp. 169-185.

Rossiaud, Jacques. 1986. Prostitution, Sex and Society in French Towns in the Fifteenth Century, in Aris, P. & A. Bjin (eds.): Western Sexuality. Practice and Precept in Past and Present Times. Basil Blackwell, Oxford, pp. 76-94.

Rossiaud, Jacques. 1988. Medieval Prostitution. Basil Blackwell, Oxford.

Rowe, Stephen. 1979. Prostitution and the Criminal Justice System - An Analysis of Present Policy and Possible Alternatives, in Ialovetta, R. G. & D. H. Chang: Critical Issues in Criminal Justice. Carolina Academic Press, Durham, pp. 391-404.

Rubington, Earl & Martin S. Weinberg. 1973. Deviance. The Interactionist Perspective. Macmillan Company, New York.

Salomon, Edna. 1989. The Homosexual Escort Agency: Deviance Disavowal, British Journal of Sociology, Vol. 40, pp. 1-21.

Salutin, Marilyn. 1971. Stripper Morality, Trans-action, Vol. 8, pp. 12-27.

Samovar, Larry & Fred Sanders. 1978. Language Patterns of the Prostitute. Some Insights into a Deviant Subculture, Et cetera, Vol. 35, pp. 30-36.

Sandberg, Liisa. 1970. Irtolaisuuden tilastollistarkastelua vuosina 1937-1966. Tutkielma sosiaalipolitiikan keskikurssia varten, Tampereen Yliopisto.

Sarlin, Bruno. 1916. Toimenpiteet kerjuun ja irtolaisuuden torjumiseksi, Köyhäinhoitolehti, Vol. 4, pp. 19-21, 25-27, 30-31.

Savitz, Leonard, & Lawrence Rosen. 1988. The Sexuality of Prostitutes: Sexual Enjoyment reported by "Streetwalkers", Journal of Sex Research, Vol. 24, pp. 200-208.

Schaepdrijver, Sophie de. 1986. Regulated Prostitution in Brussels, 1844-1877. A Policy and its Implementation, Historical Social Research, Vol. 12, pp. 89-105.

Schiøtz, Aina. 1980. Prostitusjon og prostituerte i 1880- åras Kristiania, in Gotaas, A-M. et al. (eds.): Det kriminelle kjønn - om barnefødsel i dølgsmål, abort og prostitusjon. Pax Forlag, Oslo 1980, pp. 35-79.

Schur, Edwin M. 1971. Labeling Deviant Behavior. Harper & Row, New York.

Schur, Edwin M. 1979. Reactions to Deviance: a Critical Assessment, American Journal of Sociology, Vol. 75, pp. 309- 322.

Schur, Edwin M. 1983. Labeling Women Deviant. Gender, Stigma and Social Control. Temple University Press, Philadelphia.

Seidler, Victor J. 1987. Reason, Desire, and Male Sexuality, in Caplan, P. (ed.): The Cultural Construction of Sexuality. Tavistock, London, pp. 82-112.

Sereny, Gitta. 1984. The Invisible Children. Child Prostitution in America, West Germany and Great Britain. André Deutsch. London.

Sheehy, Gail. 1973. Hustling. Prostitution in Our Wide-Open Society. Dell Publishing Co, New York.

Shoham, Shlomo. 1978. The Mark of Cain. The Stigma Theory of Crime and Social Deviation. Israel University Press, Jerusalem.

Shoham, Shlomo & Giora Rahav. 1968. Social Stigma and Prostitution. Current Survey, British Journal of Criminology, Vol. 8, pp. 402-412.

Shrage, Laurie. 1989. Should Feminists Oppose Prostitution? Ethics, Vol. 99, pp. 347-361.

Shumsky, Neil Larry & Larry M. Springer. 1981. San Francisco's Zone of Prostitution, 1880-1934, Journal of Historical Geography, Vol. 7, pp. 71-89.

Silbert, Mimi H. & Ayala M. Pines. 1981. Occupational Hazards of Street Prostitutes, Criminal Justice and Behavior, Vol. 8, pp. 395-399.

Silbert, Mimi H. & Ayala M. Pines. 1983. Early Sexual Exploitation as an Influence in Prostitution, Social Work, Vol. 28, pp. 285-289.

Simonen, Aarre E. 1937 (a): Kuka on irtolainen? Irtolaiskäsitteen selvittelyä uuden irtolaislain mukaan, Huoltaja, Vol. 25, pp. 277-282.

Simpson, Mary & Thomas Schill. 1977. Patrons of Massage Parlors: Some Facts and Figures, Archives of Social Behavior, Vol. 6, pp. 521-525.

Skipper, James K. & Charles H. McCaghy. 1971. Stripteasing: A Sex-Oriented Occupation, in Henslin, J. M. (ed.): Studies in the Sociology of Sex. Appleton Century Crafts, New York, pp. 275-296.

Snitow, Ann, Christine Stansell & Sharon Thompson (eds). 1984. Desire. The Politics of Sexuality. Virago Press, London.

Soikkeli, Sirkka. 1949. Irtolaisnainen ja hänen lähin ympäristönsä, Huoltaja, Vol. 37, pp. 177-181.

Stallberg, Friedrich W. 1983. Prostitution - ein Problem Staatlicher Kontrolle, Kriminalsoziologische Bibliographie, Vol. 10, pp. 55-80.

Stein, Martha L. 1974. Lovers, Friends, Slaves...The Nine Male Sexual Types. Their Psycho-Sexual Transactions with Call Girls. Berkeley Publishing Corporation and Putnam & Sons, New York.

Stewart, George Lee. 1972. On First Being a John, Urban Life and Culture, Vol. 3, pp. 255-274.

Stopp, G. Harry. 1978. The Distribution of Massage Parlors in the Nation's Capital, Journal of Popular Culture, Vol. 11, pp. 989-997.

Sutherland, Edwin H. 1937. The Professional Thief. By a Professional Thief. University of Chicago Press, Chicago.

Sykes, Gresham M. & David Matza. 1957. Techniques of Neutralization: A Theory of Delinquency, American Sociological Review, Vol. 31, pp. 664-670.

Symanski, Richard. 1981. The Immoral Landscape. Female Prostitution in Western Societies. Butterworth & Co, Toronto.

Sæther, Wera. 1988. Berøring forbudt. To prostituerte forteller. Gyldendal Norsk Forlag, Oslo.

Taipale, Ilkka. 1982. Asunnottomuus ja alkoholi. Sosiaalilääketieteellinen tutkimus Helsingistä vuosilta 1937-1977. Alkoholitutkimussäätiön julkaisuja n:o 32, K. J. Gummerus, Jyväskylä.

Takman, John. 1968. Prostitution, in Israel, J. (ed.): Sociala avvikelser och social kontroll. Almqvist & Wiksell, Stockholm, pp. 424-437.

Takman, John. 1970. Prostitution, in Israel, J. (ed.): Sexologi. Almqvist & Wiksell, Stockholm.

Toivola, Osmo. 1943. Alkoholisti- ja irtolaishuolto. Lainsäädäntö ja käytännöllinen huoltotyö. WSOY, Turku.

Tolkki, Mirja. 1969. Prostituutio Tampereella. Sosiologian pro-gradu tutkielma, Tampereen Yliopisto.

Trudgill, Eric. 1976. Madonnas and Magdalens. The Origins and Development of Victorian Sexual Attitudes. Heinemann, London.

Turunen, Sakari. 1965. Irtolaisista, Sosiaalilääketieteellinen Aikakauslehti, Vol. 4, pp. 23-28.
Tuulasvaara-Kaleva, Tiina. 1988. Prostituoitujen valvonta- ja rankaisusäädökset 1875-1939. Suomen historian pro-gradu tutkielma, Tampereen yliopisto.
Varsa, Hannele. 1986. Prostituution näkymätön osa: miesasiakkaat. Lehti-ilmoitteluprostituution asiakkaista. Naistutkimusmonisteita 5. Tasa-arvoasiain neuvottelukunta, Helsinki.
Varsa, Hannele & Markku Heinonen. 1984. Irtolaisrekisteri 1983. Sosiaali- ja terveysministeriön julkaisuja 12.
Velarde, Albert, J. 1975. Becoming Prostituted. The Decline of the Massage Parlour Profession and the Masseuse, British Journal of Criminology, Vol. 15, pp. 251-263.
Velarde, Albert J. & M. Warlick. 1973. Massage Parlors. The Sensuality Business, Society, Volume 11, pp. 63-74.
Vitaliano, Peter Paul, Debra Boyer & Jennifer James. 1981. Perceptions of Juvenile Experience. Females Involved in Prostitution Versus Property Offences, Criminal Justice and Behavior, Volume 8, pp. 325-342.
Walkowitz, Judith. 1977. The Making of an Outcast Group, in Vicinus, M. (ed.): A Widening Sphere. Changing Roles of Victorian Women. Indiana University Press, Bloomington, pp. 72-116.
Walkowitz, Judith R. 1980. Prostitution and Victorian Society. Women, Class and the State. Cambridge University Press, London.
Walkowitz, Judith R. 1984. Male Vice and Female Virtue: Feminism and the Politics of Prostitution in Nineteenth- Century Britain, in Snitow, A. et al. (eds.): Desire. The Politics of Sexuality. Virago Press, London, pp. 43-61.
Weeks, Jeffrey. 1981. Sex, Politics and Society. The Regulation of Sexuality since 1800. Longman Group, London.
White, Luise. 1986. Prostitution, Identity, and Class Consciousness in Nairobi During World War II, Signs, Volume 11, pp. 255-273.
Willis, Paul E. 1978 (a). Learning to Labour. How Working Class Kids get Working Class Jobs. Saxon House, Westmead, Farnborough.
Willis, Paul E. 1978 (b). Profane Culture. Routledge & Kegan Paul, London.
Winick, Charles. 1962. Prostitutes' Clients' Perception of the Prostitutes and of Themselves, International Journal of Social Psychiatry, Vol. 42, pp. 289-297.
Winick, Charles & Paul M. Kinsie. 1971. The Lively Commerce. Prostitution in the United States. Quadrangle Books, Chicago.
The Wolfenden Report. 1964. Report of the Committee on Homosexual Offences and Prostitution. Lancer Books, New York.
Women Endorsing Decriminalization. 1973. Prostitution: A Non-Victim Crime? Issues in Criminology, Vol. 8, pp. 137- 162.
Young, Wayland. 1967. Prostitution, in Gagnon, J. H. & W. Simon (eds.): Sexual Deviance. Harper & Row, New York, pp. 105-133.

Commission Reports:

Betänkande afgifvet till Finska läkaresällskapet af ett för prostitutionsfrågans behandling inom sällskapet tillsatt utskott. Helsingfors 1888.

Komitébetänkande från komitén för afgifvande af förslag rörande prostitutionen och de veneriska besiktningarna. Komitébetänkande nr 6. Helsingfors 1891.

Betänkande i prostitutionsfrågan, afgifvet af föredraganden i civil expeditionen T. J. Aminoff. Helsingfors 1892

Betänkande i fråga om anordnande af särskild kontroll i Helsingfors, Åbo, Tammerfors och Wiborgs städer öfver prostituerade personer. Afgifvet af föredraganden i civil expeditionen T. J. Aminoff. Helsingfors 1896.

Ehdotus sukupuolitautien vastustamiseksi. Komiteanmietintö n:o 10. Helsinki 1924

Ehdotus irtolaislaiksi ynnä perustelut. Lainvalmistelukunnan julkaisuja n:o 1. Helsinki 1926.

Huoltolakien tarkistamiskomitean mietintö. Komiteanmietintö n:o 4. 1946, Helsinki 1946.

Kasvatus- ja työlaitoskomitean mietintö II. Työlaitokset. Komiteanmietintö n:o 6. 1947. Helsinki 1947.

Pakkotyölainsäädäntökomitean mietintö. Moniste 1948:15.

Huolto-ohjelmakomitean mietintö. Komiteanmietintö n:o 7. 1949. Helsinki 1949.

Sosiaalihuollon periaatekomitean mietintö I. Komiteanmietintö 1968: B 86, Helsinki 1968.

Työlaitostoimikunnan mietintö. Komiteanmietintö 1966: B 66. Helsinki 1968.

Irtolaishuoltotoimikunnan osamietintö N:o 1. Komiteanmietintö 1969: B 36, Helsinki 1969.

Työlaitosten ja kunnallisten huoltoloiden kehittämistoimikunnan raportti, Helsinki 1977.

Päihdeasiainneuvottelukunnan mietintö. Ehdotus päihdeongelmaisten huollon kehittämisestä. Komiteanmietintö 1978:40, Helsinki 1978.

Irtolaislain kumoamisen vaikutuksia selvittävän toimikunnan mietintö. Komiteanmietintö 1986:46, Helsinki 1986.

Laws and Decrees:

Förordning om reglementerad prostitution 1875/20
Förordning angående lösdrifvare och deras behandling 1883/17.
Sexualbrottslagen. Strafflagens 20 kap om lägersmål och annan otukt 1889/39.
Lag om lösdrivare 1936/57.
Förordning om lösdrivare 1936/204.
Förordning om lösdrivarregister 1945/985.
Lag angående ändring av lagen om lösdrivare 1971/562.